to My Pal
Cantor Berrie Knee-
Tin
Whatta guy —
Pan Alley's #1 "Demo
Man" — a star among
his peers — a guy
you could always depend
upon — always with that
refreshing smile — never a
pain in the ass. (like me.)
* From one of the "Sunshine Boys"
Eddie White
* the other being Mack W.

Yesterday's Cake

Sketch of the Hebrew Orphan Asylum by French artist Ms. D. Guilmet. (Commissioned by Eddie White)

Yesterday's Cake

Eddie White

VANTAGE PRESS
New York / Washington / Atlanta
Los Angeles / Chicago

FIRST EDITION

Published by Vantage Press, Inc.
516 West 34th Street, New York, New York 10001

Manufactured in the United States of America
ISBN: 0-533-06428-7

Library of Congress Catalog Card No.: 84-90500

To my mother, Sophie Itzkowitz,
for her many sacrifices
and for teaching me the niceties of life and the
meaning of love;
to my son, Peter White,
for being my fishing, camping, and trail-ride buddy
and for teaching me to grow, share, and learn the meaning of
childhood;
and to Mr. Paddy Chayefsky,
for threatening, cajoling, urging, and humoring me into writing
this book
and teaching me the meaning of friendship

In the orphanage, our monitor explained that "a nickel's worth of yesterdays" was five cents' worth of "Yesterday's Cake," cake that was old, leftovers that no one wanted. In other words, we could get more for our money, and who cared if the cake was stale?

Edwin Booth in his youth heard the solemn whisper of the god of all the arts in the worshipping ear of his acolyte: "I shall give you hunger and pain and sleepless nights, also beauty and satisfactions known to few—and glimpses of the heavenly life. None of these will you have continually, and of their coming and going you shall not be foretold."

CONTENTS

CONTENTS

ILLUSTRATIONS

PREFACE

1919–21: Versailles Peace Conference and League of Nations convened; Prohibition ratified; Sacco and Vanzetti found guilty of murder; Hitler speaks in Munich; Mussolini founds the Fascidi combattimento; Dempsey defeats Willard for championship; Babe Ruth becomes New York Yankee.

How MANY TIMES have you heard about people running away with a circus or wanting to? If I heard this story once, I must have heard it a thousand times. The story goes that I ran away from the ground floor apartment where I was born, at 1033 Bryant Avenue in the South Bronx, to join a circus. This was the summer of 1921, and I was all of two years and a few moments old.

I had been left sitting in front of our apartment building and told not to get off of my little chair unless it was to come into the house, not to accept candy from strangers, not to go away with anyone, not to cross the street, and not to get dirty. Our apartment was on the ground floor front, facing the street, and every so often someone would look out the window and check on me. Suddenly I wasn't there!

It seems I had heard the enchanting strains of a calliope and was fascinated by all the funny, little people dressed as clowns and acrobats being led by a baby elephant. I had heard destiny's call and obeyed. I naturally followed my newfound friends to the corner lot and watched as they set up for business. I hadn't crossed the street.

My mother, who had originally come from Rumania, thought that I had been kidnapped by Gypsies. (Rumania is famous for Gypsies and Count Dracula.) The police were called and the search was on.

xiii

The entire neighborhood got into the act, and finally some kid found me staring wide-eyed at this beautiful outdoor party scene. I was completely mesmerized, and my mother and sister had to drag me away as I was screaming and struggling to remain with my fantastic discovery. I identified with the circus then, and I still do to this day.

The reason I tell this story is because, as I look back over the years, I think that one particular incident set me up for what was to come later on. Life to me has been one huge three-ring circus, a kaleidoscope of laughs, pathos, violence, passion, art, music, hatred, ingratitude, loyalty, rejection, and love. I guess almost anyone can make that statement, but how many people have run away with a circus? At the age of two and a fraction?

You've heard of a cat having nine lives? I've passed nine some time ago and am still going strong. Thinking about my life is almost like seeing a movie, except that, strangely, I am in the picture up there on the screen. I've ceased to think about some of the wondrous and unusual things that have occurred in my life, and I now just lean back and enjoy every experience, good and bad. I think somewhere this whole script or story has been written and I must go through with my scenes. Life started with a circus and it has remained so. The big tent I saw as a little boy is still up, and the enchanting strains of a calliope still fill the air. The only difference is, I know which part I am playing. I am one of the clowns.

ACKNOWLEDGMENTS

FOR THEIR kind words and assistance in moments of indecision, I wish to thank the following, Paddy Chayefsky, Lenny Goldstein, Marge Greene, Norman Mailer, Elaine Markson, Tanya Maria Mendoza, Missy O'Shea, Murray Schisgal, Ruth Strauss, Arthur M. Stringari, Stanley E. Tannen, Johnny Taranto, and Peter White.

Yesterday's Cake

1

Daddy Was a Baddie

LET'S SAY IT like it is, or was. My father, "Broadway" Jack White, was a petty gangster. I don't have any bad feelings toward him, although I probably should have. His picture hangs in my office, alongside my mother's, to this day. I feel complete sadness and emptiness when I think of him—for the things he did to my mother, for the things he didn't do for my sister and myself, but mostly for the things he did to himself. Jack was a Damon Runyon character, except that he was better looking than most men, dressed like a fashion plate, spoke softly, and had fine manners. Long before Sinatra, they called "Broadway" Jack White "Little Old Blue Eyes" over at the old Lindy's Restaurant.

His pals were "Good Time" Charley Friedman; Arnold Rothstein, the notorious gambler; Charley "Phil" Rosenberg; George MacManus; "Champ" Segal; "Fat the Butcher;" and some others I can't mention for personal health reasons. Some of the guys are still alive today.

Jack White was once part of a gang that all went to the electric chair. Getting married to my mother saved Jack from walking the last mile. I heard that the gang all went to the electric chair on the same day. At least they were a closer knit family than we were.

Jack swore that getting married made him a new man, that now he was "going straight." Like everything else he ever told my mother, this was a lie. My father's illustrious career included, among other things, the selling of phony stocks and bonds and gambling arrests, and he had a stint or three in jail in Lexington, Kentucky, on various drug charges. My father was into drugs before it was popular, I'll say that for him.

"Broadway" Jack White, husband, father, racketeer, and a failure at all three.

Jack White was born Max Rothenberg in New York City. His mother, my grandmother, was burned in a fire when Jack was still an infant, and my grandfather quickly remarried. Jack never got along with his stepmother and often ran away from home. He lived by his wits, but mostly he played semipro baseball. He was considered quite a pitcher, playing for the Bushwicks in his teens. One day, while he was pitching a game in Central Park, an old lady in her eighties approached him between innings and showed him a picture. It was a picture of his father, as a young man, and a young woman. Jack said that the man was his father but who was the woman? The old lady, who wanted to make trouble in the family and was a distant relative, replied, "This lady is your real mother. She died in a fire when you were a baby." Jack looked long and hard at the picture, looked at the old lady, and then slowly walked into the sunset. He never went home again. Thus began the saga of "Broadway" Jack White.

My mother and father first met at my Aunt Esther's wedding. Esther was my mother's sister and a very strong-willed, outspoken woman. My mother and grandmother had just come from Rumania for the wedding, and they stayed on for another cousin's wedding. My Aunt Esther noticed the strong attachment the handsome, glib American had for her sister Sophie. From the beginning, my aunt was dead set against the romance, but my mother just couldn't say no to this handsome, flashy sheikh. Mom never saw Rumania again!

Forget the Hungarian Gabor sisters; here come the Rumanian Itzkowitz sisters—Sophie, Adele, and Esther.

Sophie White was a diminutive Rumanian beauty barely five feet tall with a tiny, straight nose that would have been the envy of the Gabor sisters. She invariably wore only one earring, her hair done up with bangs, and a tiny spit curl, which was the style at the time. She had a sweet, honest, open face with big brown soft, searching eyes and a loving personality that endeared her to everyone. She never had an enemy in her entire life. To even think she could have one was a cruel, imagined joke. On those rare occasions, when I was a little boy, my mother laughed out loud, I would be startled. They were the first times I had ever heard music.

Mom never raised her voice; she never even knew the meaning of the word *argument*. I never remember her fighting or standing up for her common rights. She was overly kind and compassionate to the world she met, and that was her undoing.

Surely she was no match for her powerfully outspoken sister. Esther was the strong Yankee leader of the family, and my mom was the weak, very submissive greenhorn follower. Just mention my mother's name to this very day and people go into raptures. "Sally White—God only made one like her!" My mother Americanized her name to one from a song popular at the time, "I Wonder What's Become of Sally?"

I doubt if Mom ever had a secure, happy moment from the day she first arrived at Ellis Island. What son hasn't thought about his poor immigrant mother and said, "The things I could do for her if she were alive today?" With a terribly, heavy heart, I know wishing won't make it so.

Every night our little family had dinner with "Gyp" the Blood, "Dago" Frank, Jack "Legs" Diamond, and many others with names as colorful. Oh, they weren't at our dinner table, but they were mentioned over and over again. My old man worshipped these guys. He must have been a composite of all of them, but something must have gone wrong. Even with his good looks, fine manners, and dapper clothes, "Broadway" Jack White never made it. Years later, when talking to a friend of mine whose father also was a gangster, I said, "Hey, at least your father was 'Waxey' Gordon. He made it to the top. Jack White was always an 'also-ran.'" That hurt! If only my old man had pitched a no hitter or something. Or had a shootout with the cops and then given him-

My favorite aunt, "Tanta" Esther.

self up so that he could save a wounded priest. Every time I saw James Cagney and Pat O'Brien in one of those gangster pictures, I thought, *If only my father was like that.* Maybe he had his moments, but I never knew or heard about them. All the things I ever heard about "Broadway" Jack White showed that he was a man without a soul. I don't think he was cruel or vicious. As a matter of fact, I know he wasn't. But when that old hag of a woman showed him a picture of his real father and mother, something went out of Max Rothenberg, later to be known as "Broadway" Jack White.

When I really thought about it, my heart ached for the way his life started out. Like my mother, I felt love for Jack, but I suppressed it. What good would it do, where would it get me? Then too, Sister Ruth would remind me of the unkept promises and the many hurts to my mother and to us kids. My sister was stronger; she would hold the torch and banner of hatred on high. She would remind me. Much as she reminded me all these years, deep down there's something left for Jack White, now buried in Potter's Field. I even wanted to move him once, to my mother's grave, and let bygones be bygones, so I told my sister. She felt that was going too far. Still, as she is a woman, I never believed her completely. I know my sis cares like I do, but the wounds are deeper than my own.

The first few months of marriage were ecstasy to my mother, living in New York City. So it was the Bronx. So the streets weren't paved with gold. So my father never came home for weeks. So he told lies about everything. So Esther kept reminding her about the things he did. And what about the things she didn't know about? It was only the beginning. Things were bound to get better.

But better they never got; worse is more like it. Aunt Esther kept reminding her beautiful sister that she was married to a bum, a street hoodlum, and no good would ever come of the union. "Leave him while you are still young and have your looks. We'll find someone nice for you, maybe a professional man. Sophie, listen to me; I know better."

But Esther never counted on the great love my mother had for my father. No man had more but deserved less. The letters she received through the years! Always it was "Wait until my ship comes in; you'll see. We'll live in the lap of luxury. You'll be a queen." Maybe he meant it, maybe he believed it but he never even came close to the plate. Jack White, who was such a good pitcher, was now pitching Jewish blarney.

Esther prevailed and finally, triumphantly, she led my mother into a divorce court, where my mother tearfully told the judge her tale of woe. The die was cast, Sophie became a divorced woman and the children of said union, little baby Ruth and Eddie, were now fatherless. Not that we ever had our father with us, but just knowing he was around, we felt, was better than this. We've discussed it through the years, how our mother loved our father. It was Cathy and Heathcliff all over again, a Jewish *Wuthering Heights*. Bad as they were, no one could separate Mom from Jack's letters. Somehow I think she read between the lines and imagined that his letters were full of love; "Wait, wait, Sophie. You'll see. Someday my ship will come in." Somehow I don't trust ships to this day. My father's ship, like all the horses he ever picked, was the *Titanic!*

6

Somewhere, sometime, I either read or heard that "All success is only the temporary interruption of failure," also that "writing is a way of purging oneself." Both statements are truer than true as far as I am concerned.

Failure was my middle name for years. I have had more failures trying to do more things than anyone I know. I was so engrossed in trying to become something or someone that I never had time to consider my failings.

Where but in America (that old bromide) could a guy brought up in three orphanages, countless foster homes, bounced from pillar to post as a child, with failing health, with but an eighth-grade education, not only become a success but live a life no corny, third-rate writer would believe, let alone write about?

But my story is true. It happened. Who am I to write a book? Who do you have to be to write a book?

Not only did I purge myself by writing this book, but I feel that some unknown, unseen power guided me in the living and the writing of my life.

One word, *curiosity*, is the key to my personality. Curiosity makes me tick. It is who I am and what I am!

Being a true-blue Gemini, I am curious about everything that ever existed, everything I come in contact with, everything that presents any kind of a challenge. I thought I could do anything. I found out that I couldn't, but I wanted to, trying everything, anything, anywhere. And I did.

As a kid, I was so poor I thought *The Lower Depths* was about rich people. I never had three meals a day until I was twenty-one and in the army. But curiosity kept me going always. "How come I can't get a good job?" "How come that guy's got nicer clothes and a car?" "How come it's Christmas and I'm not getting any presents and I have nowhere to go?" "How come?" These were the questions I asked.

Whenever life closed in on me and it just seemed too unbearable, I would give myself the old Knute Rockne pep talk, sometimes out loud, and I would find an ounce of courage somewhere. And if I cried I would call myself a coward, a sissy, and then I would laugh and it would be all over. And then I would become curious again.

Curiosity—that's what made me run away from the orphanage. And curiosity is what got me wherever it is I am. Tell me I

7

can't do something and I'll find a way to do it! It may take me years and I may take the long way around, but somewhere it's stuck in my mind and I eventually do it. Most times, no one knows that I've accomplished what I set out to do. Only myself. That's okay; it makes me feel stronger anyway and then I scale the next mountain and the next.

One of the first things that aroused an enormous amount of curiosity in me was flying. But how could I become a flyer, I used to get airsick on a swing or a merry-go-round. I not only learned how to fly; I eventually became a first lieutenant bombardier-navigator during World War Two, and this without the benefit of an education. The odds on that happening are over a million to one!

I became enamored and curious about songwriting and show business. Without knowing anything about music, I plunged right into Tin Pan Alley and suffered rejection after rejection. It went on for years. I found out I was much too anxious, so I slowed down and learned a little of the craft. Eventually I wrote songs for Frank Sinatra, Tony Bennett, Eddie Fisher, Patti Page, Pearl Bailey, Sarah Vaughan, Billy Eckstine, Cab Calloway, and many other stars. I managed Harry Belafonte and helped start Tony Bennett's career and produced shows on Broadway and off Broadway, concerts at Carnegie Hall, and reviews in leading nightclubs.

I brought the fabulous Ella Fitzgerald to Japan for a series of concerts and we were entertained royally by the emperor and his daughter Suga. I personally brought American pop music to Japan, and now that market is number one outside of the U.S., as far as income is concerned.

Being pals with Robert Duvall and Dustin Hoffman piqued my curiosity about acting, so I went to acting school. Of course, their encouragement helped, but there I was, in my fifties trying still another thing. I've since appeared with Jimmy Caan and Robert Duvall in *The Killer Elite* and on a couple of *Kojak* episodes on TV, and you'll have to look fast to see me in *Annie Hall* and *Manhattan* with Woody Allen. I've also done a few commercials, and my face was the opening poster sequence in a "60 Minutes" episode based on the Pentagon. They made me a two-star general. Not a bad jump for a first lieutenant. (Eventually I made captain but it was for only thirty-three days, when the war was over.) In those early years when I was trying to get a break in "show biz," I hung out with a few legends—guys like Lenny Bruce, Rocky Graziano, "Toots" Shore, Tony Bennett, Harry Belafonte, Phil Silvers, et cetera, et cetera, et cetera. I think that if you have a little talent and you persist long enough, the talent will grow and you are bound to eventually get a break. I believe it and it worked for me.

But it wasn't always thus. . . .

2

Little Orphan Eddie

1923: Hitler's "Beer Hall Putsch" fails; Dada movement ends; George Gershwin writes Rhapsody in Blue; Paavo Nurmi runs first four-minute mile; Jack Dempsey knocks out Luis Firpo.

TRY AS SHE MAY, tiny, fragile, beautiful Sophie Itzkowitz, now Sally White, couldn't hold her little world together. If she worked, the baby-sisters ate up all the money, and if she stayed home, she depended on the charity of friends and family. How long could that last? Someone told her about Jewish Charities, an organization that would help place her children in an institution. At night she would cry herself to sleep at the thought of parting with her little ones. Surely a miracle would happen. Someone or something would come to her aid in this moment of anguish. Why this had to happen, my sister and I can't fathom to this very day. How come, with uncles, aunts, cousins, and friends in America, the land of opportunity, my mother had to give up her children? When I ask someone that question, someone in my family, they are dumbstruck. Why am I picking on them? Why ask them that question? They were too young, or too old, or too poor, or you name it. Like the Germans when they were told about Auschwitz, my family "didn't know what was going on"; they "didn't know it was happening." If only they knew! "Do you think we would let this happen to you two beautiful kids if we knew? If we only knew." But happen it did. Ruth and I were both placed in a charitable institution in Rockaway Park called the Convalescent Home for Hebrew Children, which was supported by The Jewish Federation, The home had three depart-

10

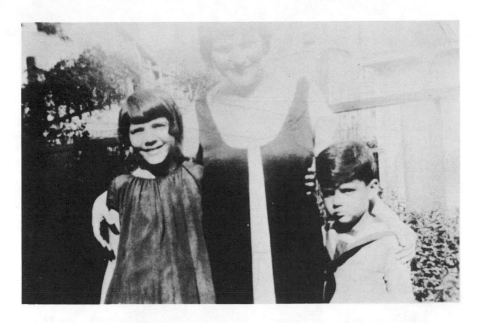

With Mom just before Ruth and I went to our first orphanage.

ments, one for children with orthopedic problems, one for poor children sent there by social agencies, and one for children recuperating from an illness.

How long we were there, I can hardly remember, but some of the friends we made there, as tiny tots, are still our friends. Cissie and Billy Cook and Henrietta Cook and Kappy Berkowitz and Nurse Godliss and her brother Al.

Somehow The SPCC (The Society for the Prevention of Cruelty to Children) got custody of the two of us, my sister and me, and we were shipped off to an institution that still sends shivers down our spines. The moment we arrived, they placed us in a large room that had glass walls. My sister still jumps up at night hearing my mother cry out, "Give me back my children!" Tearfully running to my mother, I ran right into the thick glass wall. Thank God I can't remember too much else of that institution.

The next stop was the place we stayed at the longest, the H.O.A. Those were the call letters of the Hebrew Orphan Asylum

Our first stop, the Rockaway Park orphanage. That's me on the left and my lifelong friend Billy Cook second from right.

or "H" or Academy, as we lovingly call it with reverence to this very day.

The "H" resembled a huge castle with possibly a thousand rooms. It was on 137th Street and Amsterdam Avenue in the heart of Harlem. A ghetto within a ghetto! There were 500 boys there and 500 girls. The ages were five to sixteen, and when the children reached the age when they had to leave, then they were sent to what was called The Corner House. That was a house on the corner of the next block, where the officials of the "H" could keep a paternal eye on the kids that were trying to make it on their own. Some kids were sent home, if they had a home to go to.

When we first arrived at the "H," my sister and I were put into what they called The Reception House, or Quarantine. I still remember my mother having to walk away from us, to leave us behind, and small as I was, I tried to climb the grated fence. How hard I must have made it for my mother to leave. Screaming and begging. I had gotten partially up the fence when my sister grabbed a hold of me and pulled me down. The rest is a blur and a blackout. Somehow we got through quarantine, needles, delousing, examinations, haircuts, clothes, and more needles. After a few days, we were sent to the main building. I was placed in Dormitory M-6 with the smallest children.

The dormitories were huge, with a hundred kids sleeping in alcoves in each room. For the boys, it was M-1, for the oldest up to M-6, for the youngest boys. For the girls, it was F-1 up to F-4. There was a boys' side to the "H" and a girls' side, and you weren't allowed to visit the other side unless it was visiting hours.

You weren't allowed to visit the girls' side unless you were Little Orphan Eddie. Among the thousand kids, I was the tiniest, and most of the girls found me especially cute, loveable, and huggable. I got lost all the time when I first arrived at the "H," and usually I wandered over to the girl's side to visit my sister. How could anyone say anything to such a little boy or report me for being off base? Report me to whom?

The girls didn't have any pets, so I became their pet. Many the time I had to scream out for my sister because one of the girls hugged me too tight or someone almost dropped me. They passed me around like a kitten, and although I howled I really loved it. "Let me hold him" was the hue and cry. Ugh! And all those girls kissing me. Ugh again!

School in the "H" for me was taking naps and getting a special glass of milk and a cookie. I was underweight and weak. My blood count was far less than it should have been, and the doctors and nurses thought I wasn't long for this world.

In the summer, my afternoons were spent in the lap of the most wonderful lady who ever came into my life, Mrs. Anita Desola. She was an elegant, regal-looking woman, very small and affectionate. I never saw her give an order or take charge of anything or anyone except me. She would tell me Bible stories and fairy tales, and I would fall asleep, secure and warm, in her embrace. This was just a fraction of a moment in my life, but sweet Mrs. DeSola has never left my thoughts. I'm sure she had

13

other duties to perform at the "H," but I can only remember her spending her time with me.

Then there was "Pop," Mr. Murray Sprung.

The Gentle Giant

What can you say about a warm, affectionate man who was the father image to thousands of young homeless boys? There were always 500 boys along with 500 girls in the Hebrew Orphan Asylum, but as the older children left the institution, more youngsters immediately replaced them. They came and they went, but there was always "Pop" Sprung, mostly for the boys.

Pop joined the H.O.A. sometime in 1925, as a counselor, after working at Camp Wakitan, the orphan asylum's summer camp. It was love at first sight, on all sides. The kids adored this handsome, gentle giant with the face of a male angel. The moment you met Pop Sprung, his smile somehow embraced you, and immediately we kids all found our father image, which we so desperately were searching for.

Pop had been a football player, and he looked it. Although he was only five-foot-ten, he weighed around 220 pounds and his enormous chest was fifty-four inches with a thirty-six–inch waist. To the tiniest child in the orphanage, me, "Pop" looked enormous.

Pop used to place me on his right arm, and I would proudly sit there as he paraded around the asylum. In those days, I thought I was someone very special to Pop, and I probably was, but at reunions years later, I found other guys who said and felt the same relationship with Pop. At first, like a little kid, I felt annoyed and irritated, but then I understood that Pop had shared this special warmth with every kid and it made me happier.

Pop had joined the H.O.A. as a counselor because of his abiding sense of social justice. In addition, he believed that discipline could better be achieved through understanding than through beatings. Although he himself was a powerful man, his distaste of corporal punishment was deeply felt and he dedicated himself to its removal at the H.O.A. Pop never raised a hand or his voice to a single child in the home, ever.

14

As a matter of fact, Pop went to the defense of any child who was the least bit harassed, myself included. I even saw Pop go over to the girls' side to straighten out women counselors who felt they had to use their hands in order to discipline a child. The stories we all heard about Pop coming to the defense of some child were endless.

One day, while Pop was conducting a few inspectors from the Jewish Board of Guardians on a tour of the H.O.A., a young boy cowered at the sight of Pop and his distinguished guests. When Pop asked the frightened boy what was the matter, he replied, "Please don't beat me, Mr. Sprung." A confused Pop later asked the kid why he had said something like that when Pop had never raised his hand to him. The youngster looked at Pop with a mischievious grin and said, "Hey, Pop, there's always a first time!"

Pop was eventually promoted from counselor to head counselor and then to director of the H.O.A.'s summer camp. The two weeks a year spent at Camp Wakitan were the happiest of all our young institutionalized lives. I don't think a week goes by today that I don't think of Pop and Camp Wakitan on Lake Stahahe with all the bunks named after Indian tribes, with no hot water or electricity, with the flag-raising ceremonies at the crack of dawn, with the swimming, rowing, nature hikes, the canteen where you bought candy, the campfires, the movies, and the Blue and Maroon days where the camp was evenly divided the last three days and we competed in every sport activity from sunrise to sunset and lastly, as we sleepy kids lay in our beds, smothered with citronella to ward off the mosquitoes, we would hear the haunting strains of taps away off in the distance.

The outside world was still a distant, mysterious place, but Camp Wakitan for those two wonderful weeks each year somehow allayed our fears and made us kids gloriously happy. Of course the girls had their camp, too. It was called Camp Wehaha, but being a boy, I didn't know what went on there.

One of the two memories of Camp Wakitan that stand out the most with me was of a deeply religious feeling I felt once as I sat on the edge of the dock, down at the lake one evening, and thought about my mother and life in the outside world. Somehow that one tiny moment in time still remains in my memory.

The other is of Murray Pop Sprung looking like a handsome young gladiator in nothing but shorts, standing on a raised platform and giving us sleepy-eyed kids our morning exercises. When that was over, he would bellow, "Every man down to the lake for a dip." There would be a rush down to the lake, all the kids trying to prove their manhood. Me, I ran the other way, back to the Manitoba bunk, and crawled into my cot until I stopped shivering.

Every so often, one or both of those real life replays pops into my mind and I have to smile a little. I have other rememberances of other times and places, especially some of the war, but those two memories of Camp Wakitan have remained with me through the years.

Fate played another part in my life that brought me in close touch again with Murray Pop Sprung. During the war, Pop served with much distinction as a prosecuting attorney on General MacArthur's legal staff, in both Tokyo and Manila. Pop received a commendation for his work in connection with the prosecution of the Battan Death March war criminals.

After the war, Pop became one of only forty foreign lawyers admitted to the Tokyo bar. He is also on almost every committee dealing with the rights of Japanese here in the United States, and he is a member of a distinguished law firm in Tokyo. I was to eventually go on to produce the Ella Fitzgerald concerts in Japan, along with other shows, and to become a vice-president of the huge Yamaka Nippon Gakkai industrial giant. Naturally it was my Pop and his law firm who represented me in all legal matters with the Japanese.

When we would meet in Japan, ten thousand miles away from the Hebrew Orphan Asylum, I would almost break down and weep at the thought that destiny had brought Pop and me back together again. Many a night Pop and his beautiful wife, Mary, would get together with me and one of my current Madame Butterflys and we would partake of some hot sake and sushi. Sometimes I would look at Pop and the words just didn't surface; being together in Japan was so mind boggling.

On Pop's eightieth birthday, September 24, 1983, a huge party was given at the New York Sheraton in his honor. Close to fifty thousand dollars was raised and the Pop Sprung Camp Fund,

Inc. was founded, to send underprivileged children, regardless of color, race, or creed, to summer camps. That night Murray Pop Sprung, the gentle giant, the inspiration for thousands of homeless children, a man of infinite character, an oasis of love and wisdom on this terribly difficult planet, was saluted by his very own kids. No one could have said it in more articulate words than a former member of the Hebrew Orphan Asylum and Camp Wakitan. Art Buchwald, in conclusion, said, "Murray Pop Sprung—he was our Father Flanagan!"

Although the Hebrew Orphan Asylum was a true orphanage in the way it was organized and administered, not all the children were orphans. As a matter of fact, some of the children had both parents, but they came from broken, poverty-stricken backgrounds, such as my own. Some of the children had only one parent. Some were abandoned children.

In the twenties, times were harsh for many immigrant parents. Children were neglected and something had to be done. Usually a court procedure would place the neglected or endangered child in an institution. If an emergency arose, the procedure was mercifully shortened.

The Hebrew Orphan Asylum couldn't handle all the children assigned, and over 4,000 were placed in foster homes. The city of New York helped defer the expenses incurred. Families accepting these children were paid by the city and partially by funds raised by private Jewish citizens in America.

One of the wealthy families who generously contributed was the Warner brothers of Hollywood and motion-picture fame. They not only contributed to the H.O.A's welfare but they built a large combination gymnasium-theater complex on the corner of 137th Street and Broadway, to the right of the ball field. The H.O.A. occupied one huge city block, running from 136th Street and Amsterdam Avenue to 137th Street, down to 136th street and 137th Street and Broadway. The entire block contained the main castlelike building of the home, housing one thousand children, the reception house, the tremendous ball field, greenhouses, and The Warner Memorial Gymnasium and theater.

Once a year, the Home, or "H," or Academy, the latter being our affectionate term applied to the institution, would have an outing at Tilyou's Park in Coney Island. This was the day of days

17

for the children, one of the two days a year that had our little hearts beating faster. (The other day was when we received Hannukkah or Christmas presents of our own choice. Even though the chemistry sets or games or crystal sets were too complicated for us to actually use—most presents were discarded after a few days—it was very exciting just to receive a package all wrapped in colorful paper and go to a party. It broke the monotony and complete boredom of day-to-day life in the orphanage.)

But this was my first year in the H.O.A., and my sister told me we were going to a faraway place called Coney Island where they had rides and hot dogs and the ocean and we were going to have lots of fun. For the next few days, I could hardly sleep. *This Coney Island must be the greatest place on earth,* I thought. All the other peewees in the M6 dormitory were walking around in a trance, too.

Came the eventful day and we were all herded onto buses according to our dormitories. I had a prearranged agreement with my sister that as soon as I arrived at the park, I was to take her hand and never let go. Some kids got lost on these outings, and Ruth and I were going to hang onto each other.

I had the time of my life at Tilyou Park. As soon as we arrived, an official pinned a special card on my shirt entitling me to all the free rides in the park. I never got to ride all the rides, only a few, but just the thought that I could do anything I wanted was too much for me.

Inside of an hour, I had eaten too much for a little boy; I had been shaken up by one of those milk-shake rides and I was about to fall asleep. A nice lady who had accompanied us on the trip asked my sister if she could carry me, to save my sister the trouble. My sister agreed and while we were taking in the sights, this nice lady asked my sister all kinds of questions: "What is the little boy's name?" "Where did he come from?" "Oh, you're his sister?"

Finally the nice lady popped the question, after many more questions: "Was the little boy available for adoption?" My sister was only eleven years old at the time and just barely understood what the word *adoption* meant. She grabbed me quickly and told the lady that we already had a mother who loved us very much and besides, "my brother won't ever go anywhere without me!"

The nice lady who wanted to adopt me was young Doris Warner, daughter of Harry Warner. She later married Mervyn Leroy, the famous director, and then Charles Vidor, an equally famous director of motion pictures.

Many years later, I produced a Broadway play, *The Family Way*, with Leonard Sillman of *New Faces* fame. The writer of the play, Ben Starr, suggested we have dinner with his friend Warner Leroy, the son of Doris and Mervyn Leroy and the owner of Maxwell's Plum, a popular restaurant in New York City. Upon meeting Warner, I told him the story of how we almost became brothers many years back. Sitting at our table were other couples, and Warner casually leaned over to me and said, "Well, I want you to meet your almost half-brother, Brian Vidor, and your other almost half-brother, Clinton Vidor." It was a light, happy evening, but it left me with the funny feeling of what might have been "if?" In addition to building the wonderful gymnasium, the Warner Brothers sent the orphanage their first-run pictures, even before the films were released to the general public. To a five-year-old child, movies were magic, and many nights I couldn't sleep for thinking about Douglas Fairbanks swinging on a rope escaping from the bad guys or wonderful Joe E. Brown winning a baseball game with his last pitch.

The Warner Brothers sent their movie stars to visit the "H" on occasion. As a child, I remember seeing Dolores Del Rio, Al Jolson, Tom Mix, Monte Blue, and Douglas Fairbanks. This was thrilling beyond compare, and I began to learn that there was a world outside the orphanage that was unknown to me, but I sensed I would eventually see it.

One day, Pathe Newsreel sent the idol of America, Babe Ruth, to see us. I was chosen to sit on his lap for the cameras, while all my buddies gathered around us. Fate was to step in years later when I wrote The Bambino's last public performance, a pilot radio show, "Batter Up." Co-starring on the show were the two hottest football stars of the day, Army's Felix "Doc" Blanchard and Glen Davis, and the Voice of the New York Yankees, Mr. Mel Allen. We had to use Mel more than we had expected. Everyone's idol, Babe Ruth was suffering with throat cancer at the time and could only utter a few words.

I told him that I was the little orphanage kid who had sat

on his lap for Pathe Newsreel and here I was writing his show: "Life is funny, isn't it?" Although our NBC studio was warm, The Babe had the chills and he was wearing his famous camel's hair cap and polo wraparound coat indoors. He pinched my cheek and leaned forward and whispered in my ear, "I was brought up in an orphanage, too. You'll make it, kid!" and he gave me a warm bear hug that had little strength behind it. We never did sell "Batter Up." A few days later, George Herman "Babe" Ruth died.

The Hebrew Orphan Asylum's history actually goes back to the Revolutionary War. A Jewish soldier who had served with Gen. George Washington's army meritoriously in the War of Independence was sent to City Hospital to die of old age. A call went out to New York's Jewish community, and immediately people from all over the city began visiting the elderly patriot.

A collection was taken up for his needs, and when the old soldier died and was given an honorable funeral there was $300 left. This money, collected for a Jewish hero of the American Revolution, was the beginning of organized Jewish charities in New York City. The $300 helped start the Hebrew Benevolent Society in 1822.

The Hebrew Benevolent Society merged in 1859 with The German Benevolent Society and in 1860, in a four-story—and—basement brownstone on West 29th Street, opened its first orphanage. The Hebrew Orphan Asylum. The H.O.A. had 30 children then. The "H" moved to other areas in the city and wound up on 136th and 137th Street and Amsterdam Avenue, directly across the street from City College.

The home doesn't exist anymore. Possibly orphanages are outdated today. Now that entire city block is a playground for the children of Harlem.

Ghetto within a Ghetto

That first year in the home was a little bewildering to me. I had to go to school, even though I was only a little over five years of age. Public School 192 held classes up to and including the sixth grade. P.S. 192 was approved by the New York Board of Education, and even though the school was in the orphanage, "outside" kids, children from the neighborhood, attended the school. After they had finished sixth grade, the children from the home were allowed to leave the "H" and attend schools on the "outside." The "H" kids were given twenty-five cents for the day, which included lunch and carfare. Most, if not all, of the kids would walk to school so that they could use the money for extra food. On rainy days, a teacher in the "outside" school would announce that all the children from the orphanage could receive carfare and that they could leave immediately. My sister and a lot of the children would be too embarrassed to admit that they came from the orphanage and would get soaking wet walking home from school after their classes.

The first year or two, school for me meant a class in the morning and then taking a nap in the afternoon. Then I would receive a glass of milk and a cookie upon awakening. This privileged treatment was for only a handful of the children in the home. We were all run-down and undernourished kids, terribly underweight.

I used to fall asleep holding the hand of a tiny, pretty girl with as many freckles as I had. She had long, brown hair and a sweet, smiling face. Oh, how I loved that little girl; just knowing her sustained me through many lonely hours and years. During World War II we actually became engaged, but after my release from the air force, I honestly didn't know which way to turn or actually who I was. That sweet, sweet girl, let me off the hook very easily and gently. I've always cherished the memory of my very first love, Virginia Adler.

A Nickel's Worth of Yesterdays

Every other Saturday, the orphanage would allow the children to leave for a walk on the "outside." Our monitor, who was an older boy in the "H," would bundle us peewee kids up in sweaters, overcoats and those little woolen beanies with the strap, under the chin. We used to walk by twos, holding hands

21

with the kid next to us. One freezing Saturday, we suddenly stopped at Miller's bakery a short distance across the street from the home. One of the kids said, "Let's chip in for a nickle's worth of yesterdays." After searching for a penny here and a penny there, we finally came up with the five cents.

Our monitor explained that a "nickel's worth of yesterdays" was five cents' worth of yesterday's cake, cake that was old, leftovers that no one wanted. In other words, we could get more for our money, and who cared if the cake was stale? He chose me to go into the bakery alone, as I was the smallest child. They might give me some extra cake, I was so thin, and he warned me to make sure you ask for "a nickel's worth of yesterdays."

With the five pennies clutched tightly in my little mitten, I walked into the store. There were a few women waiting to be served, so I edged under and around them, closer to the counter. But now I couldn't see above the counter; nor could I be seen.

A few times I mouthed, "Can I please have a nickel's worth of yesterday's cake?" No one heard me. I said it again whenever I thought I saw an opening. No reaction. I looked outside of the bakery and saw the kids jumping around and slapping their sides trying to keep warm.

And then it happened. I started to cry. Still no one noticed me. I cried louder and finally a large woman yelled to the woman behind the counter, "There's a small child here crying his eyes out. Whom does he belong to?"

The lady behind the counter came around the side and picked me up, saying, "I don't know who he belongs to, but he looks half starved!" Then when she kissed me with one of those wet, gooey kisses, I dropped the five pennies and blurted out, "All I want is a nickel's worth of yesterday's please."

She said, "Yesterday's cake? Oh, you must be one of the orphanage kids. I'll give you some cake, but first I've got to feed you. Here, put these pennies back in your pocket." She sat me down on the counter, then she began chucking little powdered cakes into my mouth. I ate as fast as I could, hoping she'd never stop. When she asked me if the cakes were good, I tried to talk but almost choked. The powder on the cakes was too much for me. Quickly she ran to fetch me a glass of milk.

While I was drinking the milk, I glanced out the window to

see how my buddies were doing. I could see the smoke coming out of their mouths and nostrils, it was that cold. Some of them were jumping up and down and shaking their fists at me, pleading for me to bring out the cake.

After I drank the milk and got passed around and kissed by all the women in the bakery, the nice lady who owned the bakery gave me a huge bag of cake. The bag was much larger than I was, and I knew that I couldn't carry it. I had to make a move fast, though, as the women were getting that kissy-kissy look again. They had started to gain on me when I mumbled, "Thanks" and, without trying to lift the bag, dragged it out to the street.

I became an instant hero in the peewee alcove. They had never seen so much cake before and for nothing. I still had the five pennies. The monitor carried the cake to the corner, and the kids dived into the bag. I don't know if the word *charisma* had been invented up till then, but I sure had something going for me. Even though I was the smallest kid, my advice was sought upon all matters. Naturally I always represented the Peewees in negotiating all major sales, whether they were in the bakery or the candy store.

The Storyteller

Listening to Mrs. De Sola's biblical stories must have stirred up something in my imagination. One very bad, rainy day, all the kids were just moping around, bored. I don't know what prompted me, but I suddenly said, "Anyone want to hear a story?" All the kids gathered around me and stared hungrily, waiting to be entertained. I started to tell a story about a little boy. I made it up as I went along and was quite surprised when the kids asked me to tell another story and then another.

Then when one of the kids asked me what the little boy's name was, I said, "Jimmy." Thus began the "Jimmy stories," and as I grew older, so did Jimmy. The kids never grew tired of hearing about Jimmy, the rich kid who had everything but wanted to help all the poor children in the world. Jimmy visited countries I had barely ever heard about, like Brooklyn and the Bronx. Whenever I got stuck for an idea, I'd say that I was tired and would finish the story the next day. By the next day, I would have forgotten what I had said the previous day and so would the other kids, so I'd tell a new story and no one knew the difference, not even me.

Years later, when my little son Peter would ask me to tell him a story, I would tell him a "Jimmy" story and he would be thrilled. This time Jimmy went to Africa and Egypt and China. Jimmy was all grown up now, and he could really get around.

Visiting Day

On Sundays we were allowed visitors. Then the entire orphanage would be a beehive of activity, with mothers, fathers, cousins, aunts, and uncles all over the place. It was a happy day of eating candy, cake, and fruit, and on those Sundays when my mom would visit the "H," I almost forgot I was in an orphanage.

My mother would come to see me first, and then later on we would both go over to the girls' side to visit my sister. Mom would usually arrive carrying two "Jewish packages." A "Jewish package" was the term we applied to packages of food, wonderful food, from home, whether it was brought to us or sent to us by mail. Pity the kid who didn't share his goodies with his friends, his monitor, and even his counselor. A "Jewish package" started with sandwiches, pickles, tomatoes, plenty of hard fruit, enough to last a week, candy, and cake. I can hardly remember many of the incidents that occurred in the orphanage but I sure remember every "Jewish package" my sister and I ever received. A "Jewish package" wasn't only food; it was love, it was remembering, it was belonging. Life in the home would have been nearly unbearable without them.

One Sunday my mother arrived with the beautiful two shopping bags, and I teased her a little by not running over to her immediately, as I usually did. Mom just stood there and finally I ran over, grinning ear to ear because she hadn't recognized me. Then I almost knocked her over by jumping into her arms and kissing her. Mom sadly explained that all the little boys were dressed alike and that's why she could never pick me out. I said, "Mom, all the kids have baldies. I'm the one with hair!"

It was true; all the other kids had their hair shaved off. That was something that, even though I was only a child, I just couldn't allow them to do to me. I came close many times, but somehow always managed to squirm out of having my head shaved.

When my mother visited on Sundays, all the peewees were happy. She was Mom to all of them, the same as their mothers were Mom to me. My mother would sit on one of the benches in the playroom, and all the kids in my alcove would gather around her. Each kid then received a sandwich and a pickle, and I would breathlessly await my turn. My mother always served me last, and I just couldn't understand it. One day I cried to her that she treated the other kids better than she did her own son. My little mother looked me right in the eyes and said something that rings in my ears to this day: "Always serve your friends, your guests, first when you have a party. Serve yourself last!" She also told me to take tiny bites of my pickle, because that way it lasts longer. To this day I am considered a wonderful host by all my friends. And it's true, if you take tiny bites of your pickle it lasts longer.

Once we went over to the girl's side, the party started all over again. My sister and her friends would have something to eat, and then Mom would divide all the food that was left over into two packages, one for my sister and one for myself. I got the better of the deal, though. I was always running short of candy and fruit, and being allowed on the girl's side, I could always hit my sis's locker for something to eat.

Mom loved to hear all the gossip from all the girls in my sister's group. Mom looked so young and was so small that she looked like one of the girls herself. I'd do my strutting around and load my pockets with candy from parents visiting the girl's side; after I allowed them to kiss me.

As poor as my mother was, she was always helping one of the girls with money problems or any way she could. I think the girls in my sister's group loved my mother more than anyone else they knew. Mom was a soft touch and had a sympathetic ear, and word got around to other groups and soon it was tough for me to get my mother's attention on the girls' side.

The one and only time in my life that I ever heard my mother raise her voice was on such a Sunday. The day started out as

25

Me at age eight on the lawn of the Hebrew Orphan Asylum.

usual. We were just sitting around talking when we all heard loud shouting from a distance. One of the older girls was having an argument with a counselor, a Miss Pratt, and their voices became quite agitated. I hid behind my mother and sister, thinking it was the end of the world.

Suddenly Miss Pratt struck the girl across the face. Before I knew it, my mom jumped into action like I never knew she could. She ran over to the counselor, raised her umbrella in a threatening gesture, and said, "You strike that child again, and I'll strike you. If I ever hear that you hit one of these children again, I'll report you!"

Miss Pratt, who was one of the senior or older counselors, knew how popular my mother was with all the girls, and she quickly walked away. Mom returned to us trembling and teary-eyed. All the girls surrounded Mom and hugged and kissed her, including me. I was so proud. My little mother, five feet small, couldn't stand to see any injustice perpetrated. Afterwards, the girls called Mom the Joan of Arc of the girl's side.

Upon reaching the age of sixteen, my sister, Ruth, had to leave the orphanage, as did all children reaching that age. She went to live with my mother in a tiny furnished room in the South Bronx. With heavy heart, I felt deserted by everyone I loved and whom I thought loved me, and it was then I first schemed to run away from the "H." I wanted to punish everyone I knew by disappearing and never coming back until I was a very rich man.

In the home, I was thought of as a shy quiet child who hardly ever had gotten into trouble. Sometimes I was led to it by other boys, but this was nothing to talk about. I was more a follower than a leader in my age group.

When another boy suggested running away to me, the plot was hatched. No sooner did we reach the Hamilton Grange Theatre on Broadway and 137th Street than the orphanage's house detective, elderly Pop Brady would catch us and lead us back. Out again, back again. Out again, et cetera.

All the while, word was getting back to my mother about this strange change in my nature. Finally, my sister, sensing I might hurt myself or really get lost, convinced my mother to take me out of the orphanage.

Mom just before she died.

I always looked back on the "H" with deep affection, fondness and gratitude. Also, some of the friendships I made then still exist to this day. One boy, Billy Cook, who was the very first boy I met as an infant in that first orphanage, was like a brother to me until he unfortunately passed on at too early an age.

I too joined my mother and sister in that tiny furnished room in the Bronx. The three of us slept in one bed, and Poor was our middle name. But we were proud and, more important, we were together.

Unfortunately, the pressures of daily living, hard work, worry, bad food, and two or more packs of cigarettes a day took its toll on my tiny, adorable, frail mother. In 1935, at the much too young age of forty-one, a week before mother's day, at the House of Calvary in Featherbed Lane in the Bronx, where the good sisters diligently cared for her, my mom passed away. Oedipus-shmoedipus, not a day goes by that I don't think of my mother, somehow, somewhere. Her tombstone reads: "An angel left this earth." My sister suggested *angel* for want of a better word.

"The Gentle Giant" at Pop Sprung Camp Fund reunion.

3

Carnival
(on Central Park South)

1935–38: President Roosevelt signs Social Security Act; Alcoholics Anonymous formed; Spanish Civil War begins; Amelia Earhart lost in Pacific; Jesse Owens wins four medals in Olympics; Max Schmeling knocks out Joe Louis; Hauptman convicted of killing Lindbergh baby; 20,000 television sets in service in New York City.

I ONCE THOUGHT there weren't too many redeeming features you could mention about "Broadway" Jack White. I take part of it back. Jack did help me get my very first job, other than the ones I had delivering clothes, fruit, and vegetables and hustling a little baseball game in public school. I don't consider the few days I spent in a perfume factory because I quit before I even got started.

Jack knew the superintendent of services at the Hotel St. Moritz here in New York City. At that time, it was known as the only international hotel in New York City. That meant that very few people who checked into the hotel spoke English. The guests were mostly from Greece, with a sprinkling from all over the world. The two owners were Charles and Gregory Taylor, wealthy Greeks who knew the Skouras family, Archbishop Athinagoras, champion wrestler Jimmy Londos, and any and every Greek and or half-Greek who was a celebrity or who had plenty of money. I met all of these people, and the friendships lasted only while I worked for the hotel.

The dean or warden of this establishment was a Mr. Bobby Blair, "Broadway" Jack White's friend. Mr. Blair was once a bellhop himself. He was now supervisor of bellhops, page boys, elevator operators, and lobby personnel for the very distinguished Hotel St. Moritz.

Jack had called Mr. Bobby Blair and asked if he could give his son a job, any job. Mr. Blair said he hadn't known my father had a son. I showed up at the designated time, in the basement of the hotel, where they kept the lockers. There were eight other kids there waiting to be interviewed, mostly a little older than myself.

My heart beat like a hammer, and I actually forgot my name when Bobby asked me for it. He looked at me strangely, and then he loudly asked what size shoe I wore. After he briefly spoke to each kid, he said, "Okay, that's it. You can all leave now except White. I'm sorry, but there's only one job and one pair of shoes that goes with the uniform and it's in White's size."

After the kids all left, Bobby assigned a locker to me and fitted me out with a beautiful white summer uniform. He told me to wait at the locker until the page boy on duty came down to explain all my duties. Bobby was so kind that I looked on him as a father figure and shyly asked for the shoes. He said, "What shoes?" I told him that he had mentioned the shoes' being in my size. Without smiling—Bobby never smiled—he said "Hey, kid, do you want the job or don't you? There's no shoes. I only said that to get you the job, 'ya understand!"

My friend Mr. Bobby Blair is still alive. He's in his eighties and working as the registration clerk at The Edison Hotel in New York City.

At that time of my life, I was living in a three-dollar-a-week rooming house on 160th Street and Fort Washington Avenue in Harlem. The only little joy in my life was a weekly note I received from the young girl who cleaned my room, which was smaller than a walk-in closet. The room was so narrow that I could spread my arms and touch both walls. The bathroom, down the hall, was for everyone's use on my floor. I would always stand outside the bathroom door whistling, just to let someone inside know that I was waiting to use the room. One day an old man came out and said, "Son, don't you know any song other than 'Yankee Doodle'?"

The light in my room was a tiny, dull bulb that threw hardly any light at all. My roommate was dust! The cleaning girl did her best, but in her notes she complained that cleaning two floors was too much for her. She always signed off with "Love 'ya, Ellen." This was another sad and lonely part of my life, but somehow that little note from Ellen kept me going. I imagined that she truly loved me, and I knew that I felt love for her, although I had never met her. I had a child's illusion that someday I would be rich and Ellen wouldn't have to work so hard and we would live on a farm, with chickens, horses, and cows. And I had never even seen *Of Mice and Men*.

My pay at the St. Moritz was nine dollars every ten days, plus any tips that came my way. I ate the cheapest kind of food, never a balanced diet. Breakfast was a Nedick's hot dog and an orange drink. At least once a month, I would get these attacks—an upset stomach, profuse sweating, and my eyes growing terribly weak. I could hardly see except for little white stars or flakes, and I'd feel extreme nausea. Standing on my feet all day was rough on my light frame. I only weighed around 107 pounds at the time and looked horribly thin. At night I would pour my heart out in a note that I would leave for Ellen. Her answers sustained me and she attributed the attacks I was having to the poor diet I had known as a child. I promised her I would eat more vegetables and drink milk. I tried to keep my promise, but manchild that I was and the aftermath of the orphanage, I would continue to eat all the wrong things, still wolfing everything down quickly. I still sometimes eat too quickly, I am told.

Going to work at first frightened me. What would I say to all those important people? After "Hello," I was stuck. And the thought of looking people in the eyes scared me half to death. It was all so terribly painful, but I had to work to keep myself going.

Thank God Bobby Blair was very understanding and fatherly toward me. He advised me on grooming, what to say, and how to look at people, and he always said, "Eddie, you're gonna be all right." He advised me always to take my valuables, not to leave them in the locker. My valuables? All I ever had was a skate key, a Tootsie roll, around forty cents, and the key to my furnished room.

The second day I was there, Bobby introduced me to a gentleman who became more than a father to me. He became my psychiatrist, my banker, my business advisor, my ace in the hole whenever my tiny world came crashing down around me, my everything! The man was Eddie Healy, chief bell captain and a saintly guy if ever there was one. Eddie was a hip ex-vaudevillian with a twinkle in his eyes and his feet and a heart as big as County Cork. The stories he would tell, about the time when he was on the road, doing one-night stands and true or not, I would go home and dream about being like Eddie Healy.

Eddie's brother was Dan Healy, another ex-vaudevillian and considered at that time to be The Unofficial Mayor of Broadway. Dan Healy did an act with comedian Eddie Garr at that time, and being so close to Eddie Healy, I imagined I was part of the entire vaudevillian family: Eddie Garr's baby daughter, Terri Garr, is all grown up now, and she has appeared in *Close Encounters of the Third Kind* and Mel Brooks's hysterical film *Frankenstein*. Without Eddie Healy, I was lost!

As I said, the St. Moritz Hotel in the thirties was owned by Charles and Gregory Taylor, Greek brothers who had struck it rich in America. The kitchens, dining rooms, Cafe de la Paix, and Rumplemeyer's were staffed with Greeks. Picture a young sixteen-year-old lad trying to stroll through the kitchens, as I had to do on occasion. I was half raped more than once. Eddie Healy had to come to my rescue more than once. Eddie explained what was happening, and I just couldn't or wouldn't accept the things he told me. "You mean that men actually liked other men that way?"

I didn't really believe that story until one day I was called to Room 1225, occupied by a renowned songwriter. This man was in his shorts when I arrived, and he asked me if I could get his prescription filled. I told him that I was only the page boy and couldn't leave the hotel without special permission. Whereupon he threw me on the bed and jumped on top of me. I let out an Indian yelp, squirmed out of his grasp, and ran out the door. I was so frightened that I ran down twelve flights of stairs, jumping a flight at a time.

I ran up to Eddie Healy and screamed, "Mr.——tried to kiss me! He threw me on the bed and . . . " Eddie grabbed me, held his hand over my mouth, and carried me down to the locker

33

room like a bundle of laundry. He calmed me down and then explained the facts of life to me.d It was no joke; now I believed him about what had almost happened to me in the kitchens, in the movies sometimes, and on the subway many times.

"Eddie, you mean these guys are all sissies?" Eddie said yes, there were some men who preferred other men to kiss and make love to. Now that I recall, he never told me there were women who preferred other women for the same purpose, but that wasn't my problem at the time.

I had other encounters of the weird kind at the St. Moritz Hotel, over and over again. That songwriter never left me alone for a second. He promised me a house in California and showed me pictures of himself and Robert Taylor, Barbara Stanwyck, Jack Benny, Mary Livingston, and many other stars. He tried to entice me to his room with money, and once he offered me a new car. I told him that I was only sixteen and couldn't drive and wasn't old enough to have a license.

Once he confronted me in the lobby while I was standing my post and said, "Edward, why are you avoiding me" and actually stamped his foot. He said, "I want to buy you many things and make your life easier. I truly care for you, Edward, and I can see in your eyes that you care for me." Naively I started to cry, "Please leave me alone. I'm going to lose my job if you talk to me on my post. Please." He embarrassed me by wiping my eyes; then he asked me to blow my nose into his handkerchief and said, "I won't bother you anymore, dear boy, but I want to show you something you'll be missing."

He took out a rolled-up music score from his inside coat pocket and I saw the title. This songwriter offered me two tickets to see a preview of his new movie at the Roxy Theater. Instinctively I refused, and he never bothered me again.

A few days later, I went to the Roxy and saw the movie on my day off. I went to the first show, as I could get in for a quarter and then I could get to work for my shift at the hotel. I never made it to work that day!

When the star of the film came on that screen for the first time and sang the title song, I was hooked. Actually the voice was that of a singer and the man I saw was only doing lip syn-

34

chronization. Regardless, I went ape and then and there I knew I was going to be a songwriter. I stayed in the Roxy Theater all day and couldn't sleep for a week. I could write. I always wrote short stories and poems, so why not songs? *Hey, if that sissy can do it, I can*, I thought. Little did I realize that one day I would be writing songs for Frank Sinatra, Rosemary Clooney, Tony Bennett, Pearl Bailey, Patti Page, Sarah Vaughan, and many others. Boy, life is a circus and it sure is fun!

I had many other experiences at the St. Moritz, some funny, some memorable and thrilling, and some sad. It was growing-up time. For then the St. Moritz was the big tent and I was learning all about life. Wanting to be a songwriter gave me newfound ambition, a zest for living I had never experienced before. I actually thrived on the thought. I grew taller, put on a few badly needed pounds, and actually got some color into my pale cheeks. I told everyone, "I'm going to be a songwriter. How do you like them apples?" I felt like people looked at me differently, and I kept glowing and growing.

The St. Moritz service crew. That's Bobby Blair on the extreme left. I'm fourth from the left.

Then one day I got a call to go to John Barrymore's room. I kept it a secret, afraid one of the bellhops would take this assignment away from me, but they were too busy at the time. When I knocked I could hear my heart knocking, too. Mr. Barrymore opened the door and he was in his shorts. *Please, dear Lord, not again*, I prayed. Mr. Barrymore asked me my name, and I could tell he had had a few drinks in him. Then he asked me if I could get him a Nova Scotia sandwich on pumpernickel bread with a thin slice of onion and a smidgeon of butter. I asked him if he wanted something to drink. Like Shylock in *The Merchant of Venice*, he crouched down low, rubbed his hands together, and with that unmistakable wide-eyed, maniacal Barrymore look he said, "Son, I have plenty of spirits on hand, at least until those two prison guards return."

Mr. Barrymore lived in a suite at the hotel as sort of a hostage. His girl friend, or possibly his wife at that time, was Elaine Barrie. Their escapades and arguments hit the papers often, but I don't think Mr. Barrymore knew about it or even cared. He was always mellow with drink, but polite to a fault and always very kind. Elaine Barrie's mother lived in the suite, too, and I got the feeling that the two women had taken Mr. Barrymore's clothes away so he couldn't leave the hotel on his own.

Many an hour I spent with Mr. Barrymore, telling him about the orphanage, my dreams of being a songwriter, and my prowess as an athlete. He told me many things, mainly how he hated Hollywood and the people he had to endure, about his good friend Joe Mankiewicz, and about his misspent youth. He even talked about his drinking problem and how he thought he could shake the habit someday. Sometimes something I would say would trigger him to go into a Shakespearean recitation and I would be in seventh heaven. Who would ever believe me? He treated me as an equal, and I loved him for it.

Then he would say, "Prince Edward, it's time to fetch me some repaste. Make haste before the witches return." Once or twice Ms. Barrie would be in the room and would try to take the bag out of my hands. I stood fast even though she threatened to have me fired. I had to give the sandwich to Mr. Barrymore personally. He was my very special friend, he called me Prince Valiant many times, and I had to prove that I was valiant and

36

loyal to King Richard. Years later I tried to help John Barrymore, Jr., by suggesting him as an actor for a film, but I was told that he was "strung out," a junkie, unreliable. They said he wouldn't appreciate my help and surely wouldn't show up on the set. I had suggested Barrymore, Jr., because I felt he was a fine actor, which he was. I haven't seen him in a film for years now, and I just hope he is all right.

When I reached seventeen, I was still a page boy at the St. Moritz Hotel. As a page boy, it was my job to call people to the phone, deliver messages or telegrams, and generally do anything that the bellhops couldn't or didn't want to do. As I said, I earned nine dollars every ten days, plus any tips I was lucky enough to inveigle.

At your service—page boy Eddie White at age sixteen.

A gentleman living at the hotel then was a famous impresario, man about town, producer, and cheapskate. Every day I would deliver his mail and any packages that would accumulate in the mailroom. Never did he give me a tip; nor did I ever ask for one. Then I heard the bellhops talking about foreign people thinking there was a service charge on their bills and therefore it wasn't necessary to tip for services rendered. I mentioned this to my pal Eddie Healy and told him about this famous man's never tipping me. Eddie said that he was a known cheapskate and that I should tell him I didn't get paid by the hotel and that I worked for tips.

It was Christmas week when I delivered a load of packages to the impresario's room. *Why should he tip me? I'm nobody to him*, I thought. *He's so cheap that he even washes his own long underwear and socks.* They were hanging over the shower curtain, I noticed.

Suddenly he walked into the room with his then girl friend. I started to rearrange the packages, and with my back to him I blurted out, "Merry Christmas. I just brought you your mail and these packages. I hate to mention this to you, but we page boys don't get paid well by the hotel and we depend on tips." That was the longest speech I had ever made in my life up till then.

I was scared stiff and was sure Bobby Blair would fire me if he ever found out what I had said. Something told me it wasn't right to ask for a tip. I tried to get out of the room quickly, as I was sure my face was red as a beet when the man said, "Here, boy, take this for now" and handed me a dime. I closed the door and just stood there hurt. All this anguish for a dime. I had seen how bellhops acted when they felt they were undertipped. They would say, "Here's your quarter back; you need it more than I do!" I didn't have that kind of courage. I also saw bellhops throw change under a door and let out a few epithets. I did the latter without cursing. I just threw the dime under the door and ran down the stairs to the lobby. I was too frightened to wait for the elevator. I never looked at the man again, never delivered his messages or mail. I just plain refused and I didn't get fired. All those months of delivering things to this great man and receiving one thin dime.

There were other people living at the hotel who were more

generous. There was a nice lady, Ms. Eleanor Smith, who was Ben Bernie's secretary. She was good for a quarter always, whether I did anything for her or not. She always asked about my health, if I have been reading any good books, and if I was happy. She always showed a personal interest in me, and that made me feel good.

Then there was Martha Raye, in the midst of a big buildup from the motion-picture and recording studios. She was still in her teens when I met her, and she was very pretty, with a figure close to a 10. Her brother, Buddy, was my pal, and I spent many hours in their penthouse. He died very young and I never found out how or why.

Every night Martha would come back to the hotel raving about this guy she had met at The Famous Door. She was crazy about him. His name was Louie Prima and he was breaking it up on 52nd Street with his frenetic act. Who would dream that someday I would write a song for Louie Prima and Keely Smith, "I'm Mashugga for My Sugar," that would kill them in Las Vegas. Louie and Keely recorded the song on Capitol Records, but they soon broke up their marriage and business association.

There was a nice lady with melancholy eyes and voice, Wini Shaw, who was good to one and all. They called her "The Lady in Red"—I guess, for the song she made famous. Ms. Shaw was tall, dark, and stunning. When she walked across the lobby, you couldn't take your eyes off of her.

Then there was this character out of Damon Runyon and The Dukes of Amboy, "Broadway" Sam Roth. It was my duty to bring him a boutonniere every morning and to help him dress. He was only good for a dime a day, but he was a good natured, incredible hulk, built like a hot tubful of Jell-o. He told me stories about what was going on in and around Broadway, who was going with whom, the lowdown on all the ball games and players, and most times I couldn't understand a word he was saying. I think he was a ticket speculator, as he knew which shows were going to survive and which ones were closing. They don't make 'em like "Broadway" Sam Roth anymore; he was a genuine fourteen-carat New York character.

One of the funniest incidents that happened to me was the time I had to bring the papers up to a suite on one of the higher floors. I was going off duty and was in a hurry to get out of my uniform. I knocked on the door, and a little man, just about my size, answered. I forgot that I was in a hurry; here was a man as small as I was. I was intrigued. He asked me if I could get him some food, and I took the time to run a few trivial errands for him. We became friends, but I could never get his name straight.

One day this gentleman asked me if I had ever seen a concert and I said no. Whereupon he gave me two tickets for that evening's performance of the New York Philharmonic at Carnegie Hall. It was summer and I hadn't worn a jacket to work that day. As a matter of fact, I had worn a sweater with a large "M" on the front, probably for James Monroe, although I only got to the first year of high school and had only spent a few weeks at the school.

I called a girl cousin of mine and invited her to the concert. We arrived at Carnegie Hall early, as we had nowhere to go or hang out, two sixteen-year-old kids with time on our hands. We were shown to the stairs and then escorted to the very first box on the first tier. We were all alone in Carnegie Hall for what seemed like hours, so I started to do my imitations of all the crooners around at that time, Crosby, Perry Como, Vaughn Monroe, and the like. An elderly lady came by and told me to hush up or get out.

Just then four other people looked through the door of the first box. Seeing them, my cousin and I made a beeline for the first seats in the box. Then the hall started filling up and we felt like we had company and the show would start soon.

Eventually the conductor tapped the music stand and the orchestra played an overture. The music was so different from anything I had ever heard, I was enraptured and fell in love with classical music instantly. It was love at first sight! Or sound!

At the end of the overture, the conductor was taking his bows when he looked directly up at our box and gently bowed. I almost fell out of the box. All eyes in Carnegie Hall were on me and my cousin. Everyone was nicely dressed and here I was wearing a sweater, looking like Joe Freshman from God knows where.

It was then I recognized who the conductor was. I screamed to my cousin, "That's my friend. That's my friend what's-his-name?" Most people smiled and I just hoped that they realized

40

that these were two young kids who had never seen a concert or the inside of Carnegie Hall before. I quickly looked at the program notes and found out that my friend, the man who was my size and who was so very kind to me, was Sir John Barbarolli, the world-renowned symphonic conductor. Years later, in 1963, I was to produce a three-day concert at Carnegie Hall, The Soul of Japan, featuring the top stars from Japan. I couldn't help but walk backstage during rehearsals of my concert and say a humble prayer of thanks to a little man who had a big heart and a bigger talent, Sir John Barbarolli. At my concerts, I wore a three-piece suit with a letter on my shirt cuff, but deep inside I was still that little kid sitting in that first box full of mixed emotions.

Twice while on hotel lobby duty I was beaten up by men for fooling around with their girl friends. It was mistaken identity. I can still hear Eddie Healy say, "He's only a kid. Why did you hit him?" And the guy who slugged me on the chin would say, "Oh my God, I made a mistake. Yeah, he's only a kid. Excuse me, kid. Here, let me help you up. I'm sorry." The second time this happened I tried to grow a mustache, but it's tough when when you have only three milk hairs on each side of your lip. I used a black pencil, but Bobby Blair ordered me to wash my face.

A few times I had to wake people up in the morning because they didn't answer their phones after they had left a request for a wake-up call. I would take the double-lock key just in case they didn't hear me knock. Well, let me tell you, that was an experience. Once I found a young girl who had slashed her wrists and was lying nude on the bathroom floor. I almost jumped down twenty flights of stairs in one leap. When I was told to go back and look to make sure the lady was dead, I told them, "You look! I'm going home." And I had been on duty for less than a half an hour.

Another time I had to walk into a dark suite and I found no one in the rooms. I don't know what got into me, but I opened a closet and almost left this earth at that second. A guy had hung himself in one of those walk-in closets. Why these people ever left wake-up calls is beyond me. I used to think it was just to upset me personally. But then I was just seventeen.

Then I fell in love again. A famous vaudeville star, Yvette Rugel, had her daughter visiting. As soon as I saw Mary Dooley

I was smitten. She was also the daughter of the great banjo player Eddie Dooley. I tried everything to attract her attention. I stood in front of her when she walked by and did that little hesitation step, not knowing which way to pass. I brought her her mail, letter by letter, minute by minute. I called from the lobby asking her if she needed anything. I sent her one rose every few days, which I got for nothing from the florist, and signed the card "Guess who?" She never guessed. Even though we were the same age, she treated me as if I were less than a termite. *Oh, well, I'll be big and famous someday; I'll show her.* That was exactly what I thought at that time.

If it wasn't for the girls in Rumpelmeyer's, I would have withered away. They had the most delectable cakes on display in the center of the dining room. As I was unusually thin, most of the girls who worked there agreed that I was to be fed at least once a day. They would pack up a box of napoleons and eclairs and a drink, and I would hike up to the telephone room and bother the girls up there. They all thought I was cute and funny, and I usually brought news and gossip from the lobby, front desk, and bar. It broke up a boring day, and we all got something out of the relationship. We would exchange presents around Christmas, and I got a lot of love from the telephone girls. I felt like I was part of a little family. To hear the screams of glee when I walked into that room was good for my morale. Oh, the uniform helped, but General MacArthur never received such a warm welcome.

And those guys who taught me the facts of life, the bellhops and page boys and porters and doormen. The St. Moritz may not have been the Massachusetts Institute of Technology, but it was high school and college to me. And more! I really never went further than the eighth grade, but I doubt if you can learn more about life than by working in a large hotel in Manhattan.

First there was Bobby Blair who took me under his wing. Then came Eddie Healy, who was so patient until I caught on to things. Then those other guys who all took up the slack when I needed them, Bill "Moose" Jenkins, Irish Pat Tracy, Johnny Lantigua, Timmy Crowley, Jimmy Cunningham, and fellow page boy Oscar Menendez, and then there was genial co—bell captain Harry Bartosch, who hardly ever smiled but never raised his voice. He was a little distant, but an intelligent man who left well enough alone. When Harry found fault with me, I jumped! Whereas with Eddie Healy I strolled. Yet no one ever gave me any trouble.

No one but Oscar Menendez, my fellow page boy. One day I found all the telegrams gone on an Easter Sunday. We page boys were supposed to share everything, fifty-fifty. If I couldn't deliver any telegrams, how could I earn any tips? I followed Oscar to the penthouse floor, on another elevator that I ran myself, and caught him with a pile of telegrams stuffed inside his uniform jacket. I didn't make a scene; I just told him to follow me to the elevator I worked, and then I closed the door. I asked him to explain how he wound up with all the telegrams, and he said, "Okay, okay, amigo. I fight you for them."

Well, this was a stroke of luck. I had just entered a youth program and was a pitcher on the softball team and a boxer at 108 pounds. In thirty-one fights, I had had thirty decisions and one draw. (That one draw was a fight that was stopped because my opponent was hurt real bad. I hit him a lucky shot in the neck. They thought he was done for, so to bring him back to life they declared a draw. He was okay real fast. If we won or drew, we received baseball gloves or softballs. I had to give most of the stuff away; my room was too small.)

I told Oscar Menendez to put all the telegrams on the elevator floor, and we took off our jackets. I never fought anyone as fast or knew anyone as knowledgeable about boxing as Oscar Menendez. After he beat the bejabbers out of me, he said, "Here, let's split the telegrams, amigo. You're okay."

A few days later, when my lip and eye had healed, I asked Oscar where he learned to fight. He nonchalantly said, "In the gym. With my brother, Baby Menendez. I'm his sparring partner." Baby Menendez was a ranking featherweight at that time, and I had to pick a fight with his kid brother. I made sure that Oscar Menendez and I were close amigos from then on.

During the summer months, the Skyroom up on the roof of the St. Moritz Hotel was open to the public. One day I delivered a telegram to a guy they called The Singing Cop, Phil Regan. Phil had actually been a cop at one time, but now he was trying to make it in show business. He was quite popular and I asked him for an autograph. He pinched my cheek, gave me a buck, and introduced me to his drinking buddies: "This is Mr. Ernest Hemingway, Mr. Broderick Crawford, meet Mr. Wallace Ford, and this is Mr. Quentin Reynolds." I couldn't believe it. Boy, I wish I had been old enough to drink with those guys. Years later I found out that Wallace Ford had been brought up in an orphanage and I'm sure that if I knew it then I could have stayed with those guys longer and discussed world conditions. But Mr. Regan gave me a dollar; that was almost four tips in one. It was unusual for a page boy to get a dollar tip.

Some months later, Mr. Regan's daughter got married and a batch of telegrams came into the hotel. I got this bright idea. *If he gave me a dollar for just one telegram . . .* I began figuring. I went up to his suite with one telegram, the rest tucked into my uniform jacket. I was on duty all by myself so there was no Oscar Menendez to bother me.

Mr. Regan cheerfully took the telegram and gave me a dollar. I waited on the stair landing for a few moments and then knocked on his door again. Again he cheerfully thanked me and handed me another dollar. The third time I pulled the stunt, Mr. Regan said, "Look, Eddie. I'll give you five bucks if you hand over all the telegrams." Sheepishly I opened my jacket and handed them all over to The Singing Cop, Mr. Phil Regan. He was a gentleman; he handed me the five dollars with "You're okay Eddie. No harm in trying."

If I was ever going to drink with my friend Phil Regan and his friends, I had better learn how to drink, I figured. I told all the bellhops about my predictment, and they took me around the corner to the neighborhood bar. "Moose" Jenkins was in charge of watching over me for this occasion, and he ordered "a small beer for a small boy!" While Moose, Jimmy Crowley, and Pat Tracy watched, I tried to nonchalantly drink my first beer. It must have taken me a half-hour to get that funny-tasting liquid down the hatch. One drink, one little beer, and I was king of the hill. I laughed at nothing in particular and told them how I had beaten Oscar Menendez to the punch and how those guys in the kitchen had better watch out because, I was carrying a knife now.

When it was time to go back on duty again, I started to leave the bar stool and the floor came up and hit me right on the jaw. I couldn't move my arms or legs and had to be carried down to the locker room, where I fell asleep on a bench. Moose made us all swear not to tell Eddie Healy, as "there would be the bejesus to pay!" I never said anything, I was too sick to talk for about ten days.

Years later, when I had become a flying officer in the air force, I checked into the St. Moritz Hotel just to get the feeling out of my system. Eileen in accounting asked me if I wanted to stay on the cuff or maybe I wanted a rate. I told her I wanted to pay the going rate. I just wanted to have some fun with the gang, and maybe in my heart I wanted to show off a little. I had traded one uniform in for another, but it was just like old times. We had booze and great food, and everyone I knew in the hotel came by to toast the "kid who won the war." After a few drinks, I really began to believe that MacArthur and Patton couldn't have done it without 1st Lt. Eddie White. As the boys were all leaving and saying goodnight, Eddie Healy grabbed me in a bear hug and said, "I'm real proud of you, Eddie. To think when I first met you, you weighed less than a hundred pounds and you didn't know if the sky was up or down." Then he kissed me. In my stupor I said, "Ed, I hope you're not turning into one of them sissies."

4

"Good-Bye, Dear
(I'll Be Back in a Year)"

1940: World War II; Chamberlain resigns; Churchhill becomes prime minister; Dunkirk; U.S. mobilizes, FDR selected for third time; Garbo's last film is released; Citizen Kane is produced.

THE YEAR WAS 1940 and all of Europe was in flames. Hitler's armies were rolling over the Balkan countries, and Mussolini was beginning to flex his military muscle in Greece. There was talk that President Roosevelt might institute a draft in the United States, starting with men from the Civilian Conservation Corps.

At this time of my life, I was truly alone, very confused, and full of fear. Not that I had any family to speak of, but I had had a terrible argument with my sister. My job at the McAlpin Hotel newsstand was degrading, and on top of that, my boss wouldn't allow me to go to night school. "Always concentrate on your work. If you don't want to do that, then quit and go to school. It can't be both!" My boss, Mr. Bert Flasch, was a nice guy, but he just didn't understand. How could I get anywhere in this life without some sort of an education?

My closetlike furnished room now up on West 98th Street was beginning to close in on me. Anything was better than this. I made up my mind to volunteer for the forthcoming draft. For days I went to work, my body and mind completely out of synchronization. People spoke to me, but I could hardly hear. Now I just couldn't wait to completely change my life-style. I thought, *Somewhere out there is a grand adventure waiting for me, and I'm so ready.*

The very day they announced the regulations dealing with the draft and the address of my local draft board, I showed up. Three or four kindly elderly gentlemen looked me over, asked me a few questions, and then laughed. They said it was much too early to volunteer, I should think it over, and if I still wanted to volunteer, they gave me a time and date. One old man made a remark about my being too thin, meaning I should try to put on some weight.

As I was leaving, one of the men, with a face like Judge Hardy in the Mickey Rooney movies, asked me if I wanted to volunteer for the army or the navy. I said I hadn't thought about it, and he suggested the navy, winking at me and saying, "You get better food in the navy. I know. I was a navy man myself." Then he showed me his navy ring from World War I.

That week I dreamed about the navy and the new adventure-to-be in my heretofore humdrum life. I thought those uniforms, which I never liked until now, weren't so bad. I could get used to them. I told my boss that I was quitting in a week to enter the navy, and to my surprise he was very sympathetic. Mr. Flasch had originally come from Germany, and the war and America's military buildup somehow saddened and frightened him. He had a few little prejudices, but he hated what Hitler had done to Germany and to the rest of Europe. He predicted that Hitler would come to a bad end.

Mr. Flasch gave me a week's severance pay, eighteen dollars. He also took me to lunch and treated me very warmly, almost affectionately. A Jewish kid and his German boss. He told me he was sorry for making me quit night school, but those were the orders he had received from his boss. After lecturing me on life in general and giving me a few pointers on how to conduct myself in the navy, he told me to go out and enjoy myself. I didn't have to go to work anymore; I had the week off. I had never felt such exhilaration. I kissed Mr. Flasch, thanked him, sent regards to his wife and daughter, and was off.

Off to where? I roamed the city, going from one movie to the next. Sometimes I saw three double features in one day, six movies in all, not to mention the short features, the newsreels, and the coming attractions. I was saying good-bye to New York City. Some days I would start out by walking from my furnished rooming house on West 98th Street all the way down to Battery Park and then back again. I would always stop at Grant's on West 42nd Street for a couple of their special hot dogs and a kosher pickle. For fifteen cents I had a feast.

My good buddy Stanley Adams threw a farewell chow-and-beer party for me at his father's restaurant on West 33rd Street, across the street from the back entrance to the McAlpin Hotel. I drank my first martini that night and vaguely remember Stanley mugging it up behind the bar, telling jokes, juggling bottles, which he sometimes dropped, and insulting customers. (This was long before Don Rickles.) Stanley was the funniest man I had ever met then and continued to be the funniest throughout my entire life. Later in life, this fat, lovable clown was to go to Hollywood as one of the writers on the "My Friend Irma" and "Life with Luigi" radio shows. Still later, Uncle Stanley, as almost everyone who knew him affectionately called him, was to become a fine actor. He appeared in many noteworthy films, such as *Lilies of the Field*, playing Sidney Poitier's pal; *Requiem for a Heavyweight*, playing Parelli, the wrestling promoter; and *Breakfast at Tiffany's*, with Audrey Hepburn. Uncle Stanley also appeared in films with Robert Taylor and Mickey Rooney. He was known as a character actor and was sometimes called The Jewish Thomas Gomez or The Jewish Gabby Hayes.

Uncle Stanley took his life, with a gun, in Hollywood in 1977. I don't think a week of my life goes by that I don't think of my dear friend, fat, lovable, affectionate, terribly funny, and very talented Stanley Adams.

They told me that I had another martini at Uncle Stanley's bon voyage party for me, but I can't recall ever drinking two martinis or how I ever got back to my little furnished room on West 98th Street. I do remember that I slept the entire next day and part of the day after that. If the liquor business ever depended on me for a living, they'd go broke.

I spent part of the next few days hanging around Tin Pan Alley, as it was generally know—the Brill Building in particular on West 49th Street. I tried to sell a few of my songs, but it was no luck, as usual. Lunching at the old Turf Restaurant with guys who talked music, lyrics, and such made me feel like I belonged to a very special breed or club.

Some of the real old-time songwriters like Al ("Peg O' My Heart") Bryan and Irving ("Tea for Two") Caesar had seen me so often they almost accepted me as one of themselves. They would kid me about one of my antiwar songs, "We Won't Go Over (Till It's Over, Over There)." Now that I was going into the navy, what kind of songs would I write? I told them I had two prepared already, "Let's Put the Ax to the Axis" and "There's No Yellow in the Red, White, and Blue." Al Bryan told me the story of how he had written a song titled "I Didn't Raise My Boy to be a Soldier" during World War I and the U.S government got after him to get the song out of the public eye. They felt the song was killing the morale and the entire war effort. So the song was pulled and Mr. Bryan then wrote a song titled "I Raised My Boy to Be a Soldier (in the Army of the Lord)."

Just once more he asked me to sing the lyrics to "We Won't Go Over," and I did. It went something like this:

> Oh, we won't go over
> Till it's over, over there!
> It's none of our business.
> It's their affair,
> Why should our sons on foreign soil roam,
> Away from their jobs and away from home?
> If you're one of those
> Who thinks it's better to yield,
> Think of our boys who lie
> In Flanders Field.
> We're telling them, "No,
> It just isn't fair!"
> Oh, we won't go over
> Till it's over, over there!

Now that I read these lyrics and think back, I am embarrassed, but Mr. Al Bryan, writer of so many great songs, part of the history of Americana, told me that it was clever. He said I was a great "idea" man and should keep writing during and after my service years. I think he was just being nice to me, a young, struggling songwriter. I admired Mr. Bryan for his talent, but another thing I remembered about him: In his nineties, he was living with a young woman in her twenties. A few times he introduced me to her, and she was quite pretty. What a guy Al Bryan was! I remember hoping that I had a little of his talent and some of his energy. In his nineties, he was making plans for the next twenty years. What a guy.

A couple of the wise-guy songwriters, after hearing my song, suggested that I might do better as a comedy writer. For some reason, they laughed at everything I said or did, even when I was trying to be serious. They thought I was a little flaky. One day, in the not too distant future, I would return to that very same Brill Building. Those same wise guys didn't laugh when my partner Mack Wolfson and I signed a songwriter's contract with Paramount Pictures right alongside Burt Bacharach and Hal David. They didn't laugh when Mack and I opened our own music publishing and personal management office next door to Frank Sinatra's office. Truth is certainly stranger . . .

The day before I was to report to the armory for my physical examination, leading to my induction into the navy, a sort of ecstatic euphoria came over me. After all, I asked myself, what was I leaving behind? Nothing but a meaningless job, a lousy furnished closet for a room, a rotten existence. The navy would mean a new start, nice, clean clothes, good food, an education, a new experience, new friends, an adventure. It just couldn't be nearly as bad as my life was then.

That night I packed my few worldly possessions and asked my landlady, who was from the island of Malta, to please save them for me. I told her I'd surely be back to claim the cardboard box in a year. After all, I had volunteered for just 1 year, 52 weeks, 365 days. The sweet innocence of youth. I wasn't to return for 4 years, 11 months, and 10 days.

I can recall that the only things I treasured in my little cardboard box that I had left with my landlady were my autographed picture of John Barrymore and a terribly worn pair of brown riding boots. I did try to find that nice lady, whose name I can't recall, after the war, but she had died mysteriously and no one in the neighborhood could hardly remember her or her family's whereabouts. I went to the post office but got the same answer.

Finally the big morning arrived. I reported to Draft Board

Number 28, and the nice, elderly ex–Navy man gave us all carfare and instructions on how to get to the armory for our physicals and induction. He told us that our names were in the newspapers and we were heroes. After all, we were the very first inductees in the 1940 draft. On the way down to the armory, I picked up a *New York Post* and the headline read: "GREEKS TAKE KORITZA; ITALY ADMITS BIG LOSSES" and there on the front page was a list of volunteers for the initial draft. I looked for draft Board Number 28, and there was my name heading the list. I thought this would probably be the only time I would ever come first in anything. I also read in the paper something that I hadn't known or probably had forgotten. The day I was inducted was Thanksgiving Day, 1940.

No time to feel blue or melancholy, we had to get our asses over to the induction armory. When we arrived, all hell broke loose. The place looked like Dante's Inferno. Hundreds of men in all manner of undress were waiting to be processed. It was pure mayhem. After roaming around trying to find someone who would direct us to the correct place, we were finally given our physical papers to be filled out and a number and directed to undress in the locker room. Then it was a series of getting on different lines. It was weird. I kept holding my shorts in front of me, as if anyone cared.

The first doctor, who examined my throat, eyes, nose, and ears, said everything was okay. The second doctor examined my unmentionables and gave me thumbs up and a wink. I felt a little funny about that.

Then I was weighed in and noticed the doctor shaking his head in disbelief. He consulted with another doctor and said, "Son, you're twenty-one, stand five-foot-eight, and you only weigh in at barely 117 pounds. What's wrong with you?" He gave me my papers still shaking his head.

As I headed for the next doctor, I noticed a pencil on the table. I could still see the doctor who had weighed me looking in my direction. I just knew I couldn't go back to that furnished room—with no job now—to face Uncle Stanley and tell him I had flunked out or whatever. I was thinking of joining the French

51

Foreign Legion, but I was probably underweight for them, too.

That pencil on the table got bigger and bigger in my mind. The doctor was intent on examining some guy's teeth, and now no one was looking at me. I took a deep breath, felt a stab in my heart, and grabbed the pencil, talking out loud. "Hey, guys, they got my birthdate all wrong on this form." With a prayer I changed my weight to read 127 pounds. There, it was easy. In one second I gained ten pounds. I merely made the 1 into a 2. Whenever I told this story in the service, the guys would say I was the only jerk fighting to get into uniform.

The rest of my physical was mere routine, a breeze. Then we were told to assemble before a distinguished-looking official. I was given the serial number 32000109. I think that meant that there were only 109 guys who had beaten me into the service that very first day of the draft. We were then solemnly sworn into the United States Army. A leader was assigned to us, and we were told to report to Penn Station and take the train to Fort Dix.

The United States Army? Fort Dix? Something was wrong. I had volunteered for the navy. I ran over to some guy who looked like he was in charge and said, "Hey, you can't send me to Fort Dix. I volunteered for the navy." He started to laugh, as did half the guys who had heard me. He said, "Okay, soldier, you had your little laugh; now get back in line and do your comedy routine down in Fort Dix." I started to sweat and ranted, "I'm not going and I'm not joking. I volunteered for the navy. I'm going home. I'll wait until I'm drafted. Tear up my papers; I'm not going!"

Tent City

The train ride to Fort Dix was uneventful. The only thing of interest was a large bakery truck with the name "ZITO" on it that kept following our train. People kept waving from the truck, and I guess this guy Zito waved back to them. Someone said, "Boy, this guy's family are following him right into the army latrine."

Some of the guys on the train came by my seat to pat me on the back. They said that I was a funny guy, was I a comedian, where did I work? The angrier I became, the more they laughed, so I just calmed down and figured it was best to chalk this whole thing up to a strange quirk of destiny.

Arriving at Fort Dix in freezing, snowy weather didn't help our dispositions. Then an entire comedy of errors took place. First off, the officers assigned to meet and lecture us failed to arrive on time, so we had to stand around and freeze for over two hours in the snow. This, the harsh winter of 1940, hit Fort Dix with a double vengeance.

The word *rumor* hadn't meant much to me before that day, but I was to live the next five years listening to, believing, discounting, frightened by, and following the military services favorite indoor sport: "Rumors!"

Rumor number 1 had it that we were only staying at Fort Dix for one day, but were all shipping out to Hawaii the next day. Rumor number 2 was that the United States was at war with Germany secretly and that we would soon be on a ship bound for England. Rumor number 3 had it that we were an elite-cadre who would be given special treatment, food, and lodging. We were to be trained as intelligence officers. Rumor number 4 was that we would be living in tents and roughing it, with outdoor latrines and cold mess halls.

Unfortunately, the last rumor came closest to being true. The assigned officers growled and talked down to us, and we all became an intimidated, sorrowful-looking lot. We were herded onto trucks and taken to a building where we were issued ill-fitting uniforms from World War I and given a lecture on the dangers of venereal diseases. The lecture didn't upset me that much, but the film they showed us, with men who had the actual diseases, made me sick and I started to faint. I closed my eyes and held my ears, and the feeling eventually passed. I never looked at another army VD film again.

The uniform assigned to me was three sizes too big, and the overcoat was probably made for a gorilla, and a large one at that. I was issued a pair of World War II leggings that I swore I'd never wear. It was so cold that winter that I soon changed my mind, and gladly. Everyone got a terrible fit on their uniforms. It looked like a scene out of the Keystone Kops or a Charlie Chaplin or Buster Keaton film.

Each of us was allocated either a 1918 Springfield rifle or

an English-made Enfield rifle and a bayonet. There weren't enough rifles to go around, and we were told that occasionally we would have to loan our rifles to the guys who didn't get one.

Then came the big surprise. We were told that we would be assigned to tents, not barracks. Four men were assigned to a tent with a pot-bellied soft-coal–burning stove. Some of the tents had holes in them. It was so cold that we all had to sleep with our clothes on. At night huge rats would prowl "Tent City" and I would sleep with my trusty Springfield rifle as my teddy bear. I couldn't shoot the rats, as we weren't allowed any ammunition, but maybe I could club them to death or stab them with my bayonet. I heard stories of guys getting badly bitten and saw evidence of bites when we stood reveille at five-thirty in the morning.

We were the first contingent of the 1229th Reception Center, we were told. We were put through a little halfhearted form of basic training, and then we were interviewed for assignment to our permanent outfits. No assignment was really permanent, but some were a little more than others.

When I was waiting on line for my interview, I heard someone mention that you could get a good assignment if you knew how to type or drive a truck or tractor. I was still a little mad at not being allowed to go into the navy, so I made up my mind to give them a hard time in the interview.

I laid it on real thick to the sergeant interviewing me. I told him I was a successful writer, among other things, and that I could type very well. He asked me, "Sixty words a minute?," and I laughingly replied, "Are you kidding? Sixty words a minute, ha ha ha." The sergeant looked at my face. I could see he was impressed and he wrote furiously on a long sheet of paper.

That night in the tent, I got stomach cramps. My conscience bothered me. Suppose they assign me to a typist's job? I'd wind up in the stockade for lying. And then a thought came to me. I once saw a film where this guy in prison studied law and then proved his innocence. Why couldn't I study how to type, right here and now? But how could I get or borrow a typewriter? Impossible!

While I was trying to sleep that night, a thought came to me. If I took one of my large cardboards from my shirts and copied

54

the letters and numbers on it, just like they were on a real type-writer, I could practice.

I quietly got up around 3:00 A.M., got dressed, and sneaked into our company office. Then with a quarter I copied the keyboard off an antique standard Royal typewriter.

The next morning, I was the first one up, at the crack of five, and started practicing on my new invention, the cardboard type-writer. Some of the guys in my outfit wanted to know what I was doing, and I told them I was merely trying to improve my speed. No one got wise and I practiced my typing sometimes for five hours at a time, sometimes all day, and sometimes away into the night. The day I was called for my final interview, I was pretty secure that I knew my way around a typewriter keyboard.

I knew that I had passed the final interview with flying colors, but I made one mistake. I noticed a pack of cigarettes on the interviewing corporal's desk, and I asked if I could have one. He nodded and I tried to act nonchalant and talk and smoke at the same time. I must have inhaled or exhaled incorrectly and turned green. The corporal dismissed me precisely at the right time, and I headed for the latrine, barely hearing him say, "Soldier, your resumé looks good. You're up for a cushy job." That night I was so sick I went to sleep instead of having dinner. I've never smoked a cigarette again.

As the days went by, I kept practicing on my little typewriter, and by now I could hit the letters with my eyes closed. Came the fateful day and I saw everyone running toward the bulletin board yelling, "Assignments!" It took me over half an hour to get to the board, but there it was; "Pvt. Edward R. White assigned to Post Headquarters, Fort Dix, N.J., in charge of the Message Center."

In charge? Message Center? What was that?

I asked some of the old soldiers, left over from World War I, and they told me that the Message Center was the "heart" of any military installation. It meant that all messages, letters, communi-cations, directives, and orders must go through the Message Center. Every communication coming or going off the post had to first be transcribed at the Message Center. A one- or two-line synopsis or breakdown of every piece of paper, coming or going, would be listed on a master chart together with the date and time each communication was received or sent out. This way each and every incoming or outgoing, official or unofficial document could, if need be, be traced as to date, time, destination, and existence.

The Message Center was located in a large room on the ground floor of Post Headquarters, the main artery of Fort Dix. The building was a small colonial structure situated in the very center of the military base. Across the street was a three-story very-modern red-brick building. This was the barracks for the regular army men stationed at Fort Dix. These seasoned older soldiers came from army installations in Hawaii, the Philippines and other corners of the world.

A good many of the career men drank heavily, and the more they drank, the more they resented this new volunteer-draftee army. We soon learned to stay clear of most of these veterans. I always had a few jokes ready for them if I was stopped, just to keep them off guard and in a good frame of mind. They could be ugly when drunk, but I always had a schmaltzy song ready and they usually couldn't help but join in and sing along with me. I got by all right, but a few of my buddies had rough times with the men who wore those hash marks on their sleeves. Each hash mark represented a three-year hitch. Some soldiers had as many as six, seven, or eight hash marks, and they sure wore them as marks of distinction or defiance. In a way, I couldn't blame them much, because that was all most of them had—their hash marks and their beer, if their allowances held out.

Having had some military training and a heavy dose of discipline in the orphanage, I fit into the new man's army better than most men. Some of the veteran soldiers couldn't believe that I didn't come from another planet, the way I drilled a platoon. To me, it was like acting. I was imitating the older boys who had drilled us in the H.O.A. It was a real high for me. I got a big kick out of hearing my voice boom out commands. I would just use Vaughn Monroe's voice and Pat O'Brian's grim face and bark out, "Tenshun!," "Hight face!," "Horward Harch!," and "Hup two, hup two!" Man, it was a gas. You had to make sure you never pronounced the words correctly or the men wouldn't obey you.

For eight months or so, although working at Post Headquarters, we still lived in Tent City. That first winter of 1940 had to

Private First Class White on maneuvers before World War II.

go down as one of the coldest winters ever. The snow was as "high as an elephant's eye" and higher, right to the roof of our tents. The soft coal that we were forced to burn smelled something like leaking gas and soiled our clothing and burned our eyes. What with the intense cold, the lousy food, the rats, the soft coal, the ill-fitting uniforms, and the "chicken shit" discipline that was thrown at us, I was beginning to understand what was meant when they say, "War is hell!" And we weren't even at war.

Each morning we heard a distant bugler play reveille at five-thirty in the morning. We were all practically dressed, as we slept with our clothing on. The tents were ice cold, as no one usually had enough sense to keep the stove fire going during the night. Then it was "The Charge of the Light Brigade" to the latrine, wash in ice-cold water, and off to the freezing mess hall to eat cold food. The butter was so hard that it couldn't be spread. We had to eat the butter in pieces.

Then we had to walk a half-mile in the snow to Post Head-quarters and report to work. At least, there it was properly heated, and we were all comfortable for the number of hours we spent there.

In addition to our work assignments, we were all obligated for military drilling, Headquarters Company or not. We also did our share of kitchen police, guard duty, cleaning the barracks area, and anything else the noncommssioned officers could think up.

That first memorable day we were assigned to Headquarters Company, we were told to stand by to meet our first company commander. We were told to hurry up and rush over to Post Headquarters, and once we arrived there we were told to wait. Army standard procedure: "Hurry up and wait!"

Finally a sergeant snapped us to attention, and what took place was a scene out of *Apocalypse Now,* as I look back. What seemed like an eternity of standing at attention came to an end when a tall, slightly balding officer appeared in the shadows at the top of the stairs. We were on the main floor staring innocently up at this figure wearing a World War I Sam Brown belt over his uniform and full dress boots and angrily snapping a riding crop into his left hand. Signs of Captain Queeg? Or maybe Richard Barthelmess in *Dawn Patrol?*

Anyway, this was Capt. Samuel J. Decker, fresh from the Bordentown, New Jersey, Military Academy and more recently from the CCC, or Franklin Delano Roosevelt's Civilian Conservation Corps. Captain Decker was about to make his first address to his troops.

The good captain must have known the exact amount of theatrics that would intimidate us. A small light down the hall threw a shadow over his face so that we couldn't tell exactly what he looked like, but it made him look a lot more threatening than he actually was. He scared the living shit out of all of us rookie soldiers!

Captain Decker said that we were the nucleus of the new army, in the greatest country in the world, that we could go as far up the ladder as we wanted to, that we should be proud of our uniform and our outfit, and that some changes were going to be made. For the five years I was to serve in the armed forces, every single officer eventually made that last statement, that "some changes were going to be made!" I found out that it never meant anything, but we heard it over and over again.

As Captain Decker stood at the top of the landing, looking all spit and polish in his boots and uniform, snapping his riding crop each time he tried to drive a point home, I remember it was hard for me to swallow lest I make a noise. Capt. Samuel J. Decker, that day in December 1940, sure put the fear of God, country, and the unknown into this rookie. To me, good ole Sam was Joshua at the gates of Jericho.

And he wasn't a tyrant, as we thought he might be, but a serious, fair-minded officer who always had his men's best interests at heart. After the war, whenever we had our yearly reunion of the "Piss and Growlers" club, as we called ourselves, we would mention how fortunate we were to have Captain Decker as our first commanding officer. Because we soon learned that not every officer had Captain Decker's judicious outlook. Some of our future officers actually went out of their way to make our lives, and their own, miserable.

Captain Decker finished his opening remarks to us, whipped his boots a couple of times, stared at us, and slapped his hand with the crop, and then someone yelled, "Tenshun!" and Decker disappeared into the darkened halls of Post Headquarters.

Then another memorable moment came. The sergeant who had called us to attention a moment before, appeared at the top of the stairs. He said, "At ease, men. No talking. Smoke if you wish." Then he introduced himself to us as "Master Sgt. Alphonse Sica." Sica was an old soldier in more ways than one. His voice was shot, his ruddy face had wrinkles that had wrinkles, and he had enough hash marks to really intimidate us. Here was Louis Wolheim in *All Quiet on the Western Front* or Ernest Borgnine in *From Here to Eternity*.

Surprise! This frightening-looking individual, our company's first master sergeant, was a funny, lovable pussycat. I said that Sgt. Al Sica reminded me of Louis Wolheim and Ernie Borgnine, but there was also a little bit of Jerry Lewis from the film *The Nutty Professor*.

Sergeant Sica got things done, thank God, but he also gave us more good-natured laughs than we could handle. Years later, in the '70s, whenever we had our company annual reunion at one of the hotels in New York City, Sergeant Sica, would grunt out orders and drill us potbellied relics from World War II. Excuse me, I mean Captain Sica, as our top sergeant eventually was upgraded, through the ranks, to captain. How we ever got through basic training, let alone won the war, mystifies me when I think of tough, rough, gruff Alphonse Sica. He may have made captain, but he will always be our top kick, Sergeant Sica.

As the weeks and months flew by, I became very acclimated to the discipline and routine of army life. The orphan-asylum training stood me in good stead, but now I was much better off. After all, I was now getting three square meals a day, I now belonged to an elite group of men called Headquarters Company, and I was reading and learning about everything and anything. I read every book, every manuscript, and every periodical that came my way. I took every course that was available to the GIs at Fort Dix. This hunger for an education simply overcame me, and it became somewhat of an obsession. I was accepted and liked by my peers, and for the first time in my life I had many happy and memorable moments.

I not only worked at my job as chief of the message center, but I also poked my nose into every other office up at Post Head-quarters. I tried to be of assistance sometimes, but oftentimes this got me into trouble. In the court-martial section, I would read some of the cases and ask too many questions. Why was this man convicted? Wasn't this sentence too harsh? Why is an officer's word more important than an enlisted man's word?

I sensed an unfairness in the way trials were held, and once, just once, I was able to get an enlisted man retried on a rape case and he was eventually proven innocent. This was after he was sentenced to twenty years in Leavenworth and I was told by all the people in the judge advocate's office that "If you listen to all of these guys, they'll tell you that they are all innocent!" But there it was in the trial record, and I figured it out the same way I figured out many of the Charley Chan movies. Inadequacies and errors lay on every other page.

Being the head of the Message Center, I practically read everything, sometimes out of sheer curiosity. One day, we received a letter from the office of a Mr. Stephen Early and the letter heading said "The White House." I read on and Mr. Early's letter said that an enlisted man from the Fort Dix stockade prison had written Mrs. Eleanor Roosevelt to say that he was being held there on a rape charge. He pleaded that he was innocent and that he was of Polish descent, that he was quite ugly, with hair all over his body, and that he looked like a rapist, but he swore he wasn't. I can't recall his exact name—Kazmierski or something close to it.

Anyway, I used my contacts and army knowhow to get into the stockade to visit this unfortunate soldier, and sure enough, he did look like he might be capable of a criminal act. He needed a shave and was quite agitated, too nervous to tell me everything. But he told me enough, and more than that, he convinced me of his innocence by his honesty. He told me he had had sex with the girl in question, many times, with her permission.

The next morning, I went to the court-martial office and snooped around for the file on my newfound friend. When I finally found it, I asked a personal friend of mine, Sergeant Goodman, if I could take it to the barracks to read that night. He said emphatically, "no," with a wink. "It's against army rules, American jurisprudence, and the Bill of Rights."

That night I pored over the papers, but I was too nervous and read them too fast. My heart was pounding a mile a minute. Then I slowed down and read the case slowly, page by page, and wrote my thoughts on a lined yellow pad. I knew ever so little of the procedures that had to be taken in a fair trial but enough to know that this case was one big foulup. *Snafu* was the army word.

The girl in question had come to Fort Dix from the West Side of New York City—West 72nd Street, to be exact. She came to visit a sergeant she had known, but this man had shipped out some weeks prior. She had a picnic basket and invited the private to join her, as she told the story. They spent some hours together, and then they got into the private's car and went to a bar in town. The man got angry at something and left the bar sometime after midnight, and she followed him. They argued in the car and she testified that he beat her up, scratched and punched her, and then raped her. They even had pictures made of the woman's body, and there were marks on her back and her breasts. The nurse who admitted her to the hospital testified on her behalf and said, "Only an insane butcher could have done this!"

Some of the glaring inadequacies I noted and brought to the attention of the judge advocate's office eventually held up in court, I was told. They were: Had this woman, who testified against a soldier, ever been investigated as to her credibility? The answer was an emphatic "No!" How come when she ran from this soldier's car she used a phrase only known to soldiers? She said, "I am going to report you to the P. and P. officer." P. and P. means Police and Prison, but this is army terminology, usually not known to civilians. Also, last but not least, a blade of grass was found in her vagina. No one bothered to ask her how it ever got there.

The true story eventually came out, and the soldier was cleared and set free. She was a known prostitute from the West Side of New York City. She had come to Fort Dix to pick up some extra money and had slept with a few soldiers on the grass. Being a true camp follower, she knew more than one army term than she would admit to. She had slept with the private in his car more than once that night, but when she flirted with another soldier the private walked out on her. She followed him to the car, and when he tried to make love to her again, they got into a scratching and punching match that led to her threats and his being arrested. The private had been scared and punished enough, and he was let off with a reprimand and a warning, but I am sure that he retains a few emotional scars to this day. I never went back to visit him; nor did he ever contact me after that.

I got involved with other offices, too, and I always found it fun trying new jobs and challenges. The S-2 office, Public Relations, needed someone to write copy for their poster campaigns. I volunteered and got the assignment. Huge posters went up all over Fort Dix and all over New Jersey, with Sgt. Edward Heyman getting credit for the drawing and Sgt. Edward R. White getting the credit for the copy: "A Slip of the Lip Sank This Ship!" We were both commended many times by the post commander. Then a call went out for someone to help write a radio show, "This Is Fort Dix," publicizing the work done by this new army and these new inductees. By now they didn't wait to call upon me. My name was suggested immediately, and I agreed to do my best. I wrote many of the shows, including the theme song, "Hey Ma, I Wanna Go To Fort Dix," heard by the entire country over the Mutual Network. I wrote the lyrics and my pal Cpl. Murray Gans wrote the music.

I became popular and was quite well known all over Fort Dix. When promotions were handed out, I immediately became a buck sergeant, which meant three stripes. There was much celebrating and excitement, mostly by the new army inductees or draftees, but the older veteran soldiers went around shaking their heads. They resented our promotions, as being too fast and too easy. They told us off in no uncertain terms, and they drank twice as much to forget us, this newfangled army, and their own sad past lives.

Sergeant Heyman and Sergeant White, Headquarters, Fort Dix, New Jersey. America enters the war.

The company scheduled this big party to celebrate our coming of age, and I was asked to not only supervise the party and buy the food and beer, but also to produce a little show to memorialize the handing out of ratings for Headquarters Company.

I got to work fast and wrote some skits, a few new songs, and a few parodies on some old songs and generally it all made good-natured fun of the army, ourselves, and our superior officers. Another one of my close pals, Cpl. Larry Alpert, formerly a comic from the Catskill Mountains borscht circuit, sang a parody to the music of "I Love New York in June," and it brought the house down. It was "I've Got My Corporal's Stripes (How About You?)." Larry was the hit of the evening. The rest of the cast forgot their cues and the words to the songs but everyone was so boozed up that no one noticed except me. The food I bought or had donated from the merchants of Wrightstown, New Jersey, just outside of Fort Dix, was the opposite of army fare and disappeared in minutes, and the beer flowed until the wee, small hours. I didn't drink then, but nevertheless, I became high on the excitement. Who was it who said, "War is hell?"

It was at this party, that particular night, that someone suggested that we should write an original army show and present it at the post theater. Yeah, why didn't we write a show? Let's do our own show! Shades of Mickey Rooney and Judy Garland. I tried being modest about the whole thing, but suddenly a roar went up and it was decided for me. I was going to produce and write an army show whether I liked it or not. In a million years, I wouldn't go against my outfit that night. Most of the guys had never been drunk before and I wasn't sure what the look in their eyes meant.

Then my heart started beating wildly. "Sure, I'll put the show together and write the book and lyrics, and our band piano player, Murray Gans, will do the music, and Larry Alpert will be our lead comic." It was settled then. We all went to bed and hoped that the idea would still look good to us in the morning. I don't know what Larry and Murray did that night, but I never slept a wink.

By 6:00 A.M. I already had the outline of the show, a working title, "Mistaken Identity," and a few titles for some of the songs. Within a week, we were busy casting the show and making plans and dreaming of a huge success. At every free moment, we would do rewrites of the story line, changing some of the words and music, and in three weeks it was really taking shape. Now there was no stopping us. I was so excited, I thought I would burst from the happiness and fullfillment that had now entered my life. Who would believe that I would get my big show-business break in the U.S. Army? Well, why not? Didn't Irving Berlin get his big break during World War I with a show, *Yip, Yip, Yaphank?* Hey, Mr. Berlin, here we come, White, Gans, and Alpert. Watch out, Rodgers and Hammerstein. Move over, Noel Coward. On second thought, stay where you are, Noel Coward.

As I mentioned, working at the Fort Dix Message Center I knew practically every official document that passed through my office. Call it curiosity or just being nosy, but I glanced at every communication if only for a second. I was hastily scanning papers, and sure enough, something caught my eye, the name Irving Berlin. I put the paper down and caught my breath before I could look at it again. Then I started to read carefully and slowly.

The very official letter stated that on such and such a date a detail would arrive at Fort Dix for the purpose of auditioning army talent for the forthcoming show, *This is the Army*, to be supervised and produced by Irving Berlin. Most documents were by order of this general or that, but this document was by declaration of the president of the United States.

My heart sank. This was the end of our show. Worse, it was the end of me. I called a meeting for Murray Gans, Larry Alpert, Harry Hollander, who was now our stage manager, and myself. I sadly showed them a copy of the letter from Washington, D.C. Larry thought it was my idea of a joke, but I soon convinced him otherwise by swearing on my mother's grave. He knew my mother was sacred to me and I would never say such a thing unless I was desperate.

We all agreed to a man that we wouldn't audition for *This Is the Army* and wouldn't join the show even if we were asked—nay, even if we were ordered. We went out and received strong pledges of loyalty from the rest of the cast and musicians from our show. *Mistaken Identity* was safely on its way. It wasn't easy, but didn't Mickey and Judy have trouble getting their shows produced?

The *This is the Army* contingent arrived at Fort Dix, held

their auditions, and practically wiped us out, talent wise, in one fell swoop. They took our key people, but what hurt the most was that they grabbed our best musicians. Our show was dead and so was I. All that work, planning, dreaming, praying, scheming. To add insult to injury, the day we found out our talent was transferred to *This Is the Army* was the very same day we were informed from second Corps Area that our request for permission to use the post theater had been granted.

That in itself was an unusual feat, as it was almost impossible to secure permission for a post theater for anything but films for the GIs. You had to go through all kinds of Catch-22 channels, through second Corps Area right on to Washington, D.C., and then you were usually refused.

We tried putting our little show together again, but there was just no way. When we filled the gap here, it fell apart there. I thought of joining up with some of the veteran soldiers and getting drunk, but I didn't know how to drink. I just couldn't stomach the stuff.

In my sadness and madness, I sat down and wrote a long, angry letter to Irving Berlin, full of accusations and self-pity. I told Mr. Berlin that although I have always respected him as a songwriter, an American legend in his own time, someone who had made something of himself from such humble beginnings, an inspiration to all Americans, he had an obligation, a duty to be honest with the American people. President Roosevelt, as I understood it, had appointed Irving Berlin to "supervise" a GI musical show, written and performed by GI personnel.

I further went on and asked this giant of the musical theater that since he had received his first big break in life when he wrote *Yip, Yip, Yaphank* during World War I, hadn't he received all the success and material things that life had to offer? Here I was, a young, unknown GI writer, putting my artistic guts and dreams into a show that now, "thanks to you, Mr. Berlin, will never see the light of day."

I had some doubts about sending the letter and asked Larry Alpert what he thought. He agreed I shouldn't send the letter; it might lead to my being court-martialed, maybe worse. What could be worse?

All my life, I have had this compulsion. If I write a letter, I must mail it. It's as if the letter has a power over me. Also, I have to answer every phone, especially if it rings. Even if I'm in the shower. Many times I've flooded my kitchen jumping out of the shower to answer some inconsequential phone call. I have other compulsions just like the ones I mentioned, such as answering every letter immediately, paying all bills the day I receive them, and even replying to thank-you cards that don't require an answer. I show up at airports usually an hour and a half before my flights, and I am always more than punctual for all appointments. I have a few other hangups about always trying to please everyone and that sort of thing.

So I mailed the letter the very moment I started to feel like a coward, and I waited to be court-martialed and shot at dawn. I even fantasized that I was buried in Arlington Cemetery and my tombstone read: "Mistaken Identity."

But lo and behold, a letter arrived in a few days. When I saw the envelope seal, "This is the Army," I could hardly catch my breath. I held onto the letter for hours, looking at the inscription and trying to read the letter when I held it up to the light. When all the guys in Message Center went to chow and I was alone, I opened the envelope. At first reading, I didn't understand a word. My eyes could hardly focus, and all I knew or understood was the signature. The letter was signed by Sgt. Ezra Stone. *Ezra Stone? I knew that name. Wait a while. I know this guy. Wasn't he Andy Hardy or someone? Yeah, I got it, Ezra Stone was Henry Aldrich on the radio.*

Calmly I read the letter. As I look back in slight anger, I recall thinking this was my first "Dear John" letter. In essence, Sgt. Ezra Stone said that he was in charge of production for *This is the Army*, that Mr. Irving Berlin was truly sorry for raiding our show but it was necessary, that Mr. Berlin had actually been unaware of our GI musical production personally, that Mr. Berlin might consider me for a position with *This Is the Army* if I would consider a transfer, and that whatever decision I came to, Mr. Stone and Mr. Berlin wished me luck. There was a postscript telling me where to contact Mr. Stone should I consider transferring, but under no circumstances could I write for *This Is the Army*. All songs and material were to be written by Mr. Irving Berlin.

Shirley Temple or Margaret O'Brian couldn't have shed more pathetic tears. Oh, how I cried. Why, I don't know. Was it because I felt sorry for myself, or because I got the fat cats to take notice of me, or just plain, old insecurity? I think I imagined that Irving Berlin had ruined my life, had taken something from me. I had such mixed emotions about everything, but I think that I was extremely touched that Mr. Irving Berlin, the dean of American songwriters, had actually taken the time to have someone write to me. I'm older and wiser now and consider that maybe Mr. Berlin never even knew I existed, then or now.

For a few days, I was the subject of much talk at Fort Dix. Even the officers kept asking me if I had made up my mind about the offer to transfer to *This Is the Army*. I thought it over and came to the conclusion that all I would be utilized for was a "gopher." All I was good for was as a writer of songs or sketches or jokes and that sort of thing. Again, as I look back, I think my pride was terribly hurt and that possibly I made a mistake in not going with *This Is the Army*. But another adventure awaited me, as I was soon to learn.

Then again this melancholia set in again. I felt cheated. How could Irving Berlin do this to me? Then I started feeling that this thing was getting the better of me and maybe I was building it up more than I should. Some of the older guys in Headquarters Company, guys whose opinions and advice I valued, said I might be a little paranoid. I looked the word up in the dictionary and decided I had to get off it. Sure, I had visions of having a hit army show and touring all the military installations and entertaining the troops. But this was the military service, and I could still do that in civilian life someday.

Boom! It happened. Here I had volunteered for one year and now war had been declared on Germany. I was surely in for the duration now, maybe for the rest of my life. Maybe I wouldn't even get out of this man's army alive?

I thought of making my life easier and becoming a commissioned officer. This was easier said than done, another of my pipe dreams. My education consisted of getting through the 8th grade, nothing more. Sure I went to high school for a few seconds and then to night school, but I had never received any credits because I had moved around too much. I could never dig in and really study; some calamity or event in my life would disrupt

68

everything and I had to move on. Why did I ever quit night school? My wonderful teacher, Mrs. Robinson, had written my sister that I was the best student she had ever had at Commerce High Night School. Man, it was easy to be the best in that class. Most of my classmates were immigrants who could hardly speak or write English.

One day a flyer came through the Message Center ("College graduates, join the new air corps"), and at the bottom of the flyer was an asterisk stating that students with two years of college credits could take a special test for possible acceptance into the air corps. *Could anyone take such a test?* I wondered. I called the air-corps office at Fort Dix and used my most authoritative voice. "Hey, this is Sgt. Eddie White over at post Headquarters. What's this about taking a test to get into the air corps? Let's get this goddamned war over with!" The sergeant at the other end wasn't sure about the rules and regulations, as everything was so new and the offices weren't set up as yet. I heard him talking to someone else, probably an officer, and then he asked me if I wanted to set up a time to take the test, saying that the entire ordeal would take around three hours. I had to catch my breath and asked him for his name and said I would call back soon.

I discussed the situation with a few of my college-graduate buddies, guys in high positions at Fort Dix, and they all discouraged me to a man. Was I off my nut? Didn't I realize that they threw a lot of math at you? Not to mention, you had to have a knowledge of motors and so forth and so forth. Everyone discouraged me but one guy, Cpl. Larry Alpert. Larry not only said I would win the war singlehanded, but he went out and bought me a pair of second-lieutenant gold bars. He took it for granted that I would go through with this venture, that I wouldn't back out. That did it! If I failed the test, no one would really know; I would just drop the whole thing and never mention it. I swore Larry to secrecy.

I called in my name and serial number, and the air-corps office gave me a date and time for my testing. The night before, I couldn't sleep. Why not take the easy way out? I could probably spend the entire war running the Message Center at Fort Dix. I probably wouldn't pass the test anyway—how could I? So why make waves?

I showed up at the testing office with another of my close

friends, Sgt. Arthur Smallwood, red-headed Artie, my pal. He had more than two years of college; it would go easier for Artie. He was so cool and calm about this situation, and everything else, as I recall. Artie gave me warm words of encouragement and told me that his mother and father were in my corner, too. Whenever I had a two-or-three-day pass, Artie would take me to his home in Trenton, New Jersey, and I'd stay with him. His mother fed me like I was her own son, so I always felt some sort of kinship with Artie Smallwood. A Jewish boy and a Catholic boy brought together in close friendship by earth-shaking events. I often thought about things like that.

We were all ushered into a small room with desks spaced far apart, probably so we wouldn't cheat. Remember, I had only received an eighth-grade education and the word was that one had to have at least two years of college credits in order to take the air-corps test. No one asked me any questions, and I just sat at my desk quietly waiting for the boom to fall on my head: "Okay dum-dum, take a walk. This test is for guys who are educated. Now scram!" I was all set for something to happen.

A sergeant walked around the room placing test papers on each desk and telling us to wait for a signal from him to start. The second the test was placed on my desk, I felt a surge of joy. They were multiple-choice answers. *Oh, dear Lord, let the entire test be the same*, I prayed. And so it was.

I was the very last soldier to finish taking the test, as the last ten questions had to do with motors. For all I knew, motors were wound up with rubber bands; that's how much I knew about those things. I felt I did fairly well on the rest of the test, but motors? I never looked one squarely in the face. I was sure that the last ten questions had done me in.

When I left the building, I found Artie waiting for me. He asked me how it went, and I said, "Not good." I told him I knew as much about motors as I did about women: zip!

Artie laughed and said it would be great if we were in the air corps together.

We were making our way back to Headquarters Company and we were about a mile from the air-corps building when we heard this booming voice coming from the sky: "Sergeant Smallwood, Sergeant White." The air-corps sergeant was calling us on a bullhorn. I yelled out, "What's up?" and he said some memorable words I shall never forget. "You're both in the air corps now!"

I beat Artie back to the building and grabbed the sergeant and hugged and kissed him. Then I asked him if he was kidding. Could there be some mistake? How could he be so sure so quickly? The test took close to three hours. How could he know in such a short time that we had passed?

The sergeant explained that he just places a mask over each page and only the correct answers show up. Voilà! I asked him to tell me the mark I had received, and he said it was against orders for him to say but that I had gotten a fairly good mark. Nothing was said of my lack of education, and to this day I think my getting in the corps might have had something to do with my past army record.

Artie and I congratulated each other with tears and whoops of joy and headed back to headquarters barracks just a little taller. Artie called his parents to tell them about us, and I was mobbed, shaking hands with our entire outfit. That night, I was the star of the movie *Wings*. I shot down every enemy aircraft that came my way. Eddie Rickenbacker was my buddy, Baron Richtoven my sworn enemy. I became the ace of aces, but Artie Smallwood, my buddy, was wounded. I carried him home on my shoulders, and he got better and I was the best man at his wedding.

A few days later, my little bubble burst. Word got back to me that the odds were fifty to one I'd never get past one month as an air-corps cadet. What hurt is that there weren't any takers but one. Cpl. Larry Alpert believed implicitly, more than I did, that I would make it through flight school. For the moment, I put up a great front for Larry and for my own self-esteem.

5

"Off We Go"

1942–43: Rommel retreats in North Africa; Warsaw Ghetto uprising; Allied "round the clock" bombing of Germany; penicillin introduced; zoot suits and jitterbugging popular; Count Fleet wins Triple Crown.

July 1942

THOSE FIRST FEW WEEKS in the army air corps were the most hectic and frustrating of my life. The first thing they did was change the name to the U.S. Air Force, and we became an entity unto ourselves. It was now the army, marine corps, navy, and air force, all separate but equal under the same flag and all fighting a common enemy. The next eleven months of my life was to be an adventure no one could really dream up.

I was no sooner sworn in as an aviation cadet when I was informed that I was to be a bombardier-navigator trainee. I was rather sad about this. First I had volunteered for the navy and they put me in the army; now I joined up to become a pilot and I was to be a bombardier-navigator, if I lived long enough.

My friend Sgt. Artie Smallwood was chosen for training as a pilot. It figures. Artie was smarter, more educated, stronger, and more sure of himself. I thought it over and felt quite happy and lucky to be chosen for any position in my country's air force. Can a poor, insecure Jewish kid from the South Bronx, with a limited education and a slight build, make it through adversity and the echelons of the air force to the top? You bet your ass he can!

I was issued a new dashing air-force–cadet uniform except for the shirts. No shirts? This set me up as an easy mark, because

I had to wear my old army shirts, with the stripes removed, but still visible because of many washings.

When I arrived at the first Air Force Training Base, I learned the true meaning of being a cadet. The uniforms fit well and were glamorous, almost like those of the air-force officers. We looked sharp and kind of special, and that's how we felt. We were an elite group, and we marched to a different drummer. But what really got to me was the food, and I mean food. For the first time in my life, I truly received three square, wholesome meals a day. The first time I marched into our dining room, I couldn't believe it. There was milk and fruit and cake already on the tables. And we were waited upon by other cadets and could have as much meat and vegetables as we desired, or anything else, for that matter. Uncle Sam really loved us young cadets. America the beautiful, I thought. It was really during my military service that I learned how much I respected and loved my country, and I've carried on a love affair with America ever since. Anyone who doesn't agree should be made to make a world tour to find out that this is really the best country on the globe. Sure, if we look hard enough we can find some things that may be wrong or that we don't agree with, but there is absolutely no country that can be compared with the United States.

Being the shortest cadet in my barracks, I would naturally be the first one in line to enter the mess hall. I didn't realize what I was doing, but as I came to our table I would hold my arm out and bring all the milk and fruit down to my end of the table. The guys noticed that I ate very fast and wolfed almost everything down much too quickly. I became known as a "chow hound" and was most embarrassed until a pal said something to the guys and they left me alone. After that, I tried not to take food out of the mess hall. I became secure that this wasn't all merely a wonderful dream, and I slowed down somewhat in my eating habits. When I look back now, I wonder how all those wonderful guys ever put up with me.

Next stop, Bainbridge, Georgia, was the most unorganized military installation I had ever encountered. The moment we arrived, we were told to carry our duffle bags, paraphernalia, and other belongings clear across to the other end of the air base.

73

Being put in charge, I requested trucks to expedite the matter, and a top sergeant just laughed up my nose.

Once we arrived at the other end of the base, a distance of close to two miles, we were told it was all a mistake, that we were to go back to our point of origin. I smelled a rat, but after a brief rest period we American peasants mushed on back to Point One.

This part can't be believed. Again that same top kick asked me why we had returned. After a few phone calls and some military hysterics, he ordered me and the men to report to the other side of the base again. This time I refused point blank. Shades of the Caine mutiny. I told this nameless dog to get out the firing squad and shoot me. Unless the men were fed and driven to Point Two, we weren't going anywhere. One out of two isn't bad. We got fed, but no trucks were available. The cold cuts tasted like the finest gourmet French dinner, we were so starved, but that's what we were fed at Bainbridge most times, cold cuts and grits.

At Point Two, another sergeant started talking about this being a crazy, continuous foul-up when I started screaming about my congressman and how close he was to my family. I asked the sergeant for his name and serial number and was just about to lead a mutiny when a few trucks arrived and actually delivered us to our barracks.

My stay at Bainbridge was uneventful but for two incidents that remain in my memory. One was a sign I saw in front of a church on the main drag outside of town. It read: "Nonsectarian Baptist Church." They didn't care what you were so long as you were Baptist. The other incident was my meeting a young, highly sensitive soldier who just didn't relate to military life. Someone mentioned that he was a writer, so I tried to get friendly. He just wouldn't respond (although he slept in the next bunk), and I felt sorry for him. He was lean with a young Abe Lincoln face and hauntingly penetrating eyes. I remembered his name and he was later to write one of the world's classics. That soldier was J.D. Salinger, who later was to write *Catcher in the Rye*.

A few days later, I was shipped out of Bainbridge to the psychological testing base at Nashville, Tennessee.

Nashville was a happy place. The food was better; treatment

was better; our quarters were better. Still, I almost got myself killed!

All of us air-force cadets were waiting to be assigned to a base for training as pilots, bombardiers, or navigators. Days we ran obstacle courses, jogged eight miles (which almost did me in a few times), and took psychological tests for depth perception and hearing and all these funny little tests where you put a peg in a hole et cetera.

After jogging, we usually hung around the barracks and shot the breeze, macho style. One hot afternoon, I lay on my bunk, still sweating, and grabbed the local paper. There on the front page was a picture of two twelve-year-old black boys hanging from a tree. I thought they were rag dolls, surely not children. I read the story. These two youngsters had been accused of running after a thirteen-year-old girl and pulling her dress up and teasing her. The boys were identified by the girl, but the story ended with the thought that the white girl wasn't positive these were the two black boys. I went blind for a moment and then read the story over and over again. It couldn't be!

I stood up on my bunk, without realizing it, and barked out, "Quiet, guys, quiet. Listen to this!" I read the story and emphasized the part where the girl wasn't positive that these were the two boys who had accosted her.

Then I went into an editorial about our fighting for democracy. "What the hell's going on down here in the South, and what are we going to do about all this shit?"

I yelled, "Fuck!" and then I fell down on my bed, exhausted. It was quiet for a few moments. No one said a word. Then a southern voice rang out. "Hey, New York big shot, how would you like it if this girl was your sister?"

I jumped up to see who was talking, and it was one of the guys I liked. He was from the Deep South, a good-looking kid with a drawl as long as it could be. He was defending what he thought was right, and maybe I was a little hard on him. I shouted, "What difference does it make if she was my sister? She wasn't raped or beaten. Nothing happened, you moronic college-boy asshole. These two kids are dead, and now she's not too sure these were the same kids."

The next thing I knew, there was some shouting and scuffling.

The guy I shouted at had grabbed a bayonet and was heading for me. Two of the bigger guys were all over him, holding him back. They took the bayonet away from him and held him down on a bunk until his anger subsided. Later on, we were forced to shake hands and say it was all over, forgotten and I learned that the two guys who had saved my life were also from the South.

That night, one of the cadets gave me a word of advice. If I knew what was good for me, I'd keep my mouth shut for good. Word was out that I was a New York wise guy who was a "pinko," a "commie." Luckily, in a few days, I shipped out of the Nashville Psychological Center to the Aviation Cadet Bombardier Training Base at Deming, New Mexico.

Deming, New Mexico, was situated in the middle of Nowhere, U.S.A. The cadets' barracks were long, barren cement blocks with rooms on each side of a narrow walk. There were two beds in each room and a plain, high bureau for two and a window. What could we expect in the middle of the desert? I had once seen a room such as this in a book about Vincent Van Gogh's life.

My roommate was a colorful former All-American basketball player from Baylor University, Woodrow Wilson "Whizzer" White, who hailed from Waco; Texas. A short, Jewish kid from the South Bronx put in with a skinny six-foot-six "layup" artist who was all drawl. We soon became fast friends, though. I was interested in everything the "Whizzer" had to say, and to my surprise, he found me interesting and funny. I kidded him about everything, and once he learned to understand my humor, he almost fell over himself laughing. We were inseparable, although he once threatened to throw me out of a Beechcraft plane while we were on a training mission.

It was the "Whiz" who helped me get through the Deming phase of my bombardier training. Little things he said kept me going when it all seemed too much for me to take physically. On the eight-mile runs, I was done in many times and Whizzer would say, "Eddie, just keep going up to the next clearing and I'll let you cut out then," and by the next clearing I somehow got my second wind and went on and on. This happened many times. Also, when I would have an argument with some of the guys who thought all New Yorkers were con guys, the Whiz would give me a dose of his beautiful cornball philosophy and I was okay till the next time.

I loved to hear stories about Axtell and Austin, Texas, and about his child bride, Bebe. The Whiz was such a beautiful guy, not a crooked bone or thought in his pure American makeup. And he had his own sense of humor, droll, subtle, and sometimes elusive, but I hung in there and soon found the key to his Will Rogers jokes, philosophy, and tricks. It was all "Hee Haw" and the "Farmer's Almanac," but I loved it. It was always give and take, but to this day I am close to the Whiz and his child bride, Bebe. Their son, Whitlow, another Texan, now calls me Uncle and visits me on occasion. He's just like his father, honest, forthright, full of country humor, and good-natured. The Whiz always listened to country music when he found a free moment, and he taught me some songs. He also taught me a few songs that had a country sound but big-city thoughts. One day, I was being punished for some minor infraction and stood before the entire squadron. The officer asked me to sing something funny. While I was begging off, someone yelled out, "Sing 'I Had a Little Dawg'!" The officer thereupon ordered me to sing the song, and it became my trademark or identification for the duration of my stay at Deming, New Mexico. It went like this:

> I had a little dawg
> And his name was Ring.
> Around his tail I tied a string
> I pulled the string and it closed his hole.
> Run along, little dawg, with a tight asshole.

When I finished singing, a roar went up from the squadron and the officer ordered me to sing the song again. Now whenever I was hazed I had to sing that particular song. It became mine, all mine. Then one officer devised another way for me to sing the song, with another cadet who was being hazed, a handkerchief between our noses.

This brought howls of laughter from everyone and the Whiz suggested I take it good naturedly if I wanted to graduate. My chance of graduating from the Deming bombardier training was one in a thousand and again no takers.

Here were all these college graduates, some All-American football and basketball players, all tall and Waspish-looking. Even Whizzer White would shake his head and sympathize with me because of all my problems keeping up with the squadron's flying and classroom work. Each week he would make the odds on my getting through the course, and each week the odds went down a point or two.

When we had a few hours to ourselves, I would be the life of the party, the funniest guy in the outfit, until the guys got around to singing their college songs. That depressed me. One day, someone mentioned that I never sang my college song and it was my turn. The Whiz tried to get me out of it, but it only made me look worse. So I sang "Hail To P.S. 75." Everyone thought it was a great joke, and they loved it. "Hail To P.S. 75" became my school song, and it carried me through the war years. No one ever got on my case again.

Not only were my flying and schoolwork too much for me to handle, but I suffered from an acute case of airsickness, probably the worst case in the history of the air force, if you ask Whizzer White. A couple of times I was caught throwing up in the compass cover, my favorite receptacle. I always made a joke out of it and would inform the officer assigned to my flight that I ate too much for lunch, that it was a twenty-four–hour virus, that I drank too much milk before the flight, and so forth. I prayed that no two flight training officers would talk about my airsickness or match stories. If they did, I was through; I'd be "washed out."

Each week, men were washed out for one reason or another, All-American college grads. The most important reason given was "Attitude." When they called the names of those who were "washed out," I kept my eyes closed and shuddered. Sooner or later it would be me. The Whiz would say, "Addy, you got by another week. You can do it, boy. You got by this far; keep going."

And keep going I did, with my head held high and a heavy heart! God had to be watching over me, because I had so many confrontations that "washed out" men better qualified than I and somehow I managed to squeeze through by the skin of my teeth.

On one bomb-training mission, I flew with a Lieutenant Wilson who kind of liked my jokes. He had "washed out" his share of cadets, and I was leery of getting too close to him. The whiz suggested I go to the bombing room and get the information on the winds aloft and the bombing target and all general information regarding our mission. I thought he said that he would pick up both our parachutes.

Anyway, we both showed up at the plane with information pads and no parachutes. I was furious. I screamed at Whiz and said he was trying to kill us both. Lieutenant Wilson was unaware of the chute problem, and he said, "Let's take off." The Whiz and I were too embarrassed to tell him about our chutes, so we flew without them.

We were not airborne when it was discovered that our bombsight had a malfunction. Scratch the mission! No, Lieutenant Wilson said, "Let's go ahead anyway." He needed some air time in order to get his flight pay. Flyers were paid a base monthly wage plus additional pay for flight time if they flew the minimum number of hours.

I was furious and couldn't look at the Whiz all during the flight. I had visions of the plane going down in flames. I was sure he told me to pick up the winds aloft.

When it came my turn to throw some bombs, I got behind the bombsight and blurted out, "Lieutenant Wilson, you aren't going to put these two bombs on my record, what with a malfunction and all??" He nudged me in the ribs and said, "Cadet, bombs away. We'll see about the malfunction."

I didn't believe it. "We'll see about the malfunction?" If I got this mission on my record, I'd surely wash out. I was missing the target by over a thousand feet, or so it seemed.

When we landed back at Deming, Lieutenant Wilson held out his hand and said, "Okay, fellas, see you on the next mission." The Whiz shook his hand, but I pulled back and turned away and wouldn't meet him eyeball to eyeball. Lieutenant Wilson smirked, shrugged, and walked off.

Exasperated, the Whiz watched Lieutenant Wilson for a while, looked at me, and then grabbed me by the T-shirt and some skin from my chest, lifted me up to my tippy toes, and said, "Addy, don't you ever raise your Yankee voice to me again.

D'ya hear me clear?" He gently lowered me, saying, "Now how do you feel? I don't think Lieutenant Wilson will give us marks on those bombs, what with a malfunction and all." Together we silently walked back to the barracks, his Southern arm around my Yankee shoulder.

At the time, if I had been marked on the malfunction mission, I surely would have "washed out" of cadet training. All my marks were just passable; I was barely getting through. Any slight upheaval, whether it be in my school marks, attitude, flying, bombing, or my relationship to my fellow cadets would have been enough to fail me and send me back to Fort Dix.

Lady Luck was with me, straight through cadet training. Lieutenant Wilson never mentioned my airsickness to anyone, although he had seen me get deathly sick at least three times. Nor did he mark me on "attitude" as a bad risk for the air force. As luck would have it, Lieutenant Wilson even sought me out one afternoon in the briefing room and said, "Hey, White, still mad at me?"

I grabbed him by the hand and said, "Lieutenant Wilson, you saved my life by throwing out that last bombing mission. I'm glad you overlooked everything." I'm positive he knew what I meant. Sometimes I think back, *What if Lieutenant Wilson was a bad ass, a chicken-shit officer?* Thanks, God, and thank you, Lieutenant Wilson.

The days were growing short till graduation. We had less than a month to go, and the Whiz had my odds down to 12 to 1. I was now in the top third of my cadet class in bombing, up from the bottom third. I could run the eight miles a day without getting hysterical, and my attitude was "gung ho." My marks weren't too good; still, they were passable.

It was at this point in time that my little world caved in. The director of training, Lt. Col. L.M. Gregory, called me into his office for a meeting. I told the Whiz that my time had come, it was all over. He told me to be a good soldier and not to anticipate anything.

I marched into Lieutenant Colonel Gregory's office, saluted, was told to stand "at ease," and did so, waiting for the worst. He smiled at me, offered his hand, and told me how much the men liked me, that I was a funny guy and good for the men's morale.

80

He thanked me for helping him doctor up some of his speeches, which till then had been considered quite dry and humorless. I had done this little extracurricular chore through one of our second lieutenants but had never met Lieutenant Colonel Gregory face to face.

Colonel Gregory went on. My school marks, although not good, were passable, my flying and bombing marks were exemplary, and so was my attitude. What was wrong then? I waited.

He then asked me if I remembered, when I signed up for cadet training, the "warrant officer" release form. I said I had never heard of it. Colonel Gregory said because of my very limited prior education, I had signed a "release" form allowing the air force to commission me a warrant officer instead of a second lieutenant should I graduate from cadet training. The reason he was telling me this was because he didn't want me to be embarrassed on graduation day when I received the blue bars of a warrant officer instead of the silver bars of a second lieutenant.

I asked to see the "release" form I had signed, and Colonel Gregory said it would take time to get a photo. I asked how many men signed the form in my cadet class and was told I had not only been the first and only one in my class, but I was also the very first blue bar officer in the entire air-force training program.

I requested permission to speak frankly and off the record, and Colonel Gregory agreed to this. I then strutted up and down his office pleading that I had been brought up in orphanages, always worn hand-me-down clothes, and eaten rotten food till I was in the military service, yet in spite of my lack of education, I had kept up with my fellow cadets, I was now one of the top bombardiers in our graduating class, and the air force wanted to single me out to become a warrant officer, to wear a blue bar. I said, "That's punishment, not a reward for good work."

Colonel Gregory said I would be wearing the same uniform, would receive the same treatment, and would probably be promoted to second lieutenant in no time. The only difference was the blue bars.

All the while, Colonel Gregory had a strange expression on his face, as if he was truly embarrassed by this encounter. I smelled a rat. It suddenly occurred to me that he might not know how to deal with this new, strange situation. Maybe he was testing me?

Suddenly, I told him I was taking up too much of his valuable time, that I wouldn't be singled out as the only "blue bar baby" in my class, and that I wanted to be sent back to my outfit at Fort Dix.

Colonel Gregory sympathized and agreed with me, and then, pointing a pen at me, he said, "White, I'm sending a telegram to Washington, D.C., tonight. You brought up a damned good point Your being the only one in your cadet class to graduate under the W/O Act may make a difference. I'll let you know in two days."

That night, I cried and couldn't sleep. I swore the Whiz to secrecy, but most of my class, which had been whittled down to a precious few by now because of "washouts," knew something was wrong. I made up my mind I was back at Fort Dix with my old buddies. I gave the cadet training program my all. It was an adventure. At least, now I wouldn't get killed in those crazy, fucking airplanes.

For the next couple of days, I went to class and flew my bombing missions like a zombie. I didn't sleep, couldn't eat, and wouldn't communicate to anyone except the Whizzer.

Two days went by and when I didn't hear from the colonel, I knew it was all over. The die was cast. I wasn't sure I belonged with all those Joe College fly boys anyway. I was psyching myself up for the inevitable.

The fifth day, I was shaking hands with all the guys, saying good-bye with a phony smile. There was talk about a farewell party for me.

Then it came, a booming voice from the skies. The loudspeaker barked out, "Mr. Ed White, report to Colonel Gregory's office." I was daydreaming on my bunk when I heard the announcement. As a cadet, you usually "jump to" at any command, but all the strength drained out of me. It took me minutes to just get off the bunk, get into proper uniform, and check myself out with the Whiz. He looked like he was about to slobber all over me.

I saluted Colonel Gregory and he put me at ease. Staring at the floor, I didn't notice his rising from his desk. The next thing I knew, he was slapping me on the shoulders and grabbing my hand. "You're a lucky guy, Lieutenant White. Washington says you can graduate with full honors. They agreed it was unfair to single you out as the only W/O in your class. You lucky bastard, I didn't believe it could be done."

I don't remember if I thanked the good colonel or I kissed him or what. I only remember screaming as I fell into the barracks, "Attention, men, America can now win the war. White is back and the air force has him!" or words to that effect. In ten minutes, I was the same bad New Yorkese pain-in-the-ass wise guy that all the guys loved and had missed. They said the outfit just wasn't the same without my bullshit personality. Ah, they loved me and had really missed me.

Graduation was in the air. No more flying, thank God (no more throwing up), and no more schoolwork. For the first time in my life, I was going to be something, someone. I was going to be noticed. I tingled with anticipation, with excitement. I thought, *Is this really happening to me?*

I wrote to my sister, Ruth, to come to Deming, New Mexico, on or around April 17, 1943. She could pin my wings on my uniform. It was a ritual; so they told me. My sister wrote she couldn't make it.

Then I thought of Colonel Gregory's wife. No, that was too presumptuous of me. The Whiz came up with the solution. His beautiful child bride, Bebe, would be honored to pin me.

Two nights before graduation, I heard a rumbling in the barracks. Following the noise, I came upon a friendly crap game. I had a few bucks of my own, borrowed a few from the Whiz, and dived head first into the game. Hell, I still had a $250 uniform allowance coming to me.

It was one of those rare times in my life when I just couldn't lose. Whatever I touched, whatever I did, came up magic. Bet right—win. Bet wrong—win. All night long. Luckily, I cleaned out the game. This was my first taste of house money. I must have had all of $400. Was there that much money in the world? And I still had $250 coming for my uniform allowance tomorrow. I paid the Whiz back plus some, although he didn't want to take it.

The next day, I showed up for my uniform allowance. I noticed cadets on three lines and wasn't sure which line I was to get on. I went up to a second lieutenant, told him my name, and asked where I should go. He barked, "Get the hell on any line." I froze. One of my buddies yelled out, "Hey, White, he's only a shavetail like you. Don't take that crap from a second Lieutenant." I looked at the lieutenant and gave my very first order. I said, looking the lieutenant square in the eye, "Yeah!"

Then it was off to the tailor's office to be measured for our uniforms. I was ushered into a dark room smelling of perfume. A girl was measuring another cadet and writing on a large pad. Suddenly I got horny and remembered what I had been missing for eleven months.

When it came my turn, I found I was all alone with this very pretty girl who smelled like heaven. I nervously kidded her and said, "Please don't hurt me." She giggled and went about her business, measuring and writing. When she put the tape under my crotch, I hit the ceiling. Again she giggled.

I found out her name was Lucille, she was of Mexican ancestry, she had gone to college, and yes, she would go out with me after graduation. I gave her my name and took her phone number. All the time she kept giggling.

Could this be true? Everything good was happening to me. I was on some kind of a roll.

The moment was near. I thought, *Graduation Day! Man, this was bigger than my bar mitzvah. Today I really am a man! A flight officer in the U.S. Air Force, money in my pocket, and a date with a dream girl. Don't anyone wake me up.*

Most everyone was gathering over at the huge auditorium on the base at Deming, New Mexico. I ran back to the barracks to get my new cap. Hell, I still had twenty minutes to get to the auditorium when I heard that all too familiar, "Snap to cadet!" Oh, no, not that, not now, not at this moment. I snapped to attention and saw it was the same second lieutenant who had tortured me all during my cadet training.

"What's the rush, mister? In a hurry for something? Let's hear you sing 'I Had a Little Dawg' one more time. Come on." I looked at my watch. Seven minutes to ten. Maybe my watch was slow? Here I was in the middle of the New Mexico desert, less than a hundred yards from victory, with the dragon biting at my ass.

I glanced around and not a single solitary human being was

in sight. Everyone was in the auditorium but me and this chicken-shit asshole who wanted to be amused one more time.

Something snapped in me somewhere. I measured the lieutenant just right. I smiled as I started to sing, and then I belted him right on his little mustache. I covered the hundred yards to the auditorium in nine seconds flat and never looked back once.

The Whiz wanted to know why I was all sweated up, and I said I'd tell him later. I smiled sweetly at all the wives and parents and took my seat. Bebe pinned my wings on my pocket and kissed me and I was about to shake hands with the Whiz when Lieutenant Asshole pushed his way into our midst. "Let me be the first one to congratulate you, Lieutenant." We shook hands and laughed. What the hell!

It took me a while to get used to being an officer. I got into trouble on more than one occasion. Once, while at the post theater, I sat with some of the enlisted men who worked on the base. A senior officer passed by and shouted at me; "Lieutenant, there's a section for officers. If you're not satisfied with that arrangement, we can arrange for you to stay where you are." It took a while, but I soon learned to conform. To look at me, I was a dashing officer, but in my heart I was always an enlisted man, peasant that I am.

My date with Senorita Lucille was sheer delight. I was funny and attentive, and she giggled in all the right places. Knowing I had a five-day pass coming to me prior to my reporting to my next assignment, I closed my eyes and asked Lucille to accompany me to Mexico. To my delight, she said yes, and we shared our first kiss.

The first night we stayed in El Paso, Texas, right near Juarez, over the border. The next morning we had a huge Tex-Mex breakfast replete with jalapeno peppers. We walked over to the border gate, and I was advised to change most of my money into two-dollar bills. Lucille suggested that, for safety, I put some of my money into my shoes.

Juarez was dirty, dangerous, exciting, and entertaining—poverty everywhere, brothers selling their little sisters for a pittance, cab drivers taking the *tourista Americano* to dens of iniquity. The whole town seemed to be on the hustle. Hatred for the "gringo" hung heavy in the air. Lucille cautioned me not to answer the shouts of some of the men.

The food stank in Juarez. I couldn't eat a thing. I lived on corn chips and American soft drinks. Flies were everywhere, especially in and on the food. Lucille understood and sympathized with me. I promised her a feast when we returned to El Paso, in the good old U.S.A.

Sunday was to be our last day in Mexico, so we decided to see toreador El Soldado fight El Toro in Tiajuana's main bullring.

I had never seen a bullfight, naturally, so I didn't know what to expect. Immediately I fell in love with the preliminary Mexican music, the intense trumpets blaring out the news that the bullfight was to begin. I saw many U.S. Marines and Air Force personnel in the stands, all curious and eager as I was to see what this age-old Hispanic custom was all about.

Suddenly a gigantic bull came charging into the ring. He charged at the toreadors, who mechanically sidestepped him. When they were cornered, the toreadors jumped behind small barricades. It was fun, I thought, like the clowns in the rodeo. Then I noticed as the bull approached midring and faced my side of the arena that there were gobs of blood flowing down the sides of his neck. I had noticed that as the bull entered the ring, men slapped what I thought were banners on the bull's neck. What they were doing was sticking them into the bull's neck and drawing first blood.

Lucille had assured me that the bull was not to be killed, that I shouldn't get mad or too excited. These were "mock" bullfights, imitating the bullfights in Spain, but the difference was that here in Juarez they never killed the bull.

Lucille was misinformed, she soon learned to her and my dismay. Three huge bulls were to be killed that beautiful Sunday in Juarez, Mexico. The tipoff was when a picador kept sticking the first bull with a huge, pointed daggerlike pole. He drew blood and enraged the bull so that the main matador, El Soldado, would put on a good fight and please the bloodthirsty crowd.

After the first two bulls were killed, the American soldiers in the bull arena were incensed. Every branch of the services was represented in the audience, and the GIs were quite noisy and obviously pulling for the underdog, El Toro, the bull.

By the time the main event started, all the Americans, the gringos, had already started rooting for the bull and against the toreador. The words *yellow, bully, coward, and bullshit* were heard from all sectors of the arena.

Suddenly police with billy clubs appeared on the scene. They arrested or detained an American soldier here and there, and the crowd suddenly became silent. Close to Lucille and myself I could see three policemen roughing up a marine officer. He kept yelling something about one of the picador's horses' getting killed, which had happened in the second bullfight. The bull had charged under the picador's pole and under the horse's blanket and destroyed the horse. Seeing the dead horse tied and dragged, feet first, out of the arena was too much for some of the gringos.

I identified with the marine officer and jumped up to go to his aid. Lucille grabbed me and pleaded for me to sit down, saying that I could be of no help to my comrade in arms. The people who were sitting near us were shouting epitaphs at me, and Lucille calmed them a bit in their native tongue. I asked what they were saying, but she just pleaded for me to be still.

A yell went up. The third and final bull came snorting and charging into the ring, and here was the star, El Soldado (the soldier) direct from Mexico City. We later learned that the reason El Soldado was playing the bush leagues, Juarez, was because he had screwed up in Mexico City.

The Americans started yelling, "Viva El Toro" and giving El Soldado the raspberry. Lucille tugged at my arm for me to remain quiet. Some of the spectators, especially the women, flashed hostile eyes in my direction, as if to say, "Just open your mouth one more time, gringo, and you're dead." I kept quiet.

Every time the bull charged El Soldado, he ran behind a baricade. This went on for a while, and then the crowd began to boo and yell. Finally, El Soldado faced the bull for his first pass and the bull sent Senor E.S. flying through the air.

Americanos everywhere yelled, "Yeah, come on, El Toro, go get him!" Before they could rescue El Soldado, he got gored again, as they were carrying him out of the arena—right in El Tushy, right in the ass.

I thought the bull had won, and so did Lucille. We were wrongo. Another younger toreador stepped in and finished off

El Toro to satisfy the crowd. This made me sad, as I thought it was quite unfair.

Then we all heard the commercial of commercials, both in Mexican and in English. All those wishing to visit with the brave toreador, El Soldado, in the hospital could do so. There would be a charge for such a visit to help defray the expense of the toreador's accident.

We left the arena disgusted with what had just taken place. I kept saying, "But I don't understand. The bull won. Why did they have to kill him?" Poor Lucille was torn between trying to please me and her allegiance to her people.

We left Juarez that evening and had dinner in El Paso, where the food is also El Stinko, and I said adios to my beautiful Mexican muchacha. What would my first graduation leave be without lovely, sweet, understanding Lucillita?

Carlsbad, New Mexico

I thought all my flight training was over, that I was now a full-fledged second lieutenant bombardier and that was it. The air force had other plans and shipped half of my bombardier graduation class to Carlsbad, New Mexico, for further navigational training. It was at Carlsbad that I got my very first taste of air-force country-club living.

Everything was first class, as I knew it then. The food was tops, our living quarters were almost hotel-like, our military uniforms and wings were glamorous, and our attitude and appearance were irresistible.

At the Carlsbad navigational school, except for flight and training duties, our time was our own. For training purposes, we were assigned set flight and bombing and navigation crews. That meant that each crew was a semipermanent team in training. After class or training flights, without signing out or reporting to anyone, we could merely swashbuckle downtown to the California Hotel for a drink and to play cards, shoot craps, or ogle the local coeds.

My crap-shooting streak of luck carried over from Deming to Carlsbad. We formed a close-knit group of six officers, and each one of us had an assigned function. One man was overseer at the door, another guy watched the game to make sure no one slipped in a pair of phony dice, another guy took care of the food and drinks, one of the big guys handled the money, making change, accepting or not accepting checks, and extending credit. It was my duty to handle the dice and win for the house, which, luckily, I did.

The crap game was known and allowed to function by our senior officers under one direct unwritten order. No enlisted men or civilians were allowed to play in the game! The only disruption or disturbance occurred when a few local cowboys tried to force their way into the room. First they sweet-talked us, then they challenged us, and then they started swinging from the hip. After that first encounter, whenever I saw this same group of cowboys in the hotel lobby they would nod at us with respect. They realized it was a standoff. We were just obeying orders not to gamble with civilians.

The other emotional disruption was after one of the players went broke. He asked me for a loan, saying that his wife thought I was cute (she had seen me the night before) and that he personally admired my knowledge of gambling. I didn't realize this guy had been drinking heavily, and flattery made me let my guard down completely. I nodded to the guy handling our bankroll to make the loan. After losing his money again, this man really started insulting everyone and took back that his wife thought I was cute. If I didn't step in, he would have been roughed up pretty good. That night at the California bar, his pretty wife apologized for him and asked me not to allow her husband into the game anymore.

There were other winners in our little crap game, but I was the biggest and most consistent. When you're young and carefree, you have a certain belief in yourself and a rhythm to living, and I guess that was my time at bat. I haven't felt that rhythm or been that lucky since.

The girls in Carlsbad were young and younger and younger still! One encounter I had with a gorgeous, well-developed female ended up on her porch. She said her family were all sleeping and we could smooch on the glider. As I was unbuttoning her blouse, she naively asked me for my pair of wings. At that point,

I would have given her my Norden bombsight. Then she asked if I would give her my lieutenant bars. Gladly I handed them over. I realize now that when I become passionate, my hearing and bearing become impaired. Finally her breasts came into full view and she asked if she could have my fountain pen.

This last innocent request struck me funny, and I casually asked her how old she was. Her answer sent a bolt of adrenaline through my body and destroyed my erection instantly. "Why, honey, chile, I'm going on fifteen." I buttoned up frantically without asking for my uniform paraphernalia and flew back to the air base like a marathon runner. Pacemakers hadn't been invented at that time, and I was almost a candidate for a bypass or something. Thereafter, I was sure to ask the age of any girl whose acquaintance I made. The laws in New Mexico were firm about fraternizing with underaged females.

The bar at the California Hotel was the place for everyone to meet and greet. Not being a drinker, I faked it, sidling up to the bar. I bought drinks for people I knew or liked, and no one bothered to ask me what I was drinking. One day, I bought drinks for a cowboy by the name of Buster Crabbe and his sidekick, Fuzzy St. John. They were probably between pictures at the time.

June 18, 1943, being my birthday, I had heard that a surprise party was to be thrown for me at the California Hotel. I let it be known that I couldn't attend, that I was scheduled to fly a navigational mission that night. My buddies squawked to my commanding officer, and somehow they got me excused from my flight.

The party was attended by most of my friends and a few civilians we got friendly with in Carlsbad. Not knowing how or what to drink, I made all the cardinal mistakes. At each table, when someone insisted I have a drink with them, I drank whatever they were drinking. I mixed all my drinks all evening, and then the management brought out champagne. I don't recall ever leaving the grand ballroom of the California Hotel under my own power.

The next afternoon, when I awoke in one of the rooms of the California Hotel, I was sicker than sick. I had a lot of Air-force buddies visiting me, so I just excused myself and threw up vociferously. My head was too heavy for my shoulders, and I couldn't stop drinking water. Someone said champagne did that to you.

Suddenly I became aware that everyone was staring at me. Jokingly, I asked if I were dead and was this my wake. No one answered and I knew something was wrong. Finally, one of the guys told me the bad news. My plane had crashed the night before, on my birthday, and the pilot and the two bombardier-navigators had been killed. This time I threw up bile. Fate, destiny, call it what you will, had saved my life.

It took me a week to get over mixing all those drinks. I was sick not only physically but emotionally because of the tragic occurrence. There but for the grace of God . . .

When I went back to my navigation missions, it was obvious that I became more airsick than ever. Again I was successful in covering up. I flew all my missions, got passable marks, and was popular with all my fellow officers and the enlisted men. It was just that I became airsick now and again. "Hey," I always said nervously laughing, "it could happen to anyone."

The day I made first lieutenant.

Our training at Carlsbad came to an end, and we were now officially bombardier-navigator-observers. I had three ratings, two more than I bargained for. I had never figured to get this far. A kid from an orphanage, with an eighth-grade education, sickly, with limited direction and guidance, insecure with a capital "I." Now I was a somebody, a respected officer in the U.S. Air Force. God bless America.

Little did I know when I received my shipping-out orders that I was being transferred to the most elite country-club air base of them all, Langley Field, Virginia, and not in any old outfit but in Headquarters Company. Again I came up with a pat hand in life's game of poker.

I was assigned to the BOQ, the bachelor officers' quarters, with the officers' club, dining room and bar, swimming pool, and a view of Chesapeake Bay right outside my window. We were given a food allowance at the officers' club, so outside of drinking, which I did very little of, almost everything was on the house.

The name of my outfit was the Second Sea Search Attack Squadron, one of a few antisubmarine groups on the field. We flew the Liberator planes, heavy B-24s loaded down with depth charges, fifty-calibre machine guns, and the Norden bombsight, one of America's first secret weapons. We also were the first outfit to use radar and MAD, Magnetic Aero Detection, to locate submarines in hiding.

We were somewhat successful in getting our share of German submarines, but it seemed that we constantly fought amongst ourselves more. The navy would fire at us from baby aircraft carriers sometimes, stating the next day that they had thought we were a Japanese flying boat: We were accused of firing at marine PBYs during night submarine patrol flights. This went on and on, with each branch of the service threatening to shoot the other down. I never heard of anyone being killed or hurt; it was just a tempest in a teapot. Each branch had to feel it was the best; we were playing macho.

My roommate at the BOQ was a nice-enough guy, but he was sadly lacking a sense of humor. All my jokes died a-borning. I used to hold court at a table near the bar every early evening, telling stories and jokes or imitating our senior officers. Then I'd go back to my room at the BOQ and get the silent treatment from Mr. Sourpuss.

One evening, while I was doing so-so with stories and jokes, I heard this booming laugh behind me. I turned around and there was this big, good-looking Italian lieutenant taking everything in. He said, "Hey, Lieutenant, you're funny!" I invited him to sit down and join us at our table. This handsome, good-natured Latin John Wayne turned out to be Lt. Arthur M. Stringari. Thus began one of my more solid friendships in life. Art, or "Buck," as we called him in the air force, was married to a schoolteacher and the father of a beautiful baby girl.

Through my contacts down at headquarters and the usual military finagling, I was able to transfer Buck into my room. First I had to inform the personality kid, my present roommate, and he spoke for the first time. He let out a howl and said something that sounded like "I'll kill you!" Now I could defend myself. I could fight—or rather I could box—pretty good, but my opponent was a husky middleweight. He didn't feel like boxing. Instead, he got me in a bear hug held me that way for what seemed like a decade. Finally, Buck walked in with his clothes and said, "Taking a folk-dancing lesson, Ace?" and the fight was over. From then on I was called Ace, although Buck insisted I spell it with two s's.

Buck sometimes called me Strunze and told me that meant Ace in Italian. After the war, I found out *strunze* meant shit. Buck was an educated guy, having attended college. He never tired of explaining things to me, mostly life, books, the arts, poetry, things I might be ashamed to discuss with anyone else.

We were inseparable except when we flew missions. Then we would wait for each other for dinner or whatever. My luck was still holding out in the crap games, so we had plenty of money. I owned a 1935 Packard convertible, complete with rumble seat, that we called The Green Hornet. So life was up, up, and away.

Most evenings we didn't even go to the officers' club for dinner, even though it was on the house. Money was easy come, easy go, and our tastes became more exotic. There was an Italian restaurant in a small town, Phoebus, not too far from Langley Field. The elderly Italian owner-chef maintained that he once cooked for Fiorello H. La Guardia, New York's colorful mayor.

Usually around eight of us starving flight officers would pile into the restaurant and a large table laden with antipasto would

On leave at Lake Placid.

With Betty Lou Colton of the Ziegfeld Follies and best pal Lt. Arthur (Buck) Stringari living it up in New York City.

have already been set up for us at the rear. Buck Stringari sometimes picked me up bodily and would throw me into the kitchen
as bait. Signor Chef was an obvious homosexual, and he delighted
in talking to me, pinching my cheeks, and hugging me. This
confrontation usually lasted for about three minutes, and
everyone but me agreed it was well worth the effort. The huge
amounts of food that came out of the kitchen attested to my
macho charisma. Every time the chef walked by my chair, he
would fondle me under the chin and and say, "Dis is for Lt. Don
Gentile, da Italian-American pilot. Viva Italia!" I think Buck had
told him I was Lieutenant Gentile, the great American war ace,
at that time. I had to go along with the prank to keep the guys
happy and well fed. The bills for our dinners were usually cut
in half, too. *C'est la guerre!*

Life at Langley Field was happy and carefree for the most
part, war or no war. The antisubmarine missions weren't too
dangerous. Occasionally, we lost a plane or two over water or in

My plane on the runway at Langley Field, Virginia.

flight accidents and for a time an aura of sadness hung heavy over the base. But life and the war went on.

I still got airsick but not as often. And I didn't have to maintain any secrecy about it. Most of the outfit knew about my problem, and some flight officers even admitted to being airsick themselves now and again. On long, low flight missions with heavy winds aloft, I could be totally wiped out, but on high-altitude missions I was usually okay. The trick was for me to stay relaxed and definitely not to eat anything or watch anyone eat.

One of our planes was named Showboat, and it definitely was. I was constantly on the intercom, singing songs, telling jokes, and imitating everyone from President Roosevelt to Jack Benny to Colonel Polan, our commanding officer. I insisted each enlisted man perform, even if he only read a corny poem or a silly limerick. After a while, a few of the pilots started requesting me as their bombardier-entertainer.

Buck was assigned a nice little Cape Cod house a mile outside of Langley Field, and his wife and daughter joined him. So now I had some home life, with home-cooked meals, and, being a bachelor, I was forced into baby-sitter service. I didn't want it generally known and I wouldn't admit to it, but I more than liked taking care of the children. They called me Too-Too White, as one of the kids couldn't say Lieutenant White, and the name stuck with all the kids. After a while, I realized I was becoming too attached to the children. Sometimes I prevented the parents from disciplining their own kids. A lecture from one of the wives made me understand, and I backed off.

The complex where the married officers and their families lived was a grouping of many of these small Cape Cod houses. The happiest moments I can recall at Langley Field were when some of my buddies and their wives would go out for an evening and leave me with three or four mischievous kids. As soon as their parents were out of sight, they would attack me and bounce me on the carpet. Nancy Kay Stringari and Billy Newell, Jr., and some of those other cowboys and cowgirls, where are you now and have you forgotten Too-Too White?

My car, The Green Hornet, was known by all the young WACs at Langley Field. I was considered somewhat of a ladies' man, and word spread quickly. Instead of being leery of me, the girls would all greet me cordially as soon as they saw me and the car. I could have had my pick if I wanted, but I had a huge crush on one particular girl, Cpl. Blanche Jennings—blond and petite, with the face of an angel.

When Blanche spoke to me, I practically swallowed my tongue. When I smelled her perfume, I took off without my plane. I dreamed and schemed about her at night. I was resolved she would be my girl friend or else. After all, what was this war all about? What was I fighting for? I enlisted the sworn aid of Buck Stringari. "Please help me get a date with Jennings."

One day, there was a huge bond rally at the Langley officers' club. The way they sold bonds in large amounts was to have the wealthier senior officers bid on hard-to-get items at that time— things like nylon stockings, cashmere sweaters, Evening in Paris perfume, and so forth. The bond rally was in the main ballroom, and I could hear the bidding from the bar, where I was nursing a Coke and holding court.

I suddenly felt a soft touch on my shoulder and could see in the bar mirror it was Cpl. Blanche Jennings. I almost choked on an ice cube. Blanche kissed me on the cheek and held out a form for me to sign. I signed the slip without reading it, collected my thoughts, and said to the guys, "Hey, what was that all about?"

A few moments later, Blanche Jennings returned and I quickly turned around and got my kiss on the lips. Again I signed some sort of a form. Again it happened. This time I got a kiss and a hug. Again, this time a lingering kiss standing up and a promise of a dinner date with the girl of my dreams. Whatever it was, I thought, Corporal B.J. could only resist my charms for just so long.

My dream only lasted a moment longer. Then I heard the booming voice of a chicken-shit colonel yelling, "Where's this Lieutenant White? Which one is he?" I jumped to attention and said, "I'm Lieutenant White, sir." He was standing next to a woman built of lard who was obviously his wife. She said, "Lieutenant White, I'm Colonel so-and-so's wife and you are completely out of order. You have ruined the spirit of our bond rally. All the lovely gifts that are auctioned off with the war bonds are to be spread amongst all the bidders. You are undoubtedly a spoiled brat who has no respect for money or your fellow officers."

Off they went. Other senior officers came by with their wives, gave me dirty, repelling looks, and turned on their heels.

I thought, *This is obviously some mistake. What could I have done? I never left the bar.*

Then Buck Stringari came to the bar with the biggest grin. "Well, Strunze, we did it. Corporal Jennings is all yours."

I said, "What the hell is this all about? All those majors and colonels are mad at me."

"Strunze, this will all be forgotten in a few days. Do you know what I did for you? I invested all your money, $15,000, in U.S. War Bonds. This way you'll have a stake after the war. Now with the nylons and stuff I gave to Corporal Jennings, she's flattered and very impressed with you."

I said, "Fifteen thousand dollars—that's all the money I have! No way! I'm not spending all my money on bonds. Forget it. The deal's off!"

"Okay, Ace," Stringari said. "You go tell sweet Blanche Jennings you want all those lovely gifts back, and you go tell the colonel that the deal is off!"

My dates with Blanche Jennings were heaven. I remember every lingering kiss, every fervent vow we made in the darkness of The Green Hornet. Later, those bonds helped financially get me through those first few years after the war. I hate to think how I would have made it without that money, which gave me time to get my head on straight in peacetime.

Some of the friendships I made at Langley Field and at all the other military installations where I was stationed I still retain to this day. One young lieutenant whose outfit was just passing through Langley Field touched me more than the rest. Bob Schratwieser would smile at me and say, "Roger dodger, Eddie" or "Over and out, Ace," and I would melt. I met Bob at the officers' club, and he mentioned he would love to date a certain WAC officer. On the spot I arranged the date. Then he said he didn't have use of a car, and I offered him The Green Hornet and finagled him a bottle of Haig and Haig pinch. I kept asking myself why I was looking out for this new guy—he was shipping out soon and I'd probably never see him again. I was right.

Lt. Robert Schratwieser was on the first American low-liner bombing raids over the Ploesti oil fields. The letter I received said that the flak on that mission was devastating, that only two chutes left the plane and they had come from the tail end of the ship. Bob was assumed to be dead. The WAC officer who had dated Bob for close to a month came to see me at the Langley bar, and we cried for hours. She informed me that she and Bob had become very close and expected to see each other after the war.

I thought to myself that it wasn't fair. *Young Bob Schratwieser, in the prime of his life, so good-natured, so honest about his feelings.* I remember he was Catholic and he used to take me to church on Sundays. I always came away with a wonderful spiritual feeling. Part of it was the church service, but a good part of it was Bob, too.

I couldn't shake the heavy, depressed feeling in my heart for weeks. One day, on impulse, I called Bob's mother out on Long Island. I said I was from Langley Field and had heard that her son was "lost in action." She said that she had received a telegram to that effect but she was optimistic and praying to God that Bob was still alive. I said I was praying, too, and hoped my trembling voice didn't betray my true feelings. Much as I thought about it, I never called back again.

We lost many men in training—almost as many as we did in combat. Whenever a plane went down somewhere, the fires could be seen for miles. Most of the men would run down to the fight line, out of curiosity or possibly to see if they could be of assistance. I usually ran back to the BOQ, got into bed, and pulled the comforter over my head. Hearing the names of my dead colleagues was the worst part. I'd look at their pictures over and over again in disbelief. *Where did they go? Is that it? What is life all about?* I wondered. I never could get used to death, especially when it came to someone so very young, like Lt. Bob Schratwieser.

I stayed at Langley Field for close to a year on antisubmarine patrol, and then the war started closing in. We in the Sea Search Attack Squadron were considered the number one project, from what we heard, during the war. Then word drifted down to us about The Manhattan Project, and our elite outfit utilizing radar bombing and radar landing was soon forgotten. We were then all dispersed to other outfits hastily for crew training for eventful overseas combat duty. My orders came through and I was to report to the CO at the Walla Walla Air Base in the state of Washington.

When I arrived it was raining and it rained for my entire stay at Walla Walla. I thought my back had healed from a B-18 crash at Langley Field, but now I went to bed with pains in my left and right shoulder wings and usually woke up to the same pains. The doctors called it something that sounded like "fibro myositis in the left and right trapezius" and gave me a painkiller, and I went back to flying with my new crew.

One day we were practicing takeoffs and landings on a runway some distance from the field. Before we took off, I felt a slight wave of nausea from the burnt smell of the putt-putt engine. (This is the small engine that helps get the larger engines and the propellers started.) I forgot it and carried on, but then the pilot bounced us around on his takeoffs and landings. He said he couldn't help himself, as the crosswinds were quite heavy. Finally, I started to perspire and it happened. I got airsick with a capital "A."

After the flight, I went back to the barracks to sleep the sickness off. I thought all was forgotten until the next morning, when I was told to report on sick call. *Hey, this is routine; I've been through this before,* I thought. The examining doctor asked me how long I had been getting airsick, and when I told him he looked at me with disbelief. Here was a first lieutenant with over four years of military service telling him something he probably had never heard before.

He made up a large medical report on my case and told me I was grounded till further orders. Each time I returned, the doctor revealed a little more to me. It was his contention that my acute airsickness was actually a "fear of flying" syndrome stemming from the insecurity I experienced in early life. I told him that I had been flying this long and wished to continue on flight duty till the end of the war. The good doctor stated that should I become deathly ill on a flight, I'd be jeopardizing ten men's lives. Now I was in the same situation as an enlisted man whose parachute had popped open and whom I personally grounded at Langley Field. The only difference was, I wanted to continue flying.

The doctor made an appointment for me to meet with an air-force General who was passing through the Walla Walla Air Base. I was ushered into a room filled with high-ranking officers and came face to face with Gen. "Dust to Dawn" Maughan. He got the nickname, so the story goes, because as a young officer he flew from coast to coast from morn to dawn. This had probably been unheard of in the early days of flying.

General Maughan looked me in the eyes and said, "What do we have here?" He read my report and said that if I resigned, I could be home in four weeks. "Here, just sign this resignation form, Lieutenant, and you're on your way." I said I didn't want to resign, that I wanted to be returned to my outfit and on full flight duty. The general called a huddle between himself and a few of the officers, and then he shouted at me, "Lieutenant, I don't have much time. The war is practically over. You've done your duty. Four years is a long time out of anyone's life. The U.S. government thanks you, but now you're a statistic. Sign this and you'll get an honorable discharge and all the advantages that go with it." With that he jumped up, I saluted him, and he left the room.

A colonel sat with me for a while after the general had left and explained my rights. The colonel, neglected to inform me that as a disabled officer, I should have been "retired" instead of resigning. Under duress, I signed the papers of resignation. An hour later, I went back to tear up those same papers and was refused access to them.

Within days, I was shipped to Lamour Field, California, and assigned to Squadron V. One strange coincidence is that Joe Heller, who wrote the book *Catch 22*, is now a friend of mine, and almost every character and almost every situation in *Catch 22* I personally witnessed or experienced at Lamour Field in Squadron V. Word was that the war actually was winding down and Squadron V was the first outfit organized for discharging the thousands of officers no longer needed for military duty.

Squadron V was also a pirates' cove, a den of transient iniquity. Every service con man who was caught, every thief, every rape artist, complainer, guardhouse lawyer, malingerer, and every comedian seemed to be stationed there, waiting for military discharge. It was as if I had been caught going through a red light and here I was being thrown into solitary confinement in Attica. I tried to keep my sanity, knowing this stay was only temporary. After close to two months, I was told to report for my traveling orders. Where to? Back to the base of my origin, Fort Dix, New Jersey. I was given a ticket to Trenton, New Jersey, and a roomette all to myself on the train. Sanity prevailed at last.

The train was made up of many Hollywood characters in addition to straight civilians. There were hardly any military uniforms to be seen, so as an officer, I was treated with respect, awe, and dignity. People bought me drinks, cigars, magazines, and dinner and made me feel like some sort of a celebrity. One afternoon in the club car, I met David Rose, the Hollywood producer (not the conductor) and Sammy Cohen, the comedian. We became very friendly and I quickly relaxed and they got me dead drunk. Before they carried me to my roomette, I requested they send over the young, ravishing, beautiful girl who had joined us that evening.

Anything for the war effort. Sure enough, within half an hour, there was a knock on my door. With palpitating heart I opened the door, and there was the lady of my choice with wet lips and drunker than I was. I helped her off with her clothes, and when I turned my back, she fell fast asleep. All night long we made passionate love, but all she did was grunt and burp, more from heartburn than passion.

In the morning I dressed, called the porter, and ordered breakfast for two. I tipped him and requested that he please inform me at least two hours before we reached Trenton, New Jersey, telling him that otherwise, I would be hung at dawn.

I went back to my roomette and again tested my staying power and virility. *This moment may never come for me again,* I thought. *Even if it did, this woman is exceedingly cultured, beautiful, and passionate, not to mention stacked.* The flesh was weak. I was her slave, and oh, oh, there I went again.

When the porter aroused me, I had been to the well once too often. How pale was I? Well, when I reported to Fort Dix I looked like an albino. I checked into the officers' barracks and went straight to sleep. My stay at Dix was for only three days before I would received my discharge papers. I wanted to visit my old

Fort Dix buddies at Headquarters Company before leaving military life.

After a full day's rest, I felt slightly rejuvenated and went over to the mess hall and Headquarters Company. The screams that went up were music to my hungry ears. I was embraced, picked up, kissed, pinched, punched, and all but eaten up alive. I got on line with my enlisted buddies, and when the cook questioned my credentials they all yelled, "Shaddup and serve him; he was here before you were born!"

I caught up on everything. Larry Alpert was now a sergeant in charge of the chaplain's office; Sergeant Sica was now a captain, as were Sergeants Goodman and Norris of the court-martial section. One sergeant, friend of mine Sgt. Lloyd, had received the Congressional Medal of Honor posthumously, for saving some of his men from a tank attack somewhere in Europe; Captain Decker was a full colonel off to another assignment; Sgt. Marco Rosales, our bandleader, was now in the Philipines and rumored to be engaged to President Quezon's daughter; and on and on and on.

I was home. These were my men. They knew me and accepted me as I was. Officer or not, I was still one of them. The uniform was only a coverup. I was still Sgt. Eddie White, part of the headquarters family. They didn't salute me; nor did I expect them to. It would have been most embarrassing.

The three days were gone and I was on my way to Woodmere, Long Island, New York, home of my sister, Ruth, my brother-in-law, Leon, and my nephew, Steve. I had mixed emotions, but nervously pushed all feelings out of my mind. There was enough time to make decisions and try to steer a course on the sea of life. I had had no direction before I entered the military service. Facing up to who I was and/or what I was going to do was the most frightening thing I ever had to face. I had entered the service on November 26, 1940. With my thirty-three days of terminal leave, it would be September 11, 1944, before I would be officially released from my military obligations. I had completed four years, ten months, and fifteen days of service. Those years, coupled with the thirteen years I spent in various orphanages, meant eighteen years of dead time, though not really. I had been given an education in the service, I had been paid well, I had lived well, I had been given a chance to grow into manhood, and I was rich with the many lifelong friendships I had made. When I was seventeen, I had resolved to stop feeling sorry for myself. I reminded myself over and over of the extreme self-pity I suffered as a kid.

When I arrived in Woodmere, I truly felt like a fish out of water. This wasn't exactly what I had expected. My nephew, Steve, was overjoyed to see me, which lasted for an hour or so. Then he had his friends, his games, and his TV shows.

My sister and brother-in-law were glad, too, but "What are you going to do with your life? Where are you going to live? When are you going to take off your uniform?" When, why, how, what? It wasn't their fault. I didn't blame them, but I needed time and space to figure out what this new world was all about.

That first night, I couldn't sleep. I was listless and felt a funny tickling or throbbing sensation somewhere in my body. I got up in the middle of the night to urinate but couldn't. I turned the light on and looked at my penis. There, on the tip, was a gelatin lily-white pearl, a sure sign of gonorrhea. I had seen the army VD films and knew what a clap looked like. *Oh no, that lovely, cultured lady on the train,* I thought. *It can't be!* But it was. My penis had never lied to me before.

I urinated oh so slowly and painfully, drip-dry style, and went back to bed. I was mortified. Whom could I tell or talk to? Not my sister. She thought *clap* meant applause or a board used for siding on her house. I decided to go back to Fort Dix and check into the hospital. After all, I was still officially on terminal leave for thirty-three days, therefore still under military jurisdiction.

The next day, I explained to my little family that because of a technicality I had to report back to Fort Dix. All the way back on the train, I practiced speeches as to what to say to anyone who questioned me about my embarrassing predicament. *Me, an officer, on the very first day of civilian life,* I thought. *Sure me, probably only me.* Life is a circus . . . a hectic thing. . . .

When I checked into the hospital, everything was so routine I didn't need any of my awkward speeches. Although I was the only officer in the VD ward, no one paid attention to me. I got a shot of penicillin, slept overnight, and was told I was free to go early in the morning. Years later, I learned I was allergic to penicillin, but it sure did cure me in my hour of need.

As I was leaving, a captain called my name out in the hallway and asked me to step into his office. "Lieutenant, there's a wave of gonorrhea going around. We have to have the name of the girl who gave you this dose. She probably doesn't even know she has it."

I thought for a moment, and with true phony chivalry, I said, "Do you want me to kiss and tell? I can't do that."

The captain stared at me and said, "Do you want any of your buddies to wind up with the same thing and then give it to their wives or their girl friends?"

That convinced me. I gave him my lovely donor's name and phone number, put on my dark glasses, and slinked out of the hospital. *L'amour, toujours manure.*

On my way home on the train, I thought there might be a couple of redeeming factors to this whole drama. I had learned a little lesson. Gonorrhea didn't mean the death penalty, as I once thought. Pretty girls aren't necessarily clean girls. Penicillin was a wonderful wonder drug. I felt I took care of myself like a man. "That's it!" I often heard as a kid. "You're not a man until you've had the clap!" Today I was a man. Naturally I kept my mouth shut and never told a soul about this incident.

6

Civvie Blues

1946: UN formed; guilty verdicts of Nuremberg jury; Admiral Byrd's expedition to South Pole; U.S. population 140 million; Assault wins Triple Crown.

THE NEXT FEW MONTHS were agonizing, frustrating, and inse-cure. On my terminal leave, I tried to remove my uniform, but felt naked and unsure of myself each time I put on civilian clothes. I'd run back, put on my uniform, and give a sigh of relief. It was close to three months before I could walk out of the house in civvies. Eventually, I went into New York City, and gradually I got used to wearing a sport jacket and slacks.

I was twenty-six years of age and had a degree in bombing, navigating, and observing. I could use the latter, I thought. For months I walked around the city observing the girls, eating hot dogs at Grant's on 42nd Street, seeing a double feature a day, taking in the burlesque maybe, or just walking my ass off. What else was there to do?

I went to see my old landlady, the one from the island of Malta, and heard that she had either died, moved, or gone back to Malta. All my personal things were lost. I couldn't remember what they were except for my autographed picture of John Barry-more.

I went down to the Brill Building, in Tin Pan Alley, and none of the songwriters would talk or even look at me. I stopped one writer in the office of Mills Music, Henry Tobias, and suggested we write songs together. His answer: "Would you ask Irving Berlin to write with you?"

106

Years later, Mr. Tobias changed his tune and suggested we team up as collaborators. He either forgot or didn't recognize me as the same impertinent kid who had once approached him. This time I declined without going into detail.

Eventually I found a furnished room in the West 90s, bought a wardrobe at Bond's, Howards', and Crawford's, and began trying to write songs in earnest. I heard that D'Artega, the bandleader, was searching for a theme song for the Sister Kenny Foundation. With Alphonse D'Artega, I wrote "Go Sleepy Sleep," which was a pet phrase used by my sister in putting her kids to sleep. I now had another nephew. Cary had joined our small clan.

The song was accepted and I thought I had won the Nobel Peace Prize. Actually, it meant nothing but prestige. No money, no records, and only D'Artega performed it, with his all-girl orchestra.

It was around this time of my life that my father surfaced again. I was somewhere in the West 70s when I heard someone call my name. It was Charley Phil Rosenberg, an ex–boxing champion, now a renowned bookie and a known friend of "Broadway" Jack White. He said that Jack would like to see me, that he had heard I wasn't in the service anymore. Charley Phil didn't have Jack's telephone number, so I stopped off at the old Lindy's and got the number from one of the characters who hung around there. I don't know why, but whenever I come in contact with my father's cronies they always seemed to stare at me in a holy sort of way. I felt as if I were supposed to turn their water into wine or part their chicken soup.

I called Jack and, without any emotion, he asked me how I felt and said I should come on over to his apartment, also in the West 90s. It was a large furnished room with two single couches that converted into beds when the drapes were removed. When I told him where I was living, he made a face and suggested I move into his place until I got settled. When I told my sister what Jack had said, she made the same face and said I was old enough to make my own decisions. She was expecting another child.

Living with Jack was like living at West Point and getting the silent treatment. I don't think Jack wanted it that way, but he couldn't help himself. He just couldn't express his feelings.

This very handsome, smart racketeer with the manners and dress of a matinee idol just couldn't reach out. I could make him laugh, but even then he couldn't let it all out. Laughing to me was a contagious, continuous thing; to Jack it was only a brief moment.

This time, I tried to dig in and understand my father, but he didn't like to talk about the past. I thought he had some feeling for me, but I couldn't be sure and I don't have any proof to this day. My father never embraced me, never kissed me, never put his arm around my shoulders. Yet something in the way he briefly looked at me made me think he loved me. But maybe all the love generated from my side. I remember once telling a very young, beautiful actress, "Missy, I love you enough for the two of us!" Maybe that was it. I think that if I met my old man today, I could open him up, but my feelings were still in the formative stages then.

The first thing I taught my loving son Peter, around the time I taught him to say, "Yay, Giants!," was to kiss and hug and to say, "I love you." To this day, we don't ever speak on the phone without expressing our love for each other. I may not be Dr. Spock, but I believe expressing deep, continuous love replaces many mistakes we often make. Jesus, it had better.

One afternoon I came home and found a bunch of college-type guys in the apartment and my father in handcuffs. They were detectives and Jack was charged with being a "user" and "pusher" of a white powdery substance—coke. I didn't know what the hell that was and tried to talk these nice guys out of taking Jack away. One detective looked at a picture of me in my air-force uniform on the mantle and said, "Is that you?" When I replied in the affirmative, he looked at Jack and said, "Why do bastards like you have sons like this?" Those words ring in my ears to this day.

That was the last time I ever saw my father. He was taken to the Tombs downtown and eventually sentenced to a stretch in Lexington, Kentucky, where he was to be treated for narcotic addiction. After inquiring, I found out Jack had been there twice before.

I kept the furnished room for a while, but then looked around for another place. I was embarrassed that the neighbors all knew what had happened, and I wanted a fresh start.

This was enough to stoke the fire of musical ambition in me, to keep me going. Then, too, D'Artega had me write the jingles for the Topp's Chewing Gum Company, and although he made more money than he told me, he paid me fifty dollars a jingle. Oh, lucky me. I spread the word at the Brill Building about my huge success.

D'Artega, the handsome Mexican bandleader, is now a priest somewhere in the world. Father Alphonse D'Artega went from "all girls" to "no girls"!

There wasn't any money coming in, but I still had enough left over to live on. Thank God for Buck and his war bonds. But I'd better get something going fast.

I found Stanley Adams's telephone number and called him. He was overjoyed to hear from me, and when we got together it was like we had never been apart. He was still the funniest guy in the world. He too had been in the service and he too was hungry to write—not songs, but comedy shows for radio and Broadway. We went on cheap fast-food eating binges and formulated big plans for the future. Show business was for the taking, and we were going to take over. Big Stan, Uncle Stanley, all three hundred lovable pounds of him, was back in my life. What dreams, what schemes, what plans we had. Uncle Stanley stimulated me, he made me feel ambitious, like a professional writer, but most of all he made me hysterically happy. He made me laugh till it hurt!

I broached Stanley on our writing a Broadway musical one evening by mimicking Judy Garland and Mickey Rooney in those "Why don't we put the show on ourselves?" films. Stanley scoffed until I told him I even knew who might raise the money and produce our show. Then he was interested. I came up with a working title: *Broadway Beachhead*. The main idea was to cast only professional, talented ex-GIs in the show. How could we miss? We had a waiting, locked-in audience out there. *They owed us something for the years we served our country*, we thought.

We got together with another young writer I chanced to meet, Jack Lawrence. Jack was originally from my neck of the woods, da Bronx, and he had become bored from hanging around the advertising business. Jack was a tall, and handsome, ruddy-complexioned ex–top sergeant. He was separated from the army with his share of medals. His real name was Jack Seligman, but he thought, as we all did, that he needed a more theatrical name.

Now the show started to take shape. Jack Lawrence, Stanley, and I would write the book, Murray Gans, my old Fort Dix collaborator, would compose the music to my lyrics, and two new pals of mine, Ted Seidel and Bert Knapp, would raise the money and produce the show. Ted had been in charge of a Red Cross unit overseas during the war. Bert was now an announcer with Radio Station WMCA. He had been a bombardier who had to bail out of his B-24 plane and wound up with the underground in Belgium.

Ted Seidel already had offices over at the Earle Building on 52nd Street and Broadway, and he allocated one office for *Broadway Beachhead*. Those first few staff meetings we had were very exciting to us all. This was no mere dream. We were Broadway bound.

Jack Lawrence and I would usually meet an hour before Stanley and Murray would arrive. We'd have breakfast, or rather I would eat and Jack would talk. I thought it odd that Jack never ate anything, but it soon left my mind.

Jack liked me from the moment we met, and he started telling me everything about his life. He had a crush on this nice Jewish girl who had just won the Miss America beauty Pageant. Her name was Bess Myerson, and she was meeting him in the afternoon. Would I like to meet her? She was from the Bronx, too. Her father was a house painter, she played the piano, and she was very down to earth, he told me.

Bess was everything Jack told me and more. She was still unsophisticated, tall and pretty without being overpowering— more the outdoor type, I thought at the time. Bess still had a couple of adolescent blemishes on her face. She would blush easily and was sincerely sweet.

Jack said he was going to manage Bess's career and that I was his partner. We shook on it and when I wasn't involved with our show, Jack and I would try to further the career of New York's finest Miss America.

As time went on, I had the feeling that Jack wasn't doing too well with Bess romantically. She was being pulled in all directions by other people. Most of her energies were being channeled into political endeavors. One day she was making a civil rights speech on the courthouse steps in Atlanta, Georgia, and the next she was marching in Selma, Alabama.

The first time I heard her feelings about what was wrong with the world, and especially our country, Bess Myerson's stock went up a thousand percent with me. Here was a real Jewish Joan of Arc. And this was before it was popular to be involved with unpopular causes. Bess Myerson wasn't just another bleeding heart liberal, as she was often accused of being. Bess put her young life, limbs, and time on the line. She marched, and spoke, she gave, and she suffered. Sometimes, when she appeared down south, the rednecks carried signs saying: "Messy Bessy, get out and stay out!"

Bess Myerson stimulated me politically and made me aware and interested to this day. This was before Jane Fonda and Joan Baez and Betty Friedan, whom I also respect. And Bess was all of twenty years young.

The real bleeding heart liberals I thought were Harry Belafonte, whom I knew personally, and Sammy Davis, Jr., whom I didn't know personally. They got on the bandwagon when the road was paved and it had started to become the thing. But guys like Dick Gregory pounded the dusty pavements with his people when there weren't any TV cameras grinding.

I can't recall Belafonte or Davis going up to Harlem in the old days and working the Apollo Theater so their poor brothers could see them. When Dr. Martin Luther King, probably the greatest man of this century, started to be accepted and listened to, in spite of the FBI's John Edgar Hoover, there was Harry Belafonte at the good doctor's and Mrs. King's side. Give me Dr. Ralph Bunche or Julian Bond.

I spent many months alongside Harry Belafonte and never heard him utter a profound statement of any kind. I listened to Sammy Davis time and again in interviews and always came away with the feeling that he was patronizing his own people. But "Messy Bessy"—God bless this brave woman—was there when her young voice could hardly be heard above the cannon's roar.

The next few months saw *Broadway Beachhead* start to grow.

Songs were written, sketches came together, and decisions were formulated. Jack Lawrence and I had done a concert at Carnegie Hall where Bess Myerson played the piano. She was so shy that we actually had to push her out on the stage when it came her time.

Then NBC hired Stanley Adams and me to write a pilot variety show and we chose the title "Miss America." It starred Bess, D'Artega's All Girl Band, comedian Paul Regan, and the satirist Baby Rose Marie. The show looked and sounded like a hit, but it never sold. Both Stanley and I received $500, an astronomical sum of money at the time.

Then we wrote another show, "Batter Up," starring the great Babe Ruth, Mel Allen; Davis and Doc Blanchard, et cetera. The Babe showed up for the taping of the show wearing a tan cashmere coat and peaked cap. He cut quite a handsome figure, but it was pitiful. He was starting to deteriorate physically, and his voice was completely hoarse.

Actually, Mel Allen wasn't in the original cast, but when The Bambino spoke, we learned his voice had been reduced to a whisper. We learned he had cancer of the throat, so we had to use Mel in order to hold the show together. Babe Ruth was hospitalized shortly thereafter and died, leaving us with nothing but a memorable demonstration record of "Batter Up," the Babe's last swing at life.

With these setbacks, I had to take odd jobs, writing parodies for comedians who sometimes cheated me out of my money, sketches for nightclubs that folded in the middle of an engagement, and jingles for products that were never sold. I did a little better managing a couple of aspiring young singers who worked the borscht circuit, the Catskill Mountains, and various hotel club dates. The money was small, but it was something and steady.

By this time, Ted Seidel and Bert Knapp had a live investor who wanted to keep us busy. He offered us $10,000 to finish *Broadway Beachhead*. Stupidly and proudly, we said we'd finish the show without the money. Ted Seidel thought it might be smart to show "good faith" by not taking the money up front.

This was a terrible mistake, because *Variety*, the show-business paper, came out with a story that Melvyn Douglas was producing and directing a Broadway-bound musical based on GIs entering civilian life. We were stunned. Had Mr. Douglas taken our idea? We were all paranoid. *Call Me Mister* was a Broadway hit and *Broadway Beachhead* started to lose its appeal, our interest, and our live investor. The morning meetings became few and far between, and then there was none.

When our show collapsed, I heard that Jack Lawrence was ill and inquired further. Jack showed up once for lunch, and again I noticed he wasn't eating anything. Finally, he noticed my concern and mumbled something about stomach trouble. A few months later, my handsome friend Jack Seligman Lawrence quietly passed away from cancer. That old adage about nice people going first is true. No one was nicer than Jack. He always reached out to people in every way. The world was less one sweet guy.

Managing talent usually brought me in contact with the major theatrical booking offices. Each time I visited the William Morris Agency or the General Artists Corporation or the Music Corporation of America, I thought it might be fun and very educational to work for one of these giants. One day, while securing a booking up at MCA for one of my male vocal artists who shall remain nameless, I was offered a position as an assistant to one of the top agents. I was so intent on getting the rat bastard singer a job that the job offer didn't register until that evening. The nameless singer was a young guy who never appreciated my knocking down doors for him, my placing him with a name band, securing a Columbia record contract for him, or helping him to get on "The Don McNeil Radio Breakfast Club Show." There was a young girl on that show at the same time. Her name was Anita Bryant.

The next day, I called Mr. Ervin Brabec and he repeated his offer. The money was small, the hours 10:00 to 6:00, and I'd have a beautiful office and share his secretary if need be. As a matter of fact, his secretary, Neva Conley broke me in on the job.

The opportunities were there, but my heart wasn't. Now I had the chance to come in contact with the biggies in the entertainment industry and actually get to know some of them firsthand. Still, I longed to be a songwriter. Those new songs that

113

a famous songwriter showed me when I was a page boy at the Hotel St. Moritz must have left a deep impression.

Also, the intense intrigue and power politics that went on up at MCA often left me longing for a cabin in the woods near a fishing lake. Yet I was accepted and well liked by most of the agents and a few others. I knew enough to stay out of their way. The unwritten dress of the day for MCA was dark loafers, a dark silk or knit tie, a white shirt, and a dark, conservative suit. Laughingly, we used to say MCA's slogan was "Dress British; think Yiddish."

Erv Brabec was my boss and many times my confidant and friend. He was rough and gruff on the outside to almost everyone who crossed his path, but not really to his secretary, Neva Conley, or to me. He screamed hysterically at one or both of us at times, but he never carried an argument or a grudge past the second he stopped yelling. Neva put me hip to that fact as well as many other situations that made life bearable up at Music Corporation of America.

Mr. Brabec's main position was to negotiate recording contracts for artists under contract to MCA: singers, bandleaders and such. Sometimes he took me with him when he negotiated a recording contract and then we'd go to lunch. He usually was deep in thought, so I only made conversation when I had his undivided attention or he wanted to talk. I know he liked me, even though he knew I was Jewish. I always thought he might have a thing about Jews. Once or twice he would say something about keeping MCA balanced with an equal amount of Anglo Saxons or a remark would slip and he would look at me to see my reaction. Once he said that he wasn't referring to "my kind." I let him off the hook all the time, as I thought most of my suspicions were in my head and I was making the proverbial mountain out of a molehill. After all, he did hire me and he was kind to me and knew my religious persuasion. Anyway, nothing earth-shattering was ever said or done.

Our office was mainly for negotiating record contracts, but I would drift around during the day to all the other offices. I was curious about everything: the big band department, the cocktail department, where they booked small musical groups, the drama department, where they handled Broadway, and the vaudeville circuit department. It was like when I was sergeant of the Message

114

Center in the army—I had to know what was going on in those other offices.

One of the men who was especially nice to me and sort of took me under his wing was ex-bandleader Julie Wintz. He told me which agents were approachable, who had a heart, who to stay clear of, and that sort of thing.

Erv Brabec was a former music arranger from Chicago. He had known and worked with Mel Torme and some of the great Chicago jazz musicians. Sometimes, when he forgot his MCA image and became a little mellow, he would tell me stories about how he started in the music world and eventually hooked up with MCA.

One of our bosses at MCA was Mr. Sonny Werblin of Meadowlands and Madison Square Garden fame. He was a decent, honorable sort, and I never once heard him raise his voice. Freddy Fields, the famous film producer, was an agent whose office was next to ours. Then came the office of a real character by the name of Joe Sully, and the last office was that of an infamous funny guy by the name of Jack Talan.

Jack had illusions of grandeur, that he was being groomed for the presidency of the world or something. But he was funny in a crazy sort of show-biz way. Because of his good nature, he was tolerated and the MCA brass put up with his shenanigans.

When Mr. Brabec was on a trip or out negotiating a recording contract, I sometimes sat at his desk and played "super agent." One afternoon my songwriter partner Mack Wolfson called me and said there was a girl who came to town from Georgia and she was staying at the Warwick Hotel. Someone had told Mack that the girl wanted to write songs. Why didn't I, as a single guy, call her and find out what it was all about? Might prove interesting.

I called and spoke to this girl for a few moments, and into the office walks Jack Talan. He asks me who was I talking to. Instead of telling him anything, I handed him the phone. Weeks passed and one day I suddenly got a call to report to the offices of the MCA attorneys. Innocently I went to the upper-echelon floor, knocked on the door, and walked in. There, in a large room, were all the senior big-shot agents forming a half-circle around two chairs, one being occupied by the aforesaid Jack Talan. I was told to take the other chair, and then the interrogation began.

115

One of the attorneys, Mr. Morris Schrier, asked me to tell my side of the story.

I looked around, puzzled, and inquired, "What story?"

He angrily said, "Come on, White, you know what story!"

Talan came to my rescue and said, "He's not kidding; he doesn't know what this is all about."

Schrier snapped at Talan "Okay, you begin."

Talan gulped and said, "Well, when I spoke to this girl on the phone, she invited me up to her room at the Warwick Hotel, so I went." Then Talan got cold feet and stopped. It was then that I surmised something about what this Nuremberg inquisition was all about.

Attorney Schrier taunted Talan, "Go on, Talan, go on."

Jack continued. "When I got up to the room she had just come out of the shower so I went down on her and . . . "

Schrier stopped him, saying, "You what?"

Talan, straight-faced, innocently continued. "So I went down on her and . . . "

Again Schrier stopped him. "You went down on her? You went down on her? What does that mean?"

Jack Talan couldn't believe this last question and shook his head incredulously and looked the MCA attorney right in the eyes and said, "Mr Schrier, I went down on her and sucked her pussy."

With that, Mr. Schrier let out a primal scream that reverberated throughout the hallowed halls and walls of MCA. "You what? You dirty, dirty son of a bitch!" Red-faced and holding his mouth to keep from puking, Mr. Schrier ran out of the room. Then he immediately ran back and shook a finger at both Talan and myself and said, "You young agent bastards, don't you ever mention the name MCA to anyone ever again or I'll have your jobs and your asses!" And again he ran out of the office.

Jack's head was shaking from side to side, and he was smiling as if to say, "Big deal." I looked around in back of me, and I could see one of my bosses, little Johnny Dugan, holding his mouth, too, but he was laughing and trying to hold it in. His face was as red as a beet. I tried not to laugh and waited to be formally excused. Finally everyone left except Talan and myself. Jack looked at me and said, "Eddie, you got any more women for me to meet?"

The story goes that this girl from Georgia claimed she was robbed of her jewelry and $200 and that she had written Jules Stein, president of MCA, and threatened a lawsuit. Last I heard, Jack Talan was selling Encyclopaedia Britannicas from door to door and doing great. But I never let him answer my phone after that.

Erv Brabec was a crackerjack recording negotiator and starmaker. Many artists owed their fame and fortune to his nimble guidance, but few would admit it or give him credit for their good fortune. Eileen Barton bitched when it came time for her to record "If I Knew You Were Coming (I'da Baked a Cake.)" Brabec insisted and the rest is history.

Erv signed two new kids one year—Harry Belafonte and Tony Bennett. At the weekly meetings when we discussed booking plans for many of the stars under contract to MCA, these two artists with great potential were invariably overlooked. The few times I, Little Mr. Nobody, spoke up, I was completely ignored.

Finally, I took the bull by the proverbial. I wrote my first two artist reports. A "report" was a memo that went out to all MCA agents, all over the country, and the world, for that matter. It usually consisted of one paragraph stating the artists' assets, their potential to become future stars, and the possibility of their making big commissions for MCA. It was a cry for help in bringing an artist along, and sometimes it worked. I mentioned Belafonte's going to Washington to look into the folk music archives and how good-looking, talented, and dedicated he was. At the time, I wasn't sure whether Harry wanted to be a jazz singer, an actor, or a folk singer. I do know he asked me to leave MCA and manage him, but I also know he also approached a few other agents with the same request. Mr. Brabec was one, Freddy Fields was another, Harry Rohm was another, and so on. I'm almost sure I was low man on the totem pole. Harry was probably very desperate when he got to me.

Belafonte used to come up to MCA dead broke, without a quarter in his pocket. It was a ritual. I'd have to go into Mr Brabec's office and tell him Belanfonte was outside in need of funds. Brabec would usually give me ten or fifteen dollars, and Harry would tell Neva Conley and me the current joke and leave happier than when he arrived. Sometimes Mr. Brabec wasn't in his office or he just didn't have any loose money. Then I was the patsy and had to fork over a five or ten spot. Harry Belafonte

117

never thanked me, and he never did me a kind turn, much as he promised.

One day Harry was up at MCA and one of the secretaries suggested to me we go over to The Park Central Hotel's swimming pool for some fun that evening. I turned to Harry and said, "How about it? Wanna go swimming?" Harry looked at me angrily and snapped, "Eddie, I didn't take you for a bigot. You know they won't allow my black ass in that pool." I choked on my tongue and for once was at a loss for words. Me a bigot? Little Orphan Eddie, brought up in Harlem, in an orphan asylum, a ghetto within a ghetto? I wanted to lash out, but Harry's words froze me like poison from a cobra.

As the months passed, I forgot somewhat and forgave that incident. Harry became more desperate for money for arrangements, clothes, for his wife, Marguerite, and for some records he wanted to make. He suggested I raise $30,000. Through MCA, I contacted a major jukebox owner in Cleveland, Jack Cohn, and told him that Mr. Harry Belafonte had the greatest potential to become a star in show business. Freddy Fields kept reminding me that Belanfonte couldn't miss, and I passed that information on to Jack Cohn. I suggested Mr. Cohn come into New York and Harry would audition for him. The $30,000 was on its way.

The audition took place in a small dive down in Greenwich Village. Harry looked great with his open-necked shirt and bare chest. We couldn't miss! Mr. Cohn came with a surprise for us. He showed up with Mrs. Cohn.

Harry gave out with a half-hour of pure Belafonte. I forgot why we were there and relaxed and enjoyed myself. Then it was over, and smiling, Harry came over to our table just as I asked Mr. Cohn what he thought and he was saying, "Great, great!" With that, Harry sat down while Mrs. Cohn was saying, "But Jack, he's a *schwarze*."

I cringed and hoped no one, least of all Harry, had heard that statement. I ignored Mrs. Cohn and looked at Mr. Cohn. He said he would let me know his decision in a few days, from Cleveland. The kiss of death.

Later, Harry said, "Fuck him!" He had another idea. He later on hooked up with a pretty, intelligent publicist, Virginia Wicks, who deserves most of the credit for bringing Harry Belafonte to the pinnacle of stardom. Virginia worked; she schemed; she planned; she went without for Harry.

Years later, Harry Belafonte maintained that after all was said and done, he would someday record one or more of my folk songs. After that, I could hardly ever get his secretary, Gloria Cantor, to talk to me. Harry was off to Europe or he was rehearsing for the Greek theater or he was making a picture. I was often told he would call me back. He never did.

A few times he would meet me on West 57th Street near his office and he would exclaim, "Mr. White," never calling me Eddie. I became paranoid and wondered if he wasn't putting too much emphasis on my last name.

Once I sang him a folk song by Mack Wolfson and myself: "My Heart Has Love." He said it was great. He advised me to make up a demonstration record and get the song to his office quick. Mack and I accomplished this feat the next day; I delivered the package myself. This was twenty-five years ago, and I'm beginning to become discouraged.

I sent Harry telegrams of encouragement when first he opened at Ben Marden's Riviera in the early '50s and at various other engagements early in his career. When we'd meet on West 57th Street, he would deny ever receiving any words of encouragement from me in his cool, superior manner. I felt that I had tried to be nice and helpful to this tremendously talented man, but why should he treat me any different than he did many others who helped him? I always came up with the back of Harry Belafonte's hand.

Tony Bennett came to MCA at the same time as Belafonte, but he was so insecure in those early days that he informed me he had to go through heavy Reichian therapy sessions.

Mr. Brabec signed Tony to an MCA booking contract in the early '50s. It was then I met the guiding hand behind Tony Bennett's career, his manager, Ray Muscarella. Anyone who tells me that an actor, a singer, a dancer, or any performer makes it alone on their God-given talents doesn't know anything about show business. There usually lurks someone kept in the background by the insecure artist—a manager, a lawyer, a backer, a relative, a teacher, a husband or wife, a friend who put up their hard-earned money, their time, and their blood and guts to keep the young artist's head above water in those mean, lean years. Invariably the successful artist eventually looks around one sunny day and doesn't wish to be reminded that they came out of the womb, like everyone else, and that they were nurtured on the milk of human kindness. You hardly ever see the same people around a successful performing artist that labored and were there in those formative, growing years. The slick lawyers, the sharp business managers, the new mate, or newfound friends take over. Sometimes the artist wakes up and tries to retrace his steps and clear his conscious, but usually it's too late.

To return to my story, Ray Muscarella was short, swarthy, and fat—built like a tackle on the old Chicago Bears. He looked mean, but he was considerate, kind, and generous to everyone and especially to Tony Bennett. It was Ray's guidance and money that secured Tony's contract with Columbia Records, which eventually led to his blockbuster recording of "Because of You."

Speaking of that record, three months prior to the record's release date, I wrote an interoffice memo on Tony Bennett similar to the one I wrote on Harry Belafonte. This time I chastised all of the MCA agents and offices, sayings that if we didn't get behind this young artist's career, his record would take off by itself and leave us all embarrassed. When the record became a hit, I reminded everyone who would listen to me up at MCA that I had predicted Tony's eventful stardom.

Agent Danny Welks, who worked in the office of Harry Rohm, was the first one to realize that Tony's career was skyrocketing. He came out of his office with a grin and yelled out, "I just got Tony Bennett $2,500 at Ben Maksik's Roadside Restaurant in Brooklyn." Tony's price had gone from $750 per week to $2,500, and two weeks later it was $7,500.

Ray Muscarella was Tony Bennett's lifeline from at first merely existing in show business and then slowly but surely accelerating to eventful stardom. If there was no Ray Muscarella, I doubt if there would have been a Tony Bennett. Tony would have wound up as the headwaiter at Ricardo's Restaurant out in Astoria, Long Island, where he got his first singing job.

Tony's thinking and life-style doesn't allow him to glance over his shoulder and look back at the people who had been there in the beginning. Mr. Ricardo, the man who gave Tony

Bennett his first singing job, hasn't been able to contact Tony for years. Gentleman that he is, he merely wanted to allocate one of the rooms in his restaurant as "The Tony Bennett Room," with pictures and mementos of years and times long past.

In exasperation, I finally called Tony's brother, John Bennett, in North Miami, and he gave the approval for Mr. Ricardo's Tony Bennett memento room. John Bennett liked the idea, but I never did get Tony's reaction.

When Tony was riding the crest of success in the early '50s Ray Muscarella heard that I had garnered around ten blocks of World Series tickets. The tickets actually were promised to many of my son's friends, who were obligated to pay for them. We were to go up to Yankee Stadium en masse and have a great time rooting for our Yankees. Ray looked at me sheepishly and said he needed all the tickets he could get. They were to be used as gifts for disc jockeys Ray was romancing to play Tony's new record. Sadly I handed over all the tickets. For Ray Muscarella—anything!

Ray somehow forgot to pay me for the tickets, which came to a tidy sum of money for me. I somehow made the money good, but through the years I've felt cheated, not by Ray, but by Tony, as I felt he never appreciated anyone's endeavors on his behalf.

Although Ray forgot to pay for those World Series tickets, he made it up to me in many other ways. He was always kind and solicitous to me in front of other agents and music people. He would always lift my feelings by telling people that I was one of Tony's first theatrical contacts who believed in Tony and that I wrote the first report on Tony, which brought him to the attention of all of MCA. I liked hearing all this; it was good for my ego and morale.

Ray started to pick up my dinner check whenever he saw me in a restaurant. Usually a bunch of us younger songwriters would gather at the old Eduardo's Italian restaurant on 53rd Street and Broadway. Many times the bill never arrived. Dinner, I was told, "was on the house." At first I thought someone had mistaken me for someone else, but after long, thoughtful analysis, I figured it out. Ray Muscarella was the Lone Ranger.

One day while dining at Eduardo's with Mack Wolfson, Jack Fine, Sid Wayne, Joe Sherman and a few other up-and-coming songwriters, I was told to step into a back room. There was Ray Muscarella sitting alone at a table, a bottle of red wine untouched. Ray shook my hand warmly and told me to help myself to the wine.

Ray started slowly. Tony Bennett was becoming a hot property; he was young and impressionable and he needed someone to travel with him, to act as sort of an anchor, to guide him, to be his pal. Would I like the position as Tony's road manager? I knew that "road manager" was only a fancy title for court jester, coat holder, and high-class flunkie.

Ray offered me $250 a week, plus traveling expenses. I had to think fast. How could I turn my friend Ray Muscarella down and still retain the warm feeling between us? Two hundred and fifty dollars a week was far more than I was earning with MCA, but I couldn't let Ray know this.

I looked down at my glass of wine and said, "Ray, I can't leave New York without something more tangible, without more security—say, a percentage of Tony's earnings."

Ray said, "Okay. How about 5 percent? I wouldn't give anyone a percentage deal except you, Eddie."

The offer was so inviting that I immediately choked emotionally. My life had no real direction. I was still single, and here was a chance to travel and live it up in style. I always prided myself on being an adventurer, curious about everything and anything—places, people, different life-styles. Who knew what adventure awaited me out there in Tony Bennett Land?

Then I thought of my songwriter partner, Mack Wolfson, sitting there in the main dining room—honest, sweet Mack who not only believed in me but took my every thought and opinion as the gospel, Mack who held my head and hand and dried my tears when my heart was broken over my three-year-old nephew's death. I remember hysterically throwing up all over Mack and myself and how he routinely cleaned us up and soothed my soul with words of love and compassion. Mack was a unique guy, and I wasn't about to walk away from him to better myself. I had seen too many of those Betty Grable–John Payne vaudeville-type movies.

Then, too, I got an image of me holding Tony Bennett's coat and nursing him and guiding him through and around many future theatrical discussions and involvements. I think the image of holding Tony's coat was somehow too reprehensible to me.

I looked at my good friend Ray Muscarella and whispered, "I was thinking more in terms of at least 10 percent." Ray couldn't hear me and asked me to repeat myself. I found my voice and said, "Ten percent would be more to my liking."

Up to that moment, I had never seen Ray Muscarella angry. He jumped to his feet and with that heavy sledgehammer of a fist that he had, banged the thick Italian marble table. "Nobody gets 10 percent of Tony Bennett, nobody!"

I had hurt my friend Ray Muscarella, and I was embarrassed. He told me to finish my wine and go back to my table. I thought Ray was finished with me for all time, but again the waiter said dinner was on the house. I had disappointed Ray, but he forgave me. The friendship continued up until his death. Through the years, I wondered what life would have been for me if I had accepted Ray's offer. How much money would I have made? Would I have been better off financially than I am now? And so on.

I once heard that "ingratitude" was the ultimate sin. Maybe it isn't, but to me it is—in a business surrounded by ingrates of all kinds, especially the horribly ambitious theatrical performer. I've seen artists who, the second they take a step up the ladder of success, leave their families, their friends, and their business associates. Some tolerate their families and some continue to cherish them.

There are exceptions to this rule, but those exceptions are the legends that sustain personal managers and others in the entertainment world. It's said there are isolated instances where artists and managers have worked in harmony with nothing but a handshake between them—these are few and far between. I've heard this about Kate Smith and Ted Collins. It may have been just a handshake between them, but I never bought that story.

I admit I was the epitome of the dumb Pollyanna who fell for every hard-luck story. Hardly any aritst in the '50s and the '60s ever paid a commission due me. And most times I needed the money more than they did. I think I felt like I was building goodwill, a strong bond, or a solid relationship or possibly buying love. I don't know. It never worked and I woke up much too late.

I could retire on the commissions one single act owes me. He reminded me once, from his Chicago castle, that the statute of limitations ran out a long time ago on the money he owes me.

True, but when I managed this less than human ingrate, I never took the statute of limitations into consideration. I just believed in him and worked my ass off.

Only one act ever did pay me every cent he owed me and on time, too. This was Little Tommy Edwards, the black singer, who had the hit record "It's All in the Game" in the '50s. Tommy would walk into my office and plunk down my commission in cash, pinch my cheek, and swear we were going to make millions someday. As a matter of fact, I found that black artists were, on an average, more honorable than the white artists I dealt with.

Tony Bennett became a hot act so quickly that he was immediately booked into the Paramount Theater as the star attraction. "Because of You" was number one on every disc jockey's hit parade, and my friend Ray Muscarella was all smiles. After the first show, a celebration party was given by Columbia Records upstairs in a huge gymlike hall at the Paramount Theater. It was in honor of Tony, and all his agents, record people, family, friends, and well-wishers were there. The moment Tony walked in, he was mobbed by the crowd, and he spotted me sitting by myself at the extreme end of the hall. He brushed past everyone, including his mother and his record producer, Mitch Miller, and walked toward me. As I stood up he embraced me Italian-style and said, "Eddie, I will never forget what you did for my career."

Years later, when I was telling this story, people would anxiously ask, "So what happened?" and I would glumly say, "He forgot!" and it would get a howl of laughter from everyone, including myself. That scene upstairs in the Paramount Theater was it as far as I can tell. That was my payoff—that embrace. My kiss of death, so to speak.

For a few days, I would go backstage. I always noticed a pretty little girl, about sixteen or so, in saddle shoes, socks, and skirt hovering shyly in the corner of Tony's dressing room. Finally, I walked over and said, "Hi, I'm Eddie White, Tony's friend." Tony said, "Oh, yeah, Eddie, this is Sandy from Cleveland, Ohio. Sandy is president of my fan club."

Shy little Sandy became the first Mrs. Tony Bennett, and in

time she blossomed into womanhood and had therapy sessions. She also took all the crap she could from Tony, and in his own words she called him a "hooked-nose guinea." Maybe she had reasons to get upset?

The Happiness Boys about to storm the bastions of Tin Pan Alley. We were so much alike that Mack's mother couldn't tell us apart.

7

The Real Rocky

IN THE EARLY FIFTIES, I came in contact with one of the most unique and remarkable guys it has been my pleasure to meet. At the time, I was a struggling songwriter, record producer, and part-time personal manager. Those days, juvenile delinquency was rampant and the subject was on everyone's mind.

One of the music publishers got the idea that a song about juvenile delinquency might be in the offing, and who might be the outstanding personality to sing such a song but the number-one juvenile delinquent himself, Rocco Barbella, better known as Rocky Graziano?

I was assigned to produce the recording session, and together with my writing partner, Mack Wolfson, I set out to write an appropriate song. We finally came up with "Back in My Old Neighborhood," a song about kids who were bad but grew up to be good citizens once they had people work and believe in them. That was the "A" side; we then wrote a quickie song for the "B" side.

Came the evening of the recording session, the studio was all set up, the band had been rehearsed, and in shuffles a smiling, lovable rascal who says to me, "Didn't I knock you out in Toledo?"

The Rocky Graziano charm and charisma got through to me immediately. Before I met Rocky, I thought it might be impossible to teach him to sing the song we wrote for him, I mean the way Rocky spoke and all. But Rocky was so good-natured and easygoing that the entire studio staff went out of their way to show him the utmost patience. He made the usual amount of flubs, pops, and goofs, but after a while we all finally agreed that we had what we were looking for. I thanked Rocky, he hit me playfully but softly in the kidney, and he shuffled off into the night.

I remember thinking that I would like to see the Rock again. Not only was he a very interesting guy, but I sensed a softness and kindness about the man. There was an aura of happiness about him, a light touch that emanated from this supposedly ferocious ex-pugilist.

We were just finishing editing the tapes in the record studio and the thoughts about this colorful fighter were still bouncing around in my mind when the phone rang. It was Rocky. Would I like to meet him at Patsy's Italian restaurant for dinner? I told him that I wasn't dressed to go out and besides, I didn't have too much money on me. I'll never forget what he said to me that first night. "Eddie, I always dress like a fuckin' bum. Wear what ya got on and dinner won't cost ya a fuckin' dime. Yur wid da Rock, remember dat!"

I showed up at Patsy's around eight-thirty in the evening, and when I walked in I couldn't find Rocky. A short, heavy-set man waved at me from the rear of the restaurant, and a waiter escorted me to his table. I could see there were three or four tables put together and they were set for around twelve guests.

The man shook my hand and introduced himself as Tony Corrado, a friend of Rocky's, and said he had been expecting me. He told me to sit alongside his seat and if I was especially hungry, I should order before the rest of the group arrived. He told me that there were others coming and they might be late.

I was starved, as I usually am, and this was a little late for me to be having dinner. I asked Mr. Corrado what we were having for dinner, and he stuck a finger in my chest and said, "My name is Tony, ya understand, T-O-N-Y. Forget that Mr. Corrado and whenever you're my guest you can order anything you want, anything! Now here's the waiter; give him your order."

Tony went to the front of the restaurant to greet Rocky, who was just arriving with a few other guys. I asked the waiter what this was all about, and he told me that Mr. Corrado entertained ten to twenty guests every night at Patsy's. "Go ahead, son, eat your head off. Mr. Corrado wants you to have a good time." I told the waiter to bring me anything he thought I should have. I didn't want to step out of line that first night.

Then all hell broke loose. The entire restaurant was suddenly noisy, alive and jumping. Tony was leading a parade toward our table, and everyone was shaking hands, patting backs, and drinking "salutes" all over the place. I couldn't make out what was happening, and then it became clear to me. All the guys following Tony to the table belonged to the number-one–rated TV show on the air, "You'll Never Get Rich," with Sergeant Bilko himself, Phil Silvers.

They surrounded Tony Corrado, kissing him on his bald head, yelling Italian words at the waiters, pleading with Mr. Patsy, the owner of the restaurant, to smile "for once in your life," and generally taking the restaurant over.

Hey, I was in big-time company. Here was Mr. Nat Hikan, the dean of America's comedy writers and the creator of the Sergeant Bilko series, Phil Silvers, the comedy star of the show, Herbie Faye, the little king of burlesque, and Harvey Lembeck and Jack Healy and Mickey Freeman and Allen Melvin and Maurice Gossap, who they called Doberman on the show, and bringing up the rear was my new friend, Rocky Graziano.

Immediately everyone acted as if they had known me for years. Tony Corrado sat at the head of the table, saying, "This is my pal Eddie White" and that was it; I was initiated into the group. Everyone started calling me Eddie immediately, and I felt instant friendship and acceptance. I acted very casual about the whole thing, sitting on my true emotions, like I was used to this sort of thing every day of my life. Inside I was a pressure cooker, with all these famous guys treating me as if I was their lifelong pal.

Jack Healy, one of Rocky Graziano's ex–fight managers, who acted the part of Muldoon on the Sergeant Bilko show, sat next to me. That was my first mistake. I later found out that Jack was an authority on everything in the world, so he said, but actually he was an authority on only one subject, The Kentucky Derby. He could name every winner of the Kentucky Derby going back to the year 1850 and the first derby actually didn't run until 1874. Truthfully and honestly, he could name the winning horse, the jockey, and the running time of each race going back to the Kentucky Derby's inception. Why he would want to memorize this bit of information is beyond me, but maybe he could pick up a few bets here and there in bars around town.

As I had ordered dinner first, my appetizer arrived before

the others were served. The waiter placed a plate of linguini and minced clams before me. I drooled with delight and was just about to dig in—the linguini was practically touching my lips—when the aforementioned Jack Healy grabbed my fork hand and said, "Are you going to eat that slop? I mean, are they kidding here? What's going on in this joint?"

With that he called the waiter, bawled him out, and said, "Feed this kid right! If he wants to hang out with us, he's got to be treated like us. Here, take this back to the kitchen. I want him to have linquini a la dente, whole baby clams—did ya get that?—whole baby clams, and a light touch of garlic and oil, *allia allio, pronto.*" He turned to me and said, "Don't worry, kid; Jackie Boy is here. I'll take charge from here on in." I sadly watched the waiter take my plate away, and I had tears in my heart and stomach as the plate went all the way back to the kitchen.

Of every dish that came my way—the salad, the steak, the melon—nothing was good enough for Jack Healy. He sent everything back with a grunt. This had the wrong dressing; this wasn't cooked enough; this was too hard, not ripe. Eventually I found out that all the other guys were onto Jack Healy and with them he couldn't get away with these shenanigans. I was the only one too scared, too intimidated, to say no to him. Some months later, after I had become a regular member of this Runyonesque group, I would ask where Jack Healy was going to sit and I would place myself at the other end of the table.

Practically overnight, Rocky Graziano and I were the closest of friends. We were perfect for each other—two opposites, a natural. Rocky understood every word I said; I didn't understand a word he said. Although he was a celebrity, a former middleweight champion, king of commercials, a regular on "The Martha Raye Show," and a guest on all the other variety shows, you would think that I was the celebrity when we were together. He took such pride in showing me off to everyone. "Hey, my buddy Eddie just wrote a song for Frank and Tony, whaddaya tink a dat? Yeah, Sinatra and Bennett, who d'ya tink I mean, ya bum."

Sometimes Rocky would stretch the truth and give me credit for songs written by Johnny Mercer or Sammy Cahn. He didn't do it on purpose, but he would get all the songs mixed up. I was always embarrassed and spent a lot of time correcting things he said. He would say, "What's the difference. Sixteen Tons, Sixteen

129

Teens, what's the difference?" When I wrote "C'est La Vie," he went around telling people that I wrote "C'est Si Bon," "Happiness Street" became "On the Street Where You Live," and "Flowers Mean Forgiveness," which I wrote for Frank Sinatra, became "Flowers for Your Furs."

One time, a guy got annoyed and asked Rocky if his buddy had written "Ave Maria"? Everyone started to laugh and Rocky said, "What are you guys laughing' at? That happens to be one of Eddie's best songs." I couldn't believe it, but no one took Rocky up on this; they just let it lie there. I didn't take any chances and went out and learned "Ave Maria" just in case it ever came up in conversation again.

Life became fun and games for me then. All day I would write songs with my collaborator and friend Mack Wolfson, and then in the evening I would meet Rocky and Tony Corrado and I would live it up like King Henry VIII. I kept telling people and myself that I was making up for all the meals I missed in those orphanages. It was one laugh after another. Rocky and I went everywhere. One night it was Toots Shor's, the next night it might be Ernie's Three Ring Circus down in Greenwich Village, the next night we'd have dinner with Rocky Marciano at La Scala, then over to The Latin Quarter to catch Milton Berle and Tony Corrado's latest flame, Betty George, the Greek Goddess of Song, and on and on and on. And all the time Tony Corrado kept picking up the tabs and shelling out the loot with a smile on his face. After a while, I stopped feeling guilty about Tony when he explained that "You only pass this way once. I'm having the time of my life. I like all you guys . . . and what the hell's money for anyway?" After that conversation, I relaxed and the thought never crossed my mind again.

But this staying out late at night started to get to me a bit. One day I had a serious talk with Rocky and told him I had to knuckle down and write more and better songs. Rocky sympathized with me and said he understood everything, "everything!" He even gave me a pep talk a la Knute Rockne and finished off with "Go get 'em, kid. No more parties and staying out late. I'm in your corner, kid. You write 'em; Sinatra'll sing 'em. Knock 'em dead, kid."

And then the roof caved in. Rocky would pick me up in the

morning in his white "Tunderbird," allegedly to take me downtown to work. Mack Wolfson and I were under contract to Famous Music, the publishing arm of Paramount Pictures. I'd be so engrossed in talking to Rocky, telling him our ideas, what Mack and I were writing, that I didn't realize where we were going.

Suddenly I would get the shock of my life. Looking up, I could see a sign coming at me reading "Belmont Racetrack." I'd say, "Rocky, how could you do this to me? Are you off your rocker? I'm going to lose my job. Oh please, I can't do this." Rocky would say, "Just one race, kid. One race never hurt anyone. Whaddaya say? One race?" One race usually became three races, then five, then the whole day was shot.

This went on for months. I was running out of excuses up at Paramount, and my boss started to look at me cockeyed. The only one who went along with this nonsense was my partner, Mack. He'd let me do almost anything I wanted to do; all I had to do was tell him a few jokes and I was good for another week of goofing off. One day I couldn't stand hurting Mack and I finally asked him how come he was always so understanding about my not showing up for work every day? And he told me.

It seems that the only two other contract writers up at Paramount then were a couple of guys named Burt Bacharach and Hal David. The fact was, Burt and Hal never showed up at the Paramount offices until they actually had a few songs to demonstrate to the professional manager. I asked Mack why he never mentioned this to me before, and he said that he thought I knew it all the time.

This saved the day for me. I now had the ammunition to go to my boss and explain the reason I wasn't using the office they had so nicely decorated for us. "Talented people have to write in the park sometimes, maybe at home, at night, all night, whenever the mood strikes." My boss agreed and Mack and I no longer had to punch a mental time clock anymore. We were free to come and go, like the wind and the musical geniuses we hoped to become.

A few weeks later, I read about the tragic automobile accident in which comedian Ernie Kovacs lost his life. I didn't realize then how this might affect me, but in a strange way it did. ABC Radio was in a turmoil. Ernie had been doing a six-to-nine morning show across the board, meaning from Monday to Friday.

Ernie's death left a void that had to be filled but quickly, if it could. ABC wanted to hold onto the high-rated show but needed a star, a character out of the ordinary, someone with chutzpah, like a young Arthur Godfrey or Dave Garroway or Henry Morgan. But none of these guys was available, and Don Rickles hadn't been invented as yet. "How about someone like Rocky Graziano?" "Who?" "Someone like Rocky Graziano?" "Hey, how's this for an idea? How about Rocky Graziano?" "Wow, what an idea! You're a genius! No wonder you're a top account executive."

ABC Radio called Rocky and asked him if he could do a show of this type, fifteen hours of mostly talk a week. Rocky called me; we kicked the idea around for three seconds and then went up to the offices of ABC for a meeting. Rocky was very apprehensive. He didn't care much for talking. Maybe for New York City, but to go network was another idea. The ABC people scared Rocky talking about Middle America and the Bible Belt. Rocky had thought that the Bible Belt was a guy getting socked with a Bible.

I started to get ideas about the potential of this new escapade for Rocky and me. I winked at the Rock and told the ABC mavens that I could produce and write a show of this type if we had a free hand. It was my idea to keep Rocky's conversation to a minimum, play some old-time records (mostly my own), bring on some Broadway shows, do the weather, have Rocky do an Italian recipe of the day, and generally do a radio show with a very light touch.

Actually, I was ad libbing the whole conversation, but they loved the ideas. Some of the ABC people were a little skeptical, with flashing eyes, but then they went along and agreed to try us for two weeks. Rocky kept saying he didn't think he could sustain a show for three hours a day, let alone five days a week. I stopped winking at Rocky and started stepping on his foot, but he went on saying he didn't think he could do it. Fighting was one thing but talking, "talking was for Lawrence Oliver." I told Rocky his name was Olivier, but Rocky corrected me and said it was Lawrence. Smart as I was, Rocky always made me look like a dum dum.

Before we went on the air, I rehearsed Rocky by actually doing the show myself, bit by bit. I would imitate Rocky's speech and mannerisms, and Rocky would tell me to stop doing Slapsie Maxie Rosenbloom. He kept shaking his head, saying, "Nah, let's forget dis ting. Let's go to da track and relax."

I considered the show a challenge, both to Rocky and myself. I asked him, "Rock, where's your get up and go? Where's your fight?"

Rocky looked at me and said, "Fight, I'll knock you true dat wall, ya bum."

When we arrived at the studio 5:00 A.M. on a rainy Monday, Rocky was nervous and perspiring. He kept telling me he had a tip on a horse that couldn't miss: "He's a mudder and on a rainy day like today he'll piss in." I made believe I didn't hear him, and he made believe that we weren't going to do this radio show. But in his heart Rocky knew we were committed because he had rehearsed with a seriousness I truly didn't know he possessed. Say what you will, with all his horsing around, with all his belly aching and growling, Mr. Rocco Barbella was a true thespian and trouper.

That first show was shaky, to say the least. Everything seemed to go well to the uninitiated, but Rocky wasn't very comfortable. When he got stuck or ran out of words, he would glare at me and I would immediately throw on a record. That gave me three minutes or so to explain the next thing he was going to do.

The studio ABC assigned to us was huge. At first I wasn't happy; it looked like the grand ballroom at The Waldorf Astoria. But then I found out we could use this to our advantage. I could talk to Rocky from twenty feet or so and the microphone wouldn't pick up my voice. This way, I could direct Rocky while he was on the air, and gradually he began to feel comfortable. We had signals between us, and when Rocky got stuck or confused I'd quietly tell him how to continue.

After each show, I would go home and write the next day's show on a large yellow pad. Every morning around 4:30, Rocky would come by and honk the horn and we'd be on our way.

Sometimes I would still be writing in the car and telling Rocky about some new ideas for the show. I was excited now, as I sensed that the show was coming together, but still Rocky wasn't too sure. Getting up at 4:00 A.M. and talking for three hours every day wasn't his idea of fun.

I always had this premonition that one day Rocky would say the wrong thing on the air, possibly a curse word or two. This thought nagged me no end and many times the show almost came crashing down around our heads, but good old Rocky, true-blue guy that he was, would stop dead, take a gulp, and continue on with the show. Mistakes, sure, but no big whoppers. Afterwards we would laugh ourselves silly about a close call or two, but still, I always would remind him to please watch what he said on the air.

After that first week, Rocky started to relax and really enjoy the show. I knew we were "in" when I heard him bragging to Tony Corrado about how easy it was doing this show. Rocky even suggested that maybe I should go after the "Tonight" show on NBC for him: "I'd murder dem!" Now there was no holding the Champ back.

"The Rocky Graziano Show" became Broadway open house for ex-fighters, managers, singers, theatrical agents, comics, dancers, actors—you name it. People would just amble into the studio, I'd interview them for a few moments, write down a little about what they intended to talk about, and that was it. I don't remember ever turning anyone away from the show. It was all impromptu, off the cuff, ad lib, and the ratings grew. Rocky called everyone a bum, and they and the audience loved it.

Once we got word that our ratings started to inch up, the mail came in by the bagful. At first, we got around 400 letters and cards a day, but it built up to over 1,100 pieces of mail a day, most of them telling Rocky he was great, refreshing and would he please do a benefit for some society somewhere in North Dakota?

The big hit of the show was when Rocky did the Italian recipe bit. He would say, "Ladies, get your pots ready. I'll wait. . . . " and he would hum an Italian melody for a few moments, usually "The Tarantella." Then he would go into detail on some wild Sicilian dish or Neopolitan "kook kootz," dishes that I had researched previously. He would screw the entire recipe up and finish up with "try dis on your mudder-in-law sometime. Ha! Ha! Ha!" Thank God no one ever took these recipes too seriously, or if they had, we never heard from them. Maybe they aren't alive to give testimony?

Talk about screwing up. One day, Rocky had to do one of our most important commercials. It was for an outfit called Slenderella, a chain of reducing salons. Rocky usually mangled things he said, but this time he did a hatchet job on an outfit that paid most of our salaries. He started out slow, calling the salon "a saloon," and then he lost his place and called upon all the fatsos of America to quick, join Slenderella "or I'll flatten ya!" Damon Runyon must have smiled on Rocky from on high that morning.

I threw a record on fast and told Rocky to next go into one of his stories about his fights with Tony Zale. One of the ABC secretaries started waving for me to quick pick up the phone, but I made believe that I hadn't noticed. Finally she came into the studio and handed me the phone. I said, "Oh, boy, this is it, Rock; we're fired."

The voice on the other end said he was calling from Chicago and that he was the general manager of Slenderella. I told him that I was sorry but Mr. Graziano had dropped his commercial copy and unfortunately had to ad lib the whole thing. I apologized profusely and said it wouldn't happen again.

The guy said, "Mr. White, stop kidding me. I'm hip. I know what you guys are doing up there . . . and I love it! I've been listening to the show, and I want you to keep up the good work." I started to tell Rocky about the call and got so excited I bit my tongue.

After that call, Rocky destroyed everything, every commercial, every routine, every recipe, every interview—and it was great! It all came natural to him, too; he just spoke and Shakespeare turned over in his grave. That's what they wanted, that's what they expected, and that's what they got! One of Rocky's favorite expressions to me, when I would remind him to enunciate more clearly was "Hey, kid, if I talked like you we'd both be broke!" He was right and I never told him "nuttin'" since then. As a matter of fact, I'm starting to talk like him.

"The Rocky Graziano ABC Radio Show" ran for about six

months, until Rocky started to get bigger money offers from Las Vegas and television. After appearances on "The Martha Raye Show" and then The "Dean Martin Show," the commercials started pouring in. Getting up at 4:00 A.M. was getting in the way of Rocky's nightlife. We actually quit the show at its peak. It was a good experience, both for the Rock and myself, and we proved that we could do it. We were a good team; our friendship was sealed because of our mutual dependence on each other. It started to dawn on me that this guy, Rocky Graziano, really loved me. I knew it because he methodically set out to destroy me! Everything he ever did after our radio show was a jolt to my nervous system. I sometimes wondered why he kept humming "You Only Hurt the One You Love."

After the talk about our radio show had calmed down a bit, Rocky called me one beautiful Sunday and asked if I wanted to go out for a spin in his new boat. Being a sucker for a left hook, I drove out to Long beach, where Rocky lived. *Rocky has a new boat? That's really not like the Rock at all. Oh, well.* I thought.

When I arrived, Rocky suggested we both strip down to nothing but our shorts—no shoes, no shirt, just shorts. I asked Rocky where his new boat was anchored, and he said, "Una shpett"; he had one little errand to do.

As we left Rocky's house, I could hear a military band playing in the distance; Rocky started to walk quickly, hopping every time he hit a pebble, and I did likewise, following right behind him. Finally we caught up with a band, and I could see it was a voluntary firemen's parade. Rocky hopped again, just to get in step with the marchers, and again I followed, limping a little because those damned pebbles hurt. I remembered thinking, *How come they don't hurt the Rock?* We marched on the outskirts of a brigade, and I recognized most of the voluntary firemen as Rocky's neighbors.

I felt a little self-conscious. All these guys were parading in beautiful blue uniforms, and here we were, two dopey characters in shorts making like tin soldiers. Then I heard the immortal wail of The Rock. He was yelling, "Hey, Morty, we're taking the boat. Hey, Morty, okay?"

I could see Morty in the middle of the uniformed pack, and

I could also see a painful look of anguish come over his face. Staring straight ahead like the good soldier he was, he screamed, "Rocky, don't take the boat, please, for Christ's sake. Rocky, please don't take the boat!"

Rocky gave me a shot in my ribs and said, "Okay, pal, that's the signal. Let's go." I followed Rocky, saying, "Morty said for us *not* to take the boat, Rocky. I distinctly heard him." And the ever lovable Rocky said, "Ya putz, dat's da signal between Morty and me. He don't want does udder guys to know we're taking' da boat, don't ya see? Dat's our signal, jeez." Pure of heart, I ran after Rocky. How can I be forgiven for ever doubting my close comrade, but in the distance I could still hear the faint sound of the Morty bird crying, "Please, please, don't take the boat." I thought *Jeez, they could have used a better signal than that.*

We ran to Morty's house, which was situated right on the water, and sure enough, the door had been left open. Everyone was probably out watching the parade. Rocky grabbed the boat keys, still muttering something about a "signal," and we went down to the dock. There it was in all its magnificent glory, a spanking, brand-new sixteen-foot speedboat, so new it still had the plastic wrapping paper and tarpaulin attached to it. I said something about a "Shakedown cruise," but Rocky ignored me, saying, "Come on, ya bum, give me a hand wid dis shit."

We started to pull the tarpaulin off, and then I more than raised a voice of suspicion. "Rocky, do you know anything about boats? I don't know a thing; I can't help you."

Rocky looked at me with disdain. "If there's anything I know, it's boats. I know everything there is to know about boats."

We lay the tarpaulin on the shore, and then I saw the biggest motor I've ever been close to. With a heavy heart, I just started saying, "Hey, Rocky, this motor . . . " and Rocky cut me off. "Go sit in the fuckin' front of the boat."

I made my way to the front and couldn't help noticing that the cellophane paper was still on the seats and the panels. I was trying to figure out where to sit when Rocky pulled something on the motor. It gave a loud cough, kicked, and then died. Rocky kept pulling the cord and getting the same result: a cough, a kick, and then it would die. As I looked out over the horizon to get the lay of the land, the motor kicked and didn't cough, and we shot up in the air. I went flying onto a chair, which immediately broke under me. I hurt my shoulder and ribs, but didn't have time to think about it. The boat gave another kick up, and I fell onto the bottom of the boat, breaking a couple of side panels. I held onto the bottom of the boat for dear life.

The boat kept plunging straight up in the air and then pulling back, plunging straight up in the air and pulling back, over and over again. Rocky had forgotten to untie the rope holding the boat to the dock post. By this time, I was getting sea sick and dizzy, and I stood partially up in order to throw up. Again the boat shot up and then fell back again. This time I fell toward the far end of the boat and broke a seat and a couple of varnished panels, with the cellophane paper still attached. Again I tried to squat over the side ot the boat, as I was quite nauseous by then. Again I was thrown back and this time I broke a few more things, but I was too sick to look or care if I lived or died. Then I noticed a little shpritzer shooting up on my side of the boat. We had sprung a little leak. I put my face over the leaking cold water and felt a little refreshed.

By then Rocky had the rope untied, and when he let go we really shot up in the air, not unlike a rocket. We bounced like a flat rock into the middle of the canal, and Rocky couldn't make up his mind which way we were going, so we went around and around. I started to get queasy again and pleaded for Rocky to take me back to shore. Rocky grunted. "Are you crazy? I can handle this fuckin' boat; somebody stuck a fuckin' motor on with some new shit I can't figure out. Sit back and enjoy the ride."

I sat back and Rocky yelled, "Let's head out into the ocean . . . Look, there's an opening over there." Through tearstained, bloodshot eyes I saw what looked like a huge tube leading out to the ocean. We were heading for the opening when I noticed that our boat was larger than the tube's opening. No way could our boat fit through or even squeeze through that hole.

I yelled to Rocky to jump and was just about to dive overboard when Rocky swerved the boat. Again I fell backward and broke a few more precious items. By this time I said, "Fuck it. My life is more important. The war was never like this."

Again Rocky steered us around in circles, trying to make up his mind which way to go. I was so bruised, battered, dizzy, and nauseous that I gave up all hope of being rescued. Rocky then headed for the opposite shore of our original dock and crashed into the pilings, head on. There went a few more tidbits, broken into little pieces.

Then the boat stopped, but I could hear the motor still running. I looked up and Rocky was playing Wonder Man; he had grabbed onto one of the pilings and was straining to hold on. The motor was running and Rocky was losing his grip but oh, so slowly. It looked like slow motion, and in my condition, this only made me feel dizzier. Rocky strained to hold on, but he was slipping. His arms were all scratched from the splinters, and finally he had to let go. We headed for the home shore once again.

Again, pop! We banged into the pilings head on. Now I was sure I had a concussion, too. Now I was getting soaking wet from water coming into the boat from little holes, but I was too hurt to even care. Rocky grabbed one of the pilings again and held on for dear life. His muscles bulged and strained, and his face turned a new shade of blue.

I yelped for Rocky to turn the motor off. Rocky couldn't move his arms off the pilings, so he kicked at the motor. Again he kicked. Again. Finally he must have kicked the motor in a vulnerable place, as the chugging died down. The boat settled down in the water, and we both looked at each other, too weak to move or speak.

Rocky was a bloody mess, but he showed concern for my welfare. He asked, "Are you okay, kid? I think your hair just turned white." I had pains all over my body, in places I never knew existed. I started to wash my face from the little shpritzer in front of me when from a distance we heard a plaintive wail.

At first, I couldn't make out what was being said, and then the voice got closer and we heard, "Please, don't take the boat; please, don't take the boat." Rocky quickly threw the tarpaulin over some of the broken seats near him and nonchalantly leaned on the motor. I sat down over the shpritzer and spread my arms, hoping to cover the broken panels and seats. We both tried to look like we were chatting quietly, as if we had never left the dock.

Morty appeared with two of his volunteer firemen buddies flanking him. He was still muttering, "Please, don't take the boat; please . . . " and he stopped dead. Rocky and I were afraid to look

139

up, and then we heard it. Morty let out this bone-chilling shriek, like an ostrich laying a large square egg. It echoed all over Long Beach that fateful summer Sunday, and it echoes in my dreams and memory to this very day.

Rocky, full of compassion, looked up at Morty and said, "Morty, I want everyone in the neighborhood to hear this. I give you my solemn vow, my word of honor, you, me, and Eddie, tomorrow we are going to Freeport and I'm buying' you a brand-new boat, the same as dis one, d'ya hear me? Everyone listen. I want you all to witness what I'm sayin'. Tomorrow Morty is getting a new boat from da Rock, just like dis one!"

Morty grabbed onto his two buddies for support. The light in his eyes went out, his arms went limp, and he collapsed completely. As his buddies half led him, half carried him, back to his house, I could see his lips move slightly and I could barely hear him murmuring, "Don't take the boat . . . please. . . . "

Rocky looked at me and I could see the pity in his eyes as he shrugged. I said, "No matter what happened here today, Rock, you're a gentleman. I mean, your buying Morty a new boat and all. I think you've more than risen to the occasion. This entire matter was an accident; I'll attest to that. It just couldn't be helped. Gee, a new boat Rocky, that's swell."

Rocky looked at me incredulously. "What new boat? That's bullshit!" Then he touched his head with one finger. "Don't you know dat Morty's nuts? He's off his rocker. Been like dat a long time. Come on, let's go clamming."

As we climbed up to the dock, Rocky gave me one of those familiar pokes in the ribs, "Hey, kid, look around ya, tell me, whaddaya see?" I looked around and lo and behold there were thousands of curious people lining both shores of Reynolds Channel. They had probably never seen such death-defying boat antics like they witnessed that afternoon. Rocky put up his hands, clenched together like he had just won the championship again, and a mighty roar erupted. This day Rocky Graziano was their Italian Evil Knievel. "Yuh see, ya bum, this should teach you a lesson. Now you can tell your grandchildren, wherever The Rock goes, he draws a crowd!" After that day, I became a firm believer in Rocky and the truth of the title of his book and motion picture, *Somebody Up There Likes Me.*

Rocky was right, though, about Morty. Directly after the "Don't take the boat" incident, poor Morty became bed-ridden. They said it was a nervous breakdown. Rocky said, "How do ya like dat, over a little boat?" and he would point a finger to his head. I could never figure Morty's wife, though. From then on, she would never allow Rocky or myself to come into the house to visit Morty after he was allowed to come home. Over a little boat.

In the midfifties, Paramount Pictures bought the rights to Rocky's book. The book, *Somebody Up There Likes Me*, took over a year to write. Tony Corrado donated his private office over at Corrado Electric at 100 Worth Street, in downtown New York, and every morning Rocky would meet the author, Roland Barber, for about five to eight hours a day. Roland would sift through the rough, crudely complicated life of Rocco Barbella. That was Rocky's real name. He adopted that name from his brother-in-law once when he was on the lam from the law—something about busting a captain in the nose when Rocky was in the service. Rocky had to make some money, so he fought a few four round fights under the name of Rocky Graziano. The authorities caught him, anyway, and he paid his debt to society, which turned out to be a blessing. It was in Leavenworth that Rocky made his real debut and name as a fighter.

Roland Barber did a magnificent job dissecting Rocky Graziano. Inside of this supposedly hard crust, this so-called macho Neanderthal man, was a highly sensitive and talented human being. It's my opinion that Rocky's problems were mostly because of his lashing out at his childhood and rejection because of his very limited education. You don't have to be a shrink to figure that one out. Rocky Graziano, the knockout puncher, with dynamite in both hands, was also a guy who painted beautifully, played the piano with sensitivity, sang with feeling, and was a qualified actor, among a few other attributes.

The book was finished, released, and accepted admirably by both the critics and the public. Paramount Pictures looked around for an actor to portray Rocky Graziano, and it was difficult to come even close to his likeness. They finally, after a few false starts, cast a young, serious, up-and-coming actor to play the part.

His name was Paul Newman and until then he had done only one film, *The Silver Chalice*, and that picture had failed at the box office.

Rocky called me to tell me the news. I remember saying, "Paul who?" Rocky ordered me to join him, Paul Who, and Tony Corrado for dinner at The Embers club that night. He said, "Dis guy Newman is going to hang out wid us for a while. He's got to study me so he can do me in dis picture."

Study Rocky? I thought it would be easier to study Slapsie Maxie Rosenbloom or Casey Stengel. Rocky was an original; there was only one Rocky in this world. Nobody could copy Rocky!

I met this good-looking kid, Paul Newman, that night, and after he said, "Hello," he never said another word. *What a quiet guy,* I thought, *but hell, there's ribs to be eaten and steak and cheesecake and all the rest. Let's go.*

As we were digging into this sumptuous feast, Rocky and I noticed that this new kid on the block had only ordered a chicken sandwich on white bread and a glass of milk. I said, "Hey, Paul, that's food for an old lady. Why don't you order a steak or chops?" Dorothy Donegan was banging noisily on the piano, and it was hard to be heard in the room. Paul just shook his head shyly and Tony Corrado walked over to him. "Paul, you're my guest. I want you to order anything you want. It's my pleasure."

After that first meeting, Paul relaxed a little, and without our noticing, he began to pick up on all of Rocky's mannerisms, his walk or shuffle, his voice, and the way Rocky killed the Queen's English. We were too busy with the laughs, the food, booze to notice that Paul was taking this all in. He was a guy that was determined and very serious about his assignment. It reached a point where we couldn't tell Rocky's voice from Paul's. One day, Tony Corrado said, "I've known Rocky so many years, but when they talk I don't know who's who or which is which." Tony predicted that this Paul Newman was the right choice and that he would go far as an actor.

In the spring of 1951, Rocky and his bride, Norma, were invited to go to Paris for the Friden Company, competitors of Pitney Bowes, makers of the stamp machines. Rocky represented the Friden Company in their commercials and at all their management meetings. Rocky and Norma aren't too big on flying, but after many misgivings, they went anyway. The trip was to last a week and I told him he'd have a great time. "Rocky, Paris, France—it's so historical." Rocky said, Yeah, I heard de're a little hysterical, but dose frogs better not fuck wid me!"

After a couple of days, he called me from his hotel room and said they all loved him in Paris. "Dey all talk funny, but I'm havin' a good time."

I said, "Rocky, make sure you go to see the Eiffel Tower and The Louvre."

He said, "Are ya kiddin'? I'm drinkin' beer in my room; I can always see dat shit on TV!"

Rocky called my house one day and told me to meet him in front of the building in ten minutes. It was urgent; I had to go somewhere with him. Where? "Don't ask so many questions, ya fuckin' bum. Please be dere." "Please." Rocky never said please to me, ever. It was all so vague and mysterious, and I was curious as usual.

He came by in "Da Thunderbird," and I hopped in.

"Where to?" I casually asked and Rocky quickly changed the subject to how neat I looked and was I losing weight "or sumpin'?"

We talked casually about nothing in particular, and the next thing I knew we were on Mulberry Street in the heart of Little Italy, downtown New York. Rocky stopped in front of a small old building and said, "Let's go, kid!" I followed him into a large ground-floor anteroom where a few people, with tears in their eyes, hugged and kissed Rocky.

The next thing I knew, Rocky grabbed me by the neck, pushed me down on my knees, and said, "Pray!" I saw Rocky making the Sign of the Cross on his chest and looked up and saw this very small old man lying in this tiny coffin not a foot from my face. Bewildered, I crossed myself, and copying Rocky, I started mumbling as if in prayer. I whispered to Rocky, "Who is this man?," and Rocky just shrugged like he didn't know.

Rocky then gave me the usual shot in the ribs and said, "Okay, dat's it!" I followed him down the stairs into a smaller

143

room, where an old lady handed me a cup of expresso and a cannoli cake on another plate. I tried to smile feebly at some of the guests who were staring at me, and I felt a little cold sweat rolling down the back of my neck.

Just as I was beginning to balance the expresso cup and the cake plate comfortably, a husky, grim looking guy comes over to me. He tagged me gently on my chin, loosening all my back teeth, hugs and kisses me on both cheeks and says, winking, "Kiddo, my family will never forget you for this. Anytime you need a favor, call me; you know where to reach me."

During our drive uptown, Rocky and I didn't say a word to each other. To date I've never mentioned this incident to Rocky, and he's never mentioned it to me. Sometimes I think maybe this whole thing never really happened. Maybe I saw it in a movie? And if it did happen, how could I call that guy? He never even gave me his calling card.

During the filming of *Somebody Up There Likes Me,* Tony Corrado invited two very young and beautiful people, actress Pier Angeli and her husband, singer Vic Damone, to dinner at Romeo Salta's Italian restaurant. Pier was playing Norma Graziano, Rocky's wife, in the film.

Everyone in the restaurant made quite a fuss over Pier Angeli, as she was considered a big star in Italy. I thought how beautiful and typically European she was, not acting like some stars I'd seen. Here she was, just being very sweet, down to earth, and very much in love and involved with her husband. What a lucky stiff!

We were having dinner, eating this fine Northern Italian food, when I noticed Vic Damone, a singing star in his own right, staring at me. I tried to ignore him and noticed that Pier, his lovely wife, was trying to feed him a forkful of this and that. *What a cute couple and look how wifely Pier is!* I thought.

Suddenly Vic, who appeared bored and restless, said to me, "Eddie, I envy you very much. Boy do I envy you." At that moment, I had a mouthful of pasta. I stopped eating, wiped my mouth, and cleared my throat. "Run that through for me again, Vic. Take it from the top, please."

"I envy you for a couple of reasons," he said. "The way you

enjoy your food, such gusto. You're eating like this is the Last Supper. And the way you talk about the business and life. What a zest for living you have. I never met anyone like you. You're like Zorba the Greek; you get a kick out of everything. Are you always this happy?"

I looked at Vic and said, "It's funny, your saying all this when here I've been envying you, for your beautiful wife, who is obviously very much in love with you, your talent as a singer, and your good looks, as a star in motion pictures, contemporary, always dressed to the nines. Vic, in my opinion you've got it made!"

He looked at me soulfully. "Don't envy me, buddy. I hardly get a kick out of anything anymore. I never enjoyed food the way you do; I just lost my MGM motion picture contract this week; my recording contract ran out a few months ago; my career is at an all-time low; as a matter of fact, I don't even have a single friend to my name. What do you say to all that?"

I tried giving him a little of my philosophy of life, telling him that I had come from extreme poverty and had much to be thankful for, the usual. All the time we were discussing cabbages and kings and the meaning of life, Pier was trying to feed Vic a forkful of pasta or sausage. *"Manga, manga,"* she cooed. He just turned away from her like a disinterested little boy.

I asked him what happened to his manager Lou Capone, the man who started him in the business. And what about music publisher Marvin Cane? Weren't they his close friends? Vic very matter-of-factly said, "Those guys won't ever talk to me again. I made some wrong moves a few times, and they've had it with me. I just never made any close friendships, like you and Rocky have."

Never once in our discussion did he mention his wife, Pier, or how lucky he was to be married to such a devoted wife. I thought to myself, *Man, what I wouldn't give to be married to a beautiful lady like Pier Angeli.*

Years later, Pier Angeli and Vic Damone were divorced and had a terrible knockdown custody court fight over their son, Perry. Then I sadly read somewhere that Pier took an overdose of sleeping pills and died. Sometimes I think about that evening and those two tragically young, beautiful people.

"Man, what I wouldn't give . . . "

On Wednesday, September 30, 1981, my friend, my pal, Anthony J. Corrado passed away at the young age of seventy-eight. I never knew anyone who had more fun out of life, more interests, more vitality, and a more extreme passion for living than Tony.

Rocky Graziano came over to the office as soon as he heard the news. A whole group of Tony's pals gathered, we talked about what a wonderful diamond-in-the-rough kind of a guy Tony was. I mentioned how generous Tony was to anyone who crossed his path. He sent more kids to college, paid more hospital bills, and picked up more tabs than anyone would believe. Someone sadly commented, "Tony was beyond generous!" In two words, that says it. Our friend, our pal, Tony Corrado was "beyond generous."

At the funeral, I sat with some of Tony's old pals at Saint Paul the Apostle's Church as we all said our last good-byes. Maxie Shapiro, the great featherweight and lightweight boxer of the early '40s, who was always known for his natural biting, satirical wit, mentioned that the funeral services took close to an hour. He turned to Rocky and said, "The way they're carrying on isn't for Tony; knowing him, I'd say he would have left an hour ago."

A Letter from Rocky

Everything Eddie white ever said 'bout me is a friggin' lie! Dose stories 'bout dat boat and da racetrack and all dat udder crap—pure B.S.! I never got him into any trouble either; believe me, it's the udder way 'round. I tried to get him to go to church socials wid me, to give up booze, to go wid nice friends, to go to folk dancin' classes wid me but Eddie just wouldn't see da light.

One day I heard him tellin' some people that he taught me how to fight. Hey, did you know dat Eddie White is the original "Crazy" Eddie? Once he tried to get me to take diction lessons so I could talk like him. Nuts! If I talked like him I would be broke.

He says I am too violent. The truth is I don't believe in violence and if he says it once more I'm gonna kick da stuffin' out of him.

146

Sure he wrote some songs for Frankie Sinatra and Tony Bennett and Patti Page, sure he produced some Broadway and off Broadway shows, sure he produced Ella Fitzgerald's concert tours of Japan, sure he acted in some movies—but who da hell did he ever fight?

So he was in dose orphanages. Man, I did more time on one leg—and in da hole, too!

And what's dis 'bout yesterday's cake? When I was a kid we were so poor dat we were glad to get last month's bread.

Seriously though, my best pal Eddie White is a stand up guy and I'm proud to say we been buddies for 35 years now. I love him 'cause he's a softie. Eddie is the only guy I know who has a cauliflower heart.

We got some great memories togedder and I wish him Italian "Mahzel" with dis here book. Eddie's a champ when it comes to rootin' for da underdog and many's da time he was in my corner when I was just dat—da underdog. So Eddie, now I'm rootin' for you.

Your pal,

Rocky Graziano

Two pals, Rocky and me.

147

8

Doin' My Thing

1951: General MacArthur fired; Brando opens in Streetcar; color TV is introduced; Giants beat Yanks in World Series.

LIFE WAS AT SOMEWHAT of a standstill after that meeting with Ray Muscarella in Eduardo's restaurant. I was in sort of limbo for a while. Did I make a mistake in not accepting Ray's offer? If not, when would I go out on my own and write songs full time as I longed to do? Mack Wolfson had taken odd jobs in the music business, waiting patiently for me to make up my mind.

My mind was made up for me in a terribly shocking way. One day, while making a routine afternoon call to my sister, I learned that my youngest nephew, Peter, had been run over by a school bus and had been killed.

The woman who gave me the news tried to spare me as much as she could, but I knew in my heart what had happened. I had a touch of temporary amnesia from that moment on until days later. I can't recall how I drove out to Long Island, what was said, who was there, or hardly anything. Here I was in a bed soaked with my tears for what seemed like an eternity. Peter, three years old, the apple of my and everyone else's eye, was gone. I didn't want to live, but I couldn't figure out how to get out of this life bravely.

Peter Allen Strauss was so proud of his Uncle Eddie's songs, he could almost sing them all. Peter would walk around the house all day carrying his little recorder with 45 rpm records under his other arm. He could tell all the titles by the colors on the labels, and his favorite was "If I Knew You Were Coming I'da

148

Baked a Cake." The grief of my nephew's passing still hangs as sorrowfully and heavy as if it were yesterday. I couldn't wait to name my only son Peter.

Mack Wolfson helped pull me through the next four delicate months more than anyone else. He put up with my crying jags and depressed moods. When that lady told me on the phone that something terrible had happened to my nephew, I walked out of MCA like a zombie and never walked back or called again. Mr. Brabec and Neva Conley must have found out what had happened, because they arranged for me to have separation pay and other considerations from MCA. They never questioned me.

After a few months of nothingness, I finally informed Mack it was time for him to give notice on his job because Eddie White and Mack Wolfson were ready to take on Tin Pan Alley full time.

> Let others make the nation's laws.
> Let me write its songs. . . .

I read that statement somewhere, and it always struck me as a gentle and noble thought. Each time Mack and I would finish a song, I would be mesmerized by the magic of it all. We'd start with an idea, a title, a thought, a catch phrase, a joke, a few bars of music, a statement, or a lament, and here was the finished product. Voilà! Magic! I never did get over it. But, then, I never did get over the idea of the radio. *Sound goes through the air mysteriously, from far away, and comes into this little box near my bed. Get out of here; I don't believe it. But it does. What an age we live in. Next thing you know,* I thought at the time, *people will be going under the sea or to the moon. . . . Never!*

At this time, in the early '50s, I lived at the Woodward apartments next door to the Woodward Hotel on West 55th Street off Broadway. Mack would meet me at ten o'clock in the morning, and we would write songs for five hours or so and talk and dream about the future. Mack was the ideal, dutiful son and brother, and invariably he had chores to do for his parents and sisters. I was always close to his family—they sort of adopted me as another son and brother—so I always encouraged Mack to follow through with his errands.

Then, too, money wasn't coming in, so I picked up a few acts and started managing again. One of the performers I worked with, without a signed contract, was the piano player Jose Melis. Jose and his trio were appearing at the Park Central Hotel's bar, and once in a while Jose would tell me about his army buddy, Jack Paar.

When Mack wasn't around, I would write songs with Jose Melis, advise him on some of his theatrical endeavors, and take care of all of the paperwork, involving Jose's musical copyrights. I did the same with another piano player who lived in my building, Irving Fields, and between Jose and Irving, I made enough money to barely exist.

At night my apartment was the meeting place for every out-of-work singer, musician, or actor. My neighbors were the Jack Soo family (he later became famous on the "Barney Miller" show) and a girl singer named Dolores Morgan.

Between all of us, there wasn't enough money to buy the proper food to feed us. Most nights it was two pounds of linguini number nine, which we would all eat with catsup and pepper in lieu of spaghetti sauce. Jack or his wife, Jean, had the key to my apartment, so sometimes, when I would come home late, dinner would be in progress. It was a good feeling to come home to the smell of hot catsup and the day's gossip and laughter. I felt like I had a family. Cute little Jimmy Soo would jump into my lap and ask me to tell him a story, and although none of us had any money, we all shared love.

Jack Soo's real name was Suzuki. Most people thought he was Chinese, and Jack tried, in his early days, to retain that image. When the big roundup came early in World War II and those of Japanese ancestry were herded into prison camps, Jack figured it might be a good idea to switch and become Chinese for a while, hence Soo from Suzuki. Jack kept the name for many years, but then when he secured a co-starring role in Broadway's *Flower Drum Song*, he figured it was time to change back to his real name, but he didn't figure on his co-star, Pat Suzuki. She nixed the idea. One Suzuki in the show was enough.

Jack Soo, back in the '50s, was probably the only Japanese singer-comic in show business. His singing style was more in the Dean Martin modus operandi, and his comedy was good-natured jokes, mostly kidding his ancestry—sort of Japanese-Yiddish.

Like me, Jack had a rough time making ends meet, but at least I didn't have a family. As short as I was on money, I had enough now and then to help Jack Soo and his family. Once, when I caught a terrible bug, I was treated with penicillin, since I did not know I was allergic to the drug. My fever was over 102 degrees for days, and each time I woke up there was Jackie Boy sitting or sleeping alongside my bed to reassure me. Talk about friendship—with Jack Soo and Mack Wolfson I had it made.

Jack eventually went on to do other plays, movies, and Las Vegas, and then came "Barney Miller." Now I had him back in my living room on Thursday nights, but not long enough. In 1981, Jack succumbed in a bout with the big "C." I sure hope they have catsup in heaven.

Mack and I agreed that no matter how tough things were, we should open a small office in the Brill Building, which had symbolically become Tin Pan Alley. We sold things; we borrowed; we pleaded with music publishers to give us advances on future songs; we did everything and finally signed a lease for our very own office. Some would call it a cubicle, but we called it Music Hall Songs, Inc. Now we had an office, a lawyer who never got paid, a piano, and various filing cabinets, chairs, and desks we were storing for someone else. It all looked very imposing, and we played it to the hilt. I may have had only a dollar and a half in my pocket, but every day I wore a clean white shirt, a tie, and a two-piece suit.

We were so deliciously overjoyed to have our own office, Mack and I, that we washed the floors and walls and windows ourselves. Other songwriters called us The Happiness Boys, as we exuded so much youthful enthusiasm. It was always "Tomorrow we'll get 'em!" or, on a Friday, "Wait till Monday!" I used to sing, "Maybe Tuesday will be our good news day?" There was always mañana.

Somehow, whenever we hit rock bottom—no money, no songs, no records, no nothing—a major recording company would come through and finally cut a recording of one of our songs they had previously filed away. It was as if someone was watching over us. It never failed.

Then, too, we'd get a break now and then when a top artist

151

would send us on the road with one of their records and pay all our expenses. Mack and I would visit disc jockeys, be interviewed on the air, live in nice hotels, eat well, and plug the artist's record, which happened to be our own song, too. Sometimes we'd go in different directions, each to a different city, but plugging the same artist and song.

On one of these occasions, while in Detroit, I heard a chance remark by popular disc jockey Robin Seymour, that the Ames Brothers could make a fine recording of the religious song, "Eli, Eli" if there was an English lyric available. The Ames Brothers were very popular then, having just come off one record with two hit sides—"Only You" and "You Can't Be True, Dear"! I made believe I didn't hear a thing and hoped the thought wasn't picked up by anyone. It wasn't.

When I got back to New York, I called Mack and told him what Robin Seymour had said. Mack knew the Ames Brothers very well personally, having done record promotions for them and various other favors. He was on a first-name basis with them. What could be better? Somehow this first-name–basis situation never ever worked for us. We learned that a song is a song is a song. Gertrude Stein didn't say that—The Happiness Boys did.

The Ames Brothers wouldn't even listen to the song, so we next focused on Perry Como, who we heard was due to record a religious album. Mickey Glass, Perry's major domo, told us our song wouldn't be considered. Como was doing "Eli, Eli" in Hebrew, and our song was an adaptation in English.

We left Perry Como's office more The Gloom and Doom Boys and sadly walked back to our office. A block from the Brill Building, Mack turned to me and said, "There goes Jack Rael, Patti Page's manager." I was in a deep state of self-pity and only heard my partner half-consciously. Suddenly, after a beat of maybe two minutes, I heard what Mack had actually said to me.

I turned in the direction of Jack Rael and sprinted after him, leaving Mack in the dust. I caught Jack just as he entered the elevator in his office building, and in popped Mack, huffing and puffing. Now we had Jack Rael cornered, with no distractions of any kind. He was a captive audience of one.

I screamed at him, "This is destiny. I can't believe it. Jack, we just wrote a religious song for Patti. It's based on the great 'Eli, Eli,' and you gotta hear it!"

152

Jack was amused and after I let go of his lapel he said, "Swell, I'll listen, but when will I do it? Where the hell have you two guys been? There's a nationwide recording strike on now." The impact of his words didn't penetrate and Mack and I were thrilled that Jack Rael would listen.

He had us wait a few minutes while he made some phone calls and we were able to collect our senses. A record strike? Jesus, this could ruin us if it lasted any length of time. *Why didn't I stay in the army or with MCA?* I thought.

Jack beckoned us into his office, which was supplied with a Steinway, and said, "Okay, let's hear your masterpiece, guys." I told Mack to think of the Holocaust when he sang, as this record strike could be the end of our careers.

Mack chanted like a cross between Paul Robeson and the twin Cantors. I cried and so did Jack Rael. Jack said, "Sing it again—this time slower." Jack walked to the window, and I swear I thought he was praying. When Mack finished, we heard Jack's voice as if it came from Mount Sinai: "Guys, this record strike may be a blessing in disguise. I am going to record your song with Patti Page a cappella." We asked him to repeat what he had just said, and this time Mack broke down and openly wept. We were all blowing our noses and wiping eyes and kissing and laughing. It was then we were told by Jack Rael that he had been a "Yeshiva Boocher"—a biblical student—as a youth and he had been searching for such a song for Patti.

That's how Patti Page from Oklahoma, who was known as The Tennessee Waltz Gal, came to sing "Father, Father," based on the Hebraic "Eli, Eli," for Mercury Records—a cappella. It was a stroke of fate that Patti only used voices. The union prohibited musicians from recording at that time. As "Father, Father" cried out for the Hall Johnson Choir sound, it was accorded. Immediately "The Ed Sullivan Show" booked Patti to sing "Father, Father" and Jack Rael prepared to send Mack and myself on an extended disc-jockey tour to exploit the record.

That week, Mack introduced me to a lovely divorcée from Brooklyn and I took her to the House of Chan for a Chinese dinner. What with a major record to my credit, I was well on my way in the music world, and I played the role to the hilt. I ordered the correct wine, I cut her food, I told all the right jokes, and we hit it off quite well. Somehow I missed the point where she said that she wanted to write songs, too.

Elaine and I saw each other once more, and I was off to Cleveland, Detroit, Chicago and other major disc-jockey cities to do or die for Patti Page "U." While on the road, I became depressed each time I called home and spoke to my sister. Naturally we were all still grieving for my nephew, but somehow it hit me this time even worse than when the accident occurred. Mack was his usual reassuring self, and he kept me going somehow.

One depressing evening, I called Elaine and she said, "Well, I was wondering when you would get around to calling me." We talked and I brought her up to date on our progress and other trivia. I felt better after the call, and I called again and again and made another date to see her upon our return. The days went a little better, and I surmised it had to because I met this nice girl and I was able to forget most or a little of what was bothering me.

Upon our return to New York, Elaine and I fell into each other's arms. We had our differences, but in less than three months we were married, in her parents' home. We moved to 54th Street and Eighth Avenue, and in no time at all my wife was pregnant. I told Mack that I had been warned we'd better hit it soon or I'd be way over my head financially. Somehow I got through those next harrowing, pressurized months, but I always had the feeling I wasn't earning enough to please my wife and especially my in-laws.

Then my son, Peter, was born and I was reborn. I'm sure there were other fathers who simply adored their children, but none more than I. I was in ecstasy. A son—another Giant rooter, a fishing and camping buddy, someone to carry on the name of White. Now my ambition was renewed and all would be calm with the world again.

It wasn't to be so. More arguments, more reminders regarding my inadequacy as a provider, more in-law interference. No more jokes, no more Happiness Boys, no more personality kid. People kept asking me why I had changed. I felt myself slipping.

One day, my old army pal comedian Larry Alpert came to see me in the office. He was shocked at my attitude and how I looked. I told him I wanted out desperately but I couldn't stand the thought of leaving my son. My father had deserted his wife and two children. I couldn't bear the shame of doing the same.

Still, the marital arguments in front of my son were destroying me emotionally.

Larry looked at me sympathetically and said, "Eddie, your staying unhappily married isn't good for your son. Listening to his father and mother argue all the time must be tearing him apart, too. Divorce isn't the worst thing in the world. You can start a new life while you're still young and, believe me, you won't lose your son." That last part got to me. "I won't lose my son," I repeated over and over. The die was cast.

No one was really to blame. If anything, I blame the marriage and subsequent divorce on my own stupidity. The marriage had "united" two people with opposite values and opinions on practically everything from politics to table wine. But my stupidity brought me a beautiful son who gives me the main reason for living. If there were more Peter Whites in this world, it would be the heaven on earth it can be.

After the divorce, I took a small apartment on West 58th Street. Again my home became the haven for practically every stray guy and gal in show biz. The Sunday brunches were enormous—"just help yourself. Need a job? Maybe Eddie knows someone who knows someone. Want some information on a producer, a casting director, a show? Surely someone up at the apartment can help you."

Mack and I started to get lucky. Instead of just writing a song, we figured we'd tailor the material for particular artists and it proved highly successful. We wrote "Flowers Mean Forgiveness" for Frank Sinatra, and Benny Barton, who was Frank's music manager, loved it. In a month, Frank recorded the song and it hit the top ten charts nationwide.

Then came "Happiness Street" with Georgia Gibbs having herself a hit and Tony Bennett covering the record. "Happiness Street" was one of the five most performed songs in America in 1955, according to ASCAP. We followed with Sarah Vaughn's "C'est la Vie," which was covered by Pearl Bailey and many other artists.

We were on a roll, and the future looked bright for us. Still, something was missing. Mack and I discussed it often and came to the realization that we had no management, no direction. What we needed was a powerful music organization behind us. We

155

Christmas with my son, Peter, the year of the divorce.

were still unsure of ourselves every time we finished a song. "Was it good enough? Will the publisher and artist like it? Can the song make it?" With one of the musical giants behind us, we could write our songs and let the organization carry the ball. We were doing too much, going in too many directions. Our main and primary function was to write.

Through the years, I had become friendly with Dick Stone, a song plugger and professional manager of Famous Music, the musical arm of Paramount Pictures. I asked Dick to speak to Mr. Eddie Wolpin, the general professional manager of Famous, to see if there wasn't a place for Mack and myself on their staff. They had one other songwriting team already signed—Burt Bacharach and Hal David. Burt and Hal were friends of mine, and I didn't see any conflict, as our writing styles were very different.

Mr. Wolpin called me into his office one day for an interview. Mack urged me to go alone, as he was always the "demonstrator" of our team. I was always the "negotiator." Mr. Wolpin was polite as he studied me with amusement. He asked me questions about current news events as he constantly smoked his cigarettes through a long holder. I was loose, funny, and entertaining, and I won this highly sophisticated man over. He said we had the position. He'd give us an office, a contract, a piano, but very little front money. We'd have to earn our money with our songs. When he said Cole Porter first signed the same kind of a contract when he was young, I shook Mr. Wolpin's hand and said it was a deal.

I went back to Mack and said we had no more rent money problems, no more paying for demonstration records, no more overhead, no more running to publishing and record companies. We were now under contract to Paramount Pictures. In a week, we were in our new office, having coffee breaks, going to lunch for an hour and a half, talking about what we were going to do the coming summer.

The chase was over! Now we were gentlemen songwriters, but looking back reflectively, I think signing with Paramount may have been a mistake. We became fat cats and relaxed too much. We were better off when we were hungry and running our asses off. We became somewhat lazy, hoity-toity songwriters.

The songs were written, the records were secured, and our

ASCAP rating and income gradually started to rise. But The Happiness Boys were no more. Mack and I had been the prototype and the personification of the old-time Tin Pan Alley songwriters who wrote the song, sang on the demo record or demonstrated the song live, ran to the record company or artists, secured the records, and then ran to the disc jockeys and pleaded to get the records played. We also contacted the music-business trade papers to hype them on our songs. We hyped everyone—the publishers, the record companies, the artists, the trade papers, the disc jockeys, and other songwriters. Hype was the name of the game in those days, and sometimes we even hyped ourselves into believing our own bullshit.

But it was a fun time in the music business in the '50s, when music reigned supreme and there was a certain glamor and romance involved. The big bands were still around somewhat, and more than one recording artist covered (recorded) a song and music publishers were shelling out fairly substantial advances for new songs or even ideas of songs to be written.

Mr. Eddie Wolpin, the professional manager of Famous Music, took a personal liking to me. He would take me to lunch at Lindy's or Jack Dempsey's restaurant, and it was fun meeting all the top music publishers and songwriters. I gained a lot of respect from my peers by being seen in the company of Eddie Wolpin.

Eddie was a little standoffish with almost everyone, including myself. You could only get so close to him, and I guess at times I got closer than most people.

Eddie once confessed that he was bored with life, that he had no hobbies and very little interests, and that he had never actually done anything with his hands. Immediately I suggested fishing and launched into a dissertation on the thrills and satisfaction I've always received from this sporting hobby of mine.

Before I knew it, we were both off to the Thousand Islands in Alexandria Bay and spent many weeks pursuing the elusive black bass on the Canadian border. I heard Eddie Wolpin say, many times while on the trip, that he was never happier or more relaxed.

My partner in rhyme, Mack Wolfson, encouraged my friendship with our boss, the professional manager of Famous

Music. Mack felt it surely couldn't hurt and might very well solidify our position—present and future—with Paramount. What Mack didn't realize, was that except for an occasional luncheon or dinner, I paid my own way. I didn't mind, though, meeting all the right people, going to interesting places, listening to Mr. Wolpin's stories about his theatrical past, and learning to order the correct wine with the right dish.

As for my friendship with Mr. Wolpin and solidifying our association with Paramount Pictures, it may have helped somewhat but not in the way Mack and I would have liked. Whenever Paramount was about to distribute or release a new motion picture, Mr. Eddie Wolpin would choose a songwriting team to write the title song in order to facilitate publicizing the film. That is, unless Paramount Pictures hadn't first assigned the songwriting chore to writers out in Hollywood.

The best assignments of whatever films trickled down from Hollywood didn't go to Mack and myself. They went to two young talented Paramount contract writers by the names of Burt Bacharach and Hal David. At that time in the midfifties, none of us had really made our mark—we were still relatively unknown except to our peers in the music business. We wrote pop songs for whatever recording artists were due to record. Sometimes our affiliation with Paramount Pictures helped us secure an important name artist, and sometimes it caused resentment with a recording director or producer. It was hit and miss, but it was exciting and fun.

Whereas Mack Wolfson and I were known as The Happiness Boys, Burt Bacharach and Hal David were known as The Unhappiness Boys. Although they wrote as a team, we all knew they actually wrote their songs apart. That is, Burt might write the music or Hal his lyrics and then they would get together and collaborate on the finished song. Mack and I did almost all of our writing together, spending at least twelve hours a day in each other's company. We were like two kids on a Little League baseball team—we couldn't wait to see each other every morning, and then we hated to part each evening. Many times it took us over two hours to say goodnight after writing long and diligently all day.

Through the years, the mutual dislike between Burt

Bacharach and Hal David became apparent even to the mass media and the public. Burt would go on tour with Anthony Newly or Carole Bayer Sager and run through the entire repertoire of Bacharach/David songs without mentioning his collaborator Hal David even once. Hal carried this around in his heart and gut without wanting to discuss the matter. When reminded about what was happening, he would just smile and shrug.

Mack Wolfson had gone to the same school—Brooklyn's Thomas Jefferson High School—as Hal David, had known him all through their teenage years, and said Hal had always been the same good-natured, quiet guy. My first job in life, as a fifteen-year-old boy, was for the Plymouth Thread Company. I was hired by a man named Eli Bayer who was also the owner of the company. You guessed it; he was Carole Bayer Sager's father. Mr. Bayer also tried to have a romance way back then with my sister, Ruth, but it never got off the ground. Talk about a small world.

If Burt Bacharach and Hal David weren't the best of friends or socially compatible, it never showed in their work. In these early years, there was no denying they were tremendously talented and highly thought of in the music business.

Burt was the darling of film star Marlene Dietrich, and whenever she went on her American or European tours, Burt played the piano and conducted the orchestra. It didn't hurt Burt to have a star of Miss Dietrich's magnitude plugging for him constantly, mentioning his name in the entertainment world. Sooner or later, something big had to break Burt's way, and we young fellow songwriters all envied his talents and his potential for the future. Burt Bacharach was a triple-threat guy. He not only composed wonderful music but he was a fine accompanist and a highly respected arranger. Later, Burt went on tour as an entertainer and singer, but the less said about this part of his career, the better.

Hal David came to the music business with well-respected credentials. His brother, Mack David, was already established as an important American songwriter with songs such as "La Vie En Rose," "Cherry Pink and Apple Blossom White," and "Moon Love" to his credit. I always felt that this hurt Hal more than it helped him. Whereas Mack David wasn't too well liked personally in the music-writing fraternity, Hal David was always looked on as a warm, honest, genial, likable, decent human being. Hal never knocked a fellow songwriter. He belonged to the school of writers who never said anything unless it was progressive and nice. The respect from his songwriting peers came later.

Mack David didn't open too many doors for his kid brother. Hal David wrote his butt off for years, and the recording and music publishing doors began to open gradually. Burt Bacharach and Hal David had their share of lean, struggling years, but it was evident that they would bust through with hit songs sooner or later. Hal David went on to write beautiful books of poetry and to become president of the American Society of Composers, Authors, and Publishers, but he always remained that same sweet, shy man I first met in the early fifties.

Mack and I stayed with Famous Music, Paramount Pictures, for about three years. We could have stayed on longer, but Mack started grumbling to me, and rightly so, that Burt Bacharach and Hal David were getting all the plum assignments film-wise. The only films we were allowed to write the film songs for were *The Jayhawkers*, starring Jeff Chandler and Fess Parker, and *Tempest*, starring Van Heflin and Silvana Mangano. We felt cheated. We wrote many other songs for Famous Music, but Mack and I had to hustle to the recording companies to get them to record our songs. Securing the records was supposed to be the job of the professional manager.

Mack urged me to have a meeting with Mr. Eddie Wolpin, which I promptly did. Mr. Wolpin said we were paranoid, said we were doing splendidly, urged us to hang in there, and took me to lunch at Lindy's restaurant. That day at Lindy's, I met two great songwriters, Johnny Mercer and Sammy Cahn, and came away mesmerized. I calmed Mack down and we continued to write in this vacuum for a few more months.

Then one day Mack vented his spleen on Dick Stone, the professional manager and chief song plugger for Famous Music. Mack accused Dick of not giving us a fair shake in getting our songs recorded. I intervened, calmed things down, and took Mack to lunch at Jack Dempsey's restaurant. We agreed that in a few months we should leave Famous Music. We probably could do better on our own. The experiences at Famous were invaluable, but it was time to move on.

161

Word spread through the music business of our leaving Famous Music, and before we started looking for an office in the Brill Building, then considered Tin Pan Alley, the offers started to pour in. This was something Mack and I hadn't counted on, and we had to call a huddle to reevaluate our situation.

After many weeks of visiting Belmont Racetrack, hanging out at Tony Canzoneria's Paddock restaurant, discussing our situation with some of the elder statesmen in the music field, we finally decided on signing on as writers with another music publishing firm, Gale Music.

Sheldon Music was owned by Moe Gale, whose family once owned the Savoy Ballroom, in Harlem's heyday. Mr. Gale came from a colorful theatrical family.

Moe Gale only knew about Mack and myself through his general professional manager, Aaron Goldmark, or Goldie, as he was known in the music business from coast to coast and on all the ships at sea. No more colorful human character ever took a breath on earth than this unbelievably spaced-out, outrageously funny man. He was the John Belushi of the music business, only more so.

To tell of Goldie's exploits from the time he was a bass player with Billy Eckstine's orchestra doing one-night stands until he became known as Mr. Music to those who loved and understood him would take an entire book.

Goldie was a big, heavy-set man with a mustache that matched his constantly smiling face. He could disarm you with a plaintive plea of mercy or an appeal to a tiny drop of milk of human kindness that might exist within you. No outlandish performance on his part to persuade an artist to record a song he was plugging, no monumental stretching of the truth to win a pretty girl's favor, no wild maneuvering on his part to throw the loan sharks and bookies off his trail, nothing that has ever been written, heard, or said was past our beloved Goldie.

Goldie was a Jewish Robin Hood. He would rob you blind, but only if you could afford it. If you were broke or hurting, Goldie would stake you, get you a job, or steer some outlandish good fortune your way. It was all gratuitous—Goldie only asked for your love and loyalty in return.

Goldie knew every shtick, every hype, every scam. And those who knew Goldie knew he constantly lived in this Never-Never

162

Land but hoped to coexist with him and do business with this fascinating, absolutely never boring, but terribly entertaining, wonderful walking, talking one-man band. Of no one was it better said "to know him is to love him."

One of the many outrageous things I was privy to witness was after Mack and I had written a catchy, up-tempo new song. Goldie listened as Mack and I performed the song in harmony and turned to us and said, "We've got to let Joe Carlton hear this song—it's right up his alley."

Joe Carlton was then artist and repertoire head of the RCA Victor recording company. The three of us jumped into a cab and headed for RCA Records without so much as a scheduled appointment with Mr. Carlton. As soon as Goldie's name was mentioned, we were ushered into the offices of Joe Carlton. I noticed Goldie fidgeting with the buckle on his belt, and as soon as Mr. Carlton's secretary backed out of the room, Goldie let his pants and shorts down and said, "Joe, kiss my ass, come on, kiss my ass, Joe, 'cause if you don't you don't get this song!"

P.S.: We got the record. The artists were the Crewcuts on RCA, and the song was "Hey, You Face." Years later I tried the same stunt on another A and R man at another recording label and he threw me out of his office. I really didn't have my heart in it, anyway.

Every day was a fun day with Goldie. We never knew what to expect. He wasn't our boss—he was a pal—and he stood by Mack and me through every little dissension up at Sheldon Music. Though Goldie sometimes was short on the truth or facts, he was long on friendship, loyalty, and all-around goodnaturedness.

Moe Gale still dabbled in personal management somewhat, and one of his artists was Robert Merrill, the Metropolitan Opera baritone. Bob Merrill and I became friendly, and between writing songs I would listen to him tell about his aspiration to play with the Brooklyn Dodgers. Sometimes I would go backstage at the Metropolitan Opera and be dazzled by the atmosphere, the costumes, and the temperaments of some of the divas. I remember being most impressed and thinking how this other, strange to me, show-business world hadn't changed my friend Robert Merrill. He was still a down-to-earth shortstop with the Brooklyn Dodgers at heart. After the smoke would clear at the Met and some lyric soprano had stopped cursing the tenor for upstaging

163

her, Robert and Marion Merrill and I would head for the Russian Tea Room to unwind with a plate of borscht and blintzes.

Bob Merrill loved Moe Gale like a son loves a father. Most of us at Sheldon Music felt the same way. Moe never ordered anyone to do anything. He suggested or requested you do something, and we all did our best to comply. We just couldn't stand disappointing Moe, who would stare at us with a sad, sheepdog expression. I never heard Moe raise his voice—I think he just didn't know how.

Mack and I were quite happy and content while writing for Sheldon Music. We got our fair share of records, we came and went as we saw fit, and we wrote when we felt the urge. The music world looked rosy, except for a small, dark cloud that appeared on the distant horizon and kept drifting closer and closer. The name of that cloud was "hard rock," or "acid rock."

I kept telling Mack that "hard rock" was the direction we would have to follow if we wanted to compete with these new kids on the block. Neither of us understood the music, had the stomach for it, or really wanted to write in that vein. Every time an A and R man turned down one of our songs and requested we write something "hard," we got nauseous. It was follow or die, or at least until this new sound of music ran out of steam. But it was too hard on our sensibilities, our ears, and our hearts.

It was at this time that fate, or destiny, stepped into the wings. I was doodling in my office up at Sheldon Music and looked up to notice a young Japanese man sitting in the waiting room. The next morning he was there again and the next morning, too, just sitting and quietly staring at the wall. Every so often he would turn toward me and smile.

Finally, on my way out of the office the third day, I stopped to chat with this patient young man. It seemed he was waiting to see Mr. Goldie Goldmark. I went into Goldie's office and told him that there was a Japanese guy outside who had been waiting to see him for three days. Goldie looked at me with a pained expression and asked me to please get this guy off his back.

Back I went to the waiting room, and I asked the poor fellow to state his reasons for wanting to see Mr. Goldmark. His explanation being lengthy and vague, and as I was on my way home, I asked him if he wouldn't like to take a walk. He agreed, and walking home I learned his name was Fumio Suzuki. He was from Tokyo, he represented various Japanese business firms, he was also an interpreter, and he had a love for the music industry and show business. Before I knew it, we had arrived at my apartment house on West 58th Street, and instinctively I invited my newfound friend up for dinner.

While I was preparing the pasta and salad and chilling the wine, I told Fumio about writing for Frank Sinatra, Tony Bennett, Rosemary Clooney, Patti Page, and many other artists and about my stints with Music Corporation of America as an agent and with Paramount Pictures as a writer. I guess I was trying to impress him, and I must have succeeded beyond my wildest dreams. Fumio Suzuki was my dinner guest a few more evenings, and then he was off, back to the Land of the Rising Sun. I honestly didn't think I would see or hear from him again.

Meanwhile, the record situation became stickier for Mack and myself. Then it came to a complete halt. Most music-business people stated that business was so bad because it was really a hot summer or because it was before Thanksgiving or Lent or Christmas. There was always an explanation why recordings didn't sell. Blame the songwriters, the music publishers, the record companies, the distributors, the public. Put the blame anywhere but where it belonged.

The truth is, the music business every few years stops dead in its tracks, takes a deep breath as if to take stock of itself, and looks for a brand-new direction. A new sound, a new artist, a new dance, a new fashion style, a catch phrase, or a current event can trigger the next musical trend.

While Mack and I were still writing and swimming upstream, I received a very official letter from Fumio Suzuki. I opened it and tried to read the broken English but couldn't comprehend exactly what it all meant. I put the letter in my pocket and forgot about it for a few days.

When I again read the letter, I realized that Fumio was offering me some kind of a proposition. It took two or three more letters to figure out what the deal was all about.

It seems that my inviting Fumio Suzuki to my home for dinner, without hardly knowing who he was, had opened the floodgates—heart and mind.

Fumio had gone back to Tokyo and raved about this man he had met, this *gaijin*, foreigner, who knew all the celebrities from the worlds of show business, sports, and politics. It was partially true, though Fumio, as I later learned he was prone to do, over-played his hand, but to no one's detriment. As a matter of fact, Fumio scored a direct hit, a bull's-eye.

One of the men who heard Fumio talk about this American who had thousands of contacts in all fields of endeavor was the head of the Tokyo branch of Yamaha Nippon Gakki, Japan's leading manufacturer of pianos and other musical instruments, motorcycles, and electronic equipment. From Tokyo, word spread of my fame to the president of Yamaha, Mr. Genichi Kawakami, in Hamamatsu, Japan.

President Kawakami immediately summoned his humble servant, me, to his castlelike home in Hamamatsu, where most of the main Yamaha factories belched smoke. Fumio wrote that no one disappointed President Kawakami so that I should please leave as soon as possible. Enclosed was one first-class ticket to Tokyo, Japan.

Now I had visions of going to Israel someday, or Paris in the spring, or London Town, or even Rumania, the birthplace of my parents. But Japan? This would take some deep meditation and a little soul-searching.

That night I did something that changed the whole course of my life and steered me into the wildest escapade any Jewish boy from the Bronx ever encountered. I ate a Japanese meal complete with raw fish and hot sake. Then I went to the Little Carnegie Theater to see my first Japanese film, titled *Ikiru*.

It wasn't bad enough that the raw fish was delicious and agreed with my spicy Rumanian taste, but the film thoroughly wiped me out. No other film—except maybe with the possible exception of *Stella Dallas* or *The Sin Of Madelyn Claudett*—had such an effect on me. I stayed in my seat, paralyzed, and saw the picture again, in the last performance that night.

I don't remember going home, but I remember staying up all night thinking and agonizing. Did God help me make my decision about going to Japan by having me see this particular film, *Ikiru*? I went back to the theater early the next afternoon and saw the picture four more times. During intermission I called Goldie Goldmark and with a hoarse voice told him I had laryngitis and

166

had lost my voice. He glibly stated that I sounded like I had lost my will to live. On the contrary, I was on to something but I didn't know just what.

Ikiru was a film about a widowed man who had just been told he had only six more months to live. He keeps this information from his son and daughter-in-law, who live in his home and haven't been showing him the proper respect, and sets out in search of some purpose, some meaning, for his life. With his life savings, this sad, bewildered man hires a sophisticated but drunken writer, thinking surely he must possess the secret meaning of life, to teach him how to live. They visit many bars, restaurants, and houses of prostitution, and finally the writer tires of the endless round of dissipation, but mostly of seeing the sad, expressionless face of the widower. The writer, although personally sympathizing with his strange companion, finally tells the widower that he can't help him, that he doesn't know the meaning of life and never did.

The widower drifts off and eventually finds a chubby teen-aged girl with a pretty face who works in a stuffed animal factory. He buys her lunch and, without eating himself, enchantedly watches her eat and laugh with youthful enthusiasm. After a few lunches and gifts from the widower, who merely stares at her all the time, she becomes suspicious of his motives. She questions him and when he doesn't respond to her satisfaction, she runs away screaming she doesn't want to see him anymore.

Having nothing to do and nowhere to go, he reports to his old job, where he did nothing but stamp papers as a low-level clerk in a dead-end bureaucratic municipal office. He chances to overhear two mothers bemoaning the fact that a small area near their homes, promised to the children as a park, has now been turned over to gangsters for a bar. They are screaming and ranting about the injustice of the mayor and all the petty politicians when the widower asks to see this area.

After seeing the land originally promised for a children's park and examining the original petition, the widower visits the mayor. The mayor refuses to see this strange, somber man, but the widower waits for him day after day. Soon, some gangsters get wind of the widower's purpose and threaten to kill him. The widower just stares at them.

Finally, the mayor can take it no longer and nervously invites

Walter Winchell
of New York

The Broadway Lights

Celebs In The Crowd: Jack Dempsey at his Broadway oasis looking like he could take on anybody...Warren Beatty studying a script in a limousine along Park Avenue at 9 a.m....Ava Gardner getting the up-and-down from hackies parked near her abode, the Hotel Elysee...Sinatra Senior and Junior strolling along Central Park South looking very father&sonatra...Gordon and Sheila MacRae obliging autographers in the foyer of the Waldorf...they start their 5th return booking Friday eve...Barbara Bel G skirt being defeated by the wind at 7th Avenue and 59th St Novelistocrat John Steinbeck, recovered from recent surger zling the Mediterranee crowd with his Black Cape, Top H glittering cane...Robert Preston, one of the few actors who pretty steady, exciting the belles at One Fifth Avenue... Cugat (escorting his Abbe Lane to the "Girl Talk" show) loud laughs with his brown suit and red sox.

Sallies In Our Alley: Showfolks dining at Teddy's w caking F. Sinatra Jr's good notices following his Ameri miere. "It must make his father feel old," someone s father?" chuckled another. "You mean his father's girl fr Two Copa show-gels were gossiping about a newcomer s backstage with her first mink coat...."Oh, well," meow'd goes another halo."

Las Vegas Story: Gamblers back from the desert eye-witnessed it...Ray Ryan, the multi-oilionaire, wh tacular gambler, gave the usually placid casino bosses a place a big scare the other night...They raised the l at a dice table...He wagered on the Eleven twice (1! it came up both times...He had about $20,000 of th asked the management if they'd let him bet their Eleven once more...After a brief huddle they decline them...It came up 11 again!

Times Square Circle: Federal subpenas will be Cosa Nostra chiefs any day. The ones named by n All will "take the 5th"; Sen. McClellan and B. K more publicity and nothing will be solved...Toots the Copa audience ending a 15 year feud with the s The Sardi's crowd fear the Kim Stanley-Alfred R static...Merle Oberon must wonder. The N.Y. Tin her new film "Love and Desire," noted: 'Her came her to look downright pitiful"...The Trib's reviewer reported: Oberon is lovely...rest assured that age hasn't withered a thing" ...Ticket brokers still rate "Succeed" the top show. Some get $45 per pair...Carlos Aruzza, Mexico's star matador, is here making passes at the Little Club's prettiest faces...The Norman Rosemonts (he's Robert Goulet's manager) are imaging...Reporter J. Hyams' next book will be an "as-told-to" with Barbara Stanwyck...The Stork Club had its busiest weekend in 2 years...Isabelle Farrell, featured dancer in "Boys From Syracuse," and Avon Cosmetics heir actor Wayne Rooks are a Romeo-Julietching.

Novelet: For 13 years he was in the Hebrew Orphan Asylum n New York...He was in the Air Force as a combat flier 5 years ...For 18 years, you see, he was out of circulation...Never went ast the 8th grade in school...He was a page boy at the St. Moritz Hotel here when drafted...Never had 3 squares a day until he was 1 in the Services...He was elevated from the ranks to Captain and after a tour of combat wound up teaching "Theory of Bombing" and 'Weights and Balances"...He also wrote several song hits including "C'est La Vie" and "Happiness Street"...He is producing the I. George Carnegie Hall Concerts on Oct. 8, 9, 10...Ditto the Ella Fitz- gerald shows in Japan next January...He is the top importer of Japanese films and he owns several record and music firms...His name is Eddie White, who would like to borrow part of today's col'm just to say "Thank you America."

Eddie White Sets U. S. Publishing Co. For Yamaha, Ltd.

NEW YORK — Writer Eddie White has set up a sub-publishing firm in the U. S. for the Japanese company Yamaha Music, Ltd. White, who just returned from a summer trip to Japan, is the U. S. representative for the Japanese company, whose president, Genichi Kawakami, is also head of Nippon Gakki, large manufacturing concern.

In addition to inboard motors, pianos, motorcycles and organs, Nippon Gakki owns 1,200 music schools, 9 music-department stores, and controls 500 music store outlets. General professional manager of Yamaha is Fumio Suzuki, former key deejay on radio KANTO.

White has already started to sign U. S. catalogs for the Japanese market, including Spanka Music, the Paul Anka publishing firm, and writer Aaron Schroeder's three publishing outfits. He is also negotiating for a number of other catalogs for immediate Japanese exposure.

According to White, while the main area of activity for Yamaha here will be the exposing of American copyrights and catalogs to the Japanese market, the firm will also import Japanese classics and current hits for U. S. audiences. In addition, plans are under way to start a record label within the next few months.

EDDIE WHITE — BROADWAY'S NICE GUY

Eddie White is a fellow you've probably never heard of, but everyone in show business has because he's one of the fastest-rising young men along Broadway. Eddie's Brill Building office is always packed with show people wanting advice or asking him to use his vast number of contacts to help them get recording contracts, personal appearances etc.

Eddie White was born in the Bronx, N. Y. June 18, 1919 and spent 13 years of his life in orphan asylums. A teacher at one encouraged him with his poems and Eddie was off! He began work as a bellboy at the swank St. Moritz, where he met many show business people. He worked at the cigar counters of many hotels, but always wrote. Next he worked in a perfume factory (and couldn't stand the smell!) Music publishers kept ing down his material. He even aged a prize fighter, but the gym sphere made him even sicker the perfume factory!

n World War II came along ddie volunteered so speedily he No. 1 at Board 28, New York! November, 1940 and he volun- r a year, but it was five years at he got out as Captain the AAF. In the Army he plicity material, as well as d staging shows. He also Army Hit Kit, a booklet of sang. Many of them ho pt" before they could be

e joined the Sea Search ron where he met a fel-

low he cherishes as his best friend, Lt. Art Stringari. Art convinced Eddie that show business was "it." Art later became one of the best-known labor relations counselors in the country.

Eddie was discharged September 11, 1945 and began writing material for comedians and jingles for radio use. He got an offer from MCA and joined them for three years as an agent. He switched to Mercury Artists for another two years, but meanwhile kept writing songs. About this time Mack Wolfson came in, asking advice on managing talent. He and Eddie realized they had much in common. Eddie explained he wanted to quit agenting to open a manage office and write songs Mack thought it was the boys made plans.

They began by Eddi ent and both of them jingles and special m has managed Dick Noe ren, Eddie "Piano" Mi Russell, Tommy Edward more. He's currently ha McLaurin and Ken Cars whom are going very well

Together Mack and E written such top notch tune piness Street, C'est La Vie Mean Forgiveness, Crazy (etc. They've written for Gibbs, Tony Bennett, Sarah V Frank Sinatra, Patti Page, D nell and Billy Eckstine.

Eddie's main ambition is t duce musicals and stage sho Broadway. He says his second i tion is "to make enough mone become a full-time beachcomber!

Advice to youngsters intereste show business? Eddie says, "F have a genuine love for whatever part of show biz you pick. Learn every phase, take any job you can get." To succeed? "Maintain a good reputation, keep appointments consistently, pay your bills on time and always be willing to lend a helping hand whenever it's needed."

It's easy to see why Eddie White is becoming a success. He's taking his own very good advice!

the widower into his office. The widower just stares at the mayor, and finally, in a Kabuki monotone, speaking like some high priest, he requests the mayor to comply with the petition of the parents for a children's playground.

The mayor screams and insults the widower, but after many such meetings, the mayor relents and agrees to the park, either out of consciousness or the fear of the unknown. The widower dies during a snowstorm, singing a plaintive song and sitting on a swing in the children's park.

After his funeral, the people in the community come to his home to pay their respects to this gallant man who had the courage to stand up to the mayor, gangsters, and the immense bureaucracy. The mothers lament that a saint had left this earth and that the park means so much to the children. All the townspeople, his fellow clerks, the police, and the press tell little anecdotes about the widower—like tiny pieces of a jigsaw puzzle that is finally completed. And we realize that our hero has truly given meaning to his life. My description of *Ikiru* doesn't give justice to this unusually fine film. The widower was splendidly played by Takashi Shimura, and this film was directed by the great Japanese director Akira Kurasawa.

To say that *Ikiru* changed my life is to put it mildly. If it didn't help me make up my mind to go to Japan, it surely helped me decide on a course for the rest of my life. In a few days, I knew I would never work for anyone else as long as I lived. I knew that heretofore I would only do the things that were personally satisfying to me. Somehow I knew that from this day forward I was going to be my own man as much as I possibly could. It would take some doing and some earth shaking, but by God, I too wanted to give my life some meaning.

Now to tell Mack, my partner, my brother, whom I loved more than he knew. I planned what to say—that the music business as we knew it was shot through with holes, that it was going in a direction we fully didn't understand, that we'd have to get into other things, possibly another business. We would always be close; we could still write our songs; we would always see each other and would stay in daily contact, as always.

I never got to say much of anything, because as soon as Mack heard what was on my mind he let out a scream that made Tarzan sound like a hummingbird. We both started to cry and choke and pant, and stuff came out of our noses. Maxela, to use my pet name for him, was hurt, and I was scared, because I didn't know how to quickly undo the hurt, how to make it go away. Today I think it was mostly the element of surprise that upset Mack, because, in time, he fully understood everything, and we are now closer friends than ever. We still call each other partner, and we are. We have so many old songs coming up for renewal, and occasionally we write a special song if the spirit moves us. We're still The Happiness Boys—a little older, a little heavier, a lot smarter. To me, the thought of breaking up with Mack would have been more than I could bear.

The next couple of months were a blur. I'd go to the office at Sheldon Music, but mostly to break the news to Goldie Goldmark, who, in turn, told our boss Mr. Moe Gale, who then told the entire office staff, that Eddie White was a great kidder, that the closest he was ever going to get to Japan was Coney Island.

No one except Mack believed me. Moe Gale thought I had an ulterior motive, that I wanted more money, a bigger office, more time off. He started taking me to lunches at fancy restaurants and picking my brains to find out what made me tick. Moe kept saying, "Come on, you're not going to Japan. We need you here."

I bought a new wardrobe, including new pairs of shoes, and started to lose weight. Still Moe Gale didn't believe I was serious until I flashed my passport. That afternoon he took me to the 21 Restaurant, ordered some fine French wine, and offered me a partnership in his personal-management firm. I asked about Mack, my partner, and Moe said we could each have 15 percent. I asked about a participation in Sheldon Music, and Moe said that could be worked out, too, in time. I realized I was only teasing Moe Gale and jerking myself off. I wanted to go to Japan—I *had* to go to Japan—to clear my head, to find out if there was more to my life than just writing pop songs. I finally told Mr. Moe Gale that I was leaving for Japan on a certain date, that if I returned empty-handed and empty-hearted and he still wanted Mack and me as partners, we could talk then. Moe gave me an ultimatum. If I went to Japan, the deal was off and all bets were cancelled. The die was cast.

I got my affairs and head in order, called all the music

171

businesses and theatrical papers to tell them what I was doing, and headed for Kennedy Airport. My itinerary was to fly to Los Angeles, stay at the home of my old pal and writing partner Stanley Adams, who had now become a legend in Hollywood, then board my Japan Airlines flight to Hawaii. Then I would visit Hawaii for three days and head on to Japan.

Stanley Adams was now a fine actor who had appeared in *Breakfast at Tiffany's, Lilies Of the Field, Requiem for a Heavyweight*, and many more noteworthy films. Stanley and Harriet Adams made a fuss over me with the usual chicken in the pot, home cooking, and abundance of love. Stanley took me to the studios to show me off, and I couldn't get over the high regard big stars had for my fat friend. They actually stopped shooting scenes on "Wagon Train," "Dr. Kildare," and "Combat" when Stanley walked on the set. Someone would invariably yell out, "Cut! Uncle Stanley is here!"

Stanley was one of the world's funniest men, in my opinion and in the opinion of such stars as Elizabeth Taylor, Audrey Hepburn, the late Robert Taylor, Mickey Rooney, the late Buster Keaton, Keenan Wynn, and so many other Hollywoodites.

He and I did so many improvisational comedy routines and threw away so many hilarious situations and ideas that today I am sad that I didn't take notes or make some audio-cassettes. We were the poor man's Mel Brooks and Carl Reiner, so to speak. One of our oldest routines was so like the Brooks/Reiner "2,000-year-old Man" that we never did get over the similarity. It had to be a coincidence, though. Mel Brooks and Carl Reiner are my comedy idols, along with Lenny Bruce and, of course, Stanley Adams.

Stanley's weight was a source of concern for his family and friends for years. He weighed in the vicinity of 300, pounds and he hardly ever ate sensibly. Pasta, sushi, and sausages with a side of ribs was considered an afternoon snack.

On this trip, Uncle Stanley wanted me to meet his next-door neighbors. Harriet Adams had just cooked us a huge meal, and off we went. The squeals of laughter and the hugs and kisses were things I had become accustomed to in Stanley's company. He wasn't just loved; Stanley was adored and worshipped by adults, children, animals, and plants.

I noticed a large dining-room table set for about eight people and felt embarrassed that we might be intruding on these nice people at their dinner hour. Stanley said, "I want you all to meet my very best friend, Eddie White" and sat down at the table, but with his back to it. The grandmother immediately invited us to dinner, but Stanley waved her off with "No, no, no, we just had dinner and we're stuffed!" I sat in a soft chair off in the living room.

The grandmother first brought out a salad and a stuffed fish course and set the food at everyone's place, including Stanley's. As the family started to eat, Stanley glanced at the food at his setting and, with his back still to the table, picked up a fork and said, "I'll just pick."

In time, Stanley finished all the salad and fish. Then the grandmother brought out bowls of soup and Stanley picked at that until it was all gone, too. Then the main course was served— chicken fricassee, potatoes, and vegetables. Again, Stanley picked and picked until that was all gone. Up to this time, not a word was said by anyone, except for Stanley's words of protest that Grandma shouldn't serve him, that he just couldn't eat another thing.

Finally, there was much applause and sighs from the family sitting at the table. I looked up to see Grandma entering the dining room with a large pan of kugel. Kugel is a heavy Middle European potato dish sometimes jokingly referred to as Jewish cement. Stanley was applauding, too, and he stood up and kissed Grandma, saying, "Wait awhile; kugel I'll have!" The years have come and gone, but I haven't stopped laughing.

I stayed with Stanley and Harriet Adams in their little house in Santa Monica for three days. My insides hurt from all the belly laughs and the abundance of home-cooked food. Like two kids, Stanley and I made plans for the future. We were going to be the fair-haired boys of Hollywood, writing films, producing plays, and forming a company.

Stanley made me promise to move to California, and I think I gave him him the idea that I would. With Stanley Adam's moral support and love, I felt there was a place for me out in Hollywood. Most of my theatrical friends usually would tell me, "They'll eat you up out there in Never-Never Land!" I always thought that

173

was true, that Los Angeles and its environs and people had some sort of cult mentality. I honestly feared making the move, although I had so many friends and past business associates now residing there.

Teary-eyed, Stanley and I drove to the airport. Unashamedly we kissed good-bye and Stanley screamed to anyone who would listen that I was leaving him to have a sex-change operation. We laughed some more, with heavy hearts, and with all the Japanese men staring at me I walked toward Japan Air lines.

Meeting
Notice

We
Pa

The HOA Assn. RISING

Vol. 9, No. 1, January 1965

LT. EDWARD R. WHITE'S "BRAINCHILD" CHEERS WEARY CREWMEN

A novel idea was born in the mind of one Lt. Edward R. White, a bombardier in the 3rd Search Attack Squadron. Deviating from his regular job due to the lack of ground personnel, he temporarily took charge of Shellbank mess hall T-269 and con-

Lt. Eddie R. White Leads Luncheon Swing

sequently changed this Army structure from an ordinary chow house into a jumpin' luncheon rendezvous. With the able assistance of Leo J. Neissen, CO of the First Aviation Squadron, mess hall each noon to accommoved its music widely acclaimed swing band pany the boy mid-day chow. So appealing did this m halls were quite vacant during th

White stated: "When ose face, but he

Eddie White in Debut On Broadway as Producer

Eddie White, who has produced television, concert, and variety shows, makes his debut as a Broadway producer with the opening of "The Family Way," on Wednesday, January 13th, at the Lyceum Theatre.

The production of "The Family Way" represents the fulfillment of a long cherished dream for Eddie, who has been in show business for twenty-five years. He was a song and comedy writer before turning to producing some years ago.

Among the big investors in his play, one—Charles Tuckman—is an HOA alumnus, and two—Irving Kaster (Kastrinsky) and Charles Lester (Loesberg) are BHOA graduates.

Eddie's interest in show business began when he was a boy in the HOA. At the age of eleven he submitted a poem to the Rising Bell and became its youngest contributor. Getting his work in print at so early an age was a heady start and a spur to his creativity.

It took years, though, before he got the breaks he needed. When he was discharged from the HOA, Eddie worked at a variety of jobs while trying to find publishers for the songs he was writing. None would buy them.

His chance came during World War II. While in the Army, he wrote publicity material, turned out more songs, and authored a GI song booklet called "The Army Hit Kit." He held the rank of captain in the Army Air Force by the time he left the service, in 1945.

Returning to show business, he wrote songs, comedy material, even jingles—anything that singers or comics could use.

He became an agent for Music Corporation of America and later opened a talent management office of his own. Producing was the next inevitable step upward in his career and he took it some years afterward. Last year, he toured

EDDIE WHITE

Feiler Re-Elected Preside At December Meeting; Recruiting Unit Formed

Morris Feiler was re-elected to a se ond term as president of the association at the December meeting at the Park Sheraton Hotel. Frank Nassberg, who has been a second vice-president, w elected first vice president. Hy Kamp succeeded Frank as second vice pr dent.

All the other officers—Al Lang gina Moser, David Goldberg, and Begelman—kept their posts. M Roback was again named Hono retary.

The Chanukah Bazaar dr many customers and realize able sum from the sale merchandise.

Ways and means of members provided the discussion during the b meeting. Mac Mod

Ed White Appears At Popular Film Symposium

By Andre Stepankowsky

Eddie White, the well-known producer, writer, and actor, appeared at a film symposium sponsored by the English Society last Wednesday and kept the discussion of various popular films in the real world. As a member of a four man panel that included Professors Thomas Stavola Professors Violi, all from the English Department, Mr. White's comments to an audience of about 100 were down-to-earth, giving his listeners an interesting glimpse of the behind-the-scene activities of film and Broadway drama. However, Prof. Stavola, the dramatic and aesthetic perspective of Prof. Nelson, and Dr. Violi's neomarxist interpretation were equally interesting.

The films that received the attention were On the Cukon must

and answer period should have been given more attention.

Another common criticism common among the students was that Prof. Stavola, who acted as chairman, allowed the professors to speak at too great a length and, by doing so, prevented Mr. White from offering his opinions as often as he and the audience would have liked. The three professors were, as expected, very articulate and interesting; but as an invited guest, Mr. White should have been given the role of primary speaker. Mr. White was kind enough to appear at FDU-he even returned his $250 fee-and should have been given more attention.

The English officers, Donna Lynn Albi Socia fashion.

9

Japan

1960: Russia shoots down U-2 plane; Kennedy and Nixon debate; the Twist introduced; John F. Kennedy elected president; "Never on Sunday" number one hit.

FROM THE MOMENT I boarded my JAL flight to Hawaii, I felt I was in the Orient—the stewardess called me White-san, gave me a pair of slippers, some hot sake, seaweed crackers, and the warmest smile of welcome it was ever my pleasure to receive. The more sake I drank, the more enticing and welcome the stewardess's smile became.

The food served on JAL was Japanese, naturally, and by now I knew all the dishes by their names. What wonderful adventure awaited this Marco Polo from the Bronx, this Jewish Lieutenant Pinkerton? I leaned back and dreamed about Anna Mae Wong and Charlie Chan and Dr. Fu Man Chu. I knew they were all Chinese, but that's about as close as I could get. I actually tingled with excitement and anticipation.

The first stop was Honolulu, Hawaii. I stayed in a bungalow on the lagoon at the Hawaiian Village for three days. I felt I owed it to myself to rest up, see Hawaii a bit, and get a little color, which would help me make an impression in Japan.

At another hotel's piano bar, I actually heard a couple of the Hawaiian songs Mack and I wrote with Johnny Pineapple and Hal Aloma back in our lean salad days. I started to tell the people that I had co-written "I Hear Hawaii Calling" and "Hawaiian Love Chant" but thought better of it. I remember that time in the Hotel Astor bar when I inferred that I had written the song Frank Sinatra was singing on T.V. A woman who was obviously drunk and

175

with tears in her eyes turned to me and said, "Hey, fuck off, kid—man, that Frankie boy is so beautiful."

The lagoon in front of my bungalow was three feet deep, no matter how far out into the ocean I went. Lunchtime I'd walk fifty yards out with a chair, a hat, sunglasses, and a rack of baby barbequed ribs. I was one happy Caucasian.

Again with heavy heart, I had to leave this tropical paradise and follow my secret destiny. I boarded my third and last leg of my flight, again on JAL, to Honeda Airport, in Tokyo, Japan.

Somewhere in flight, the stewardess approached to inform me we had reached the International Date Line, the point of no return. I had no intentions of returning, but if I filled out the form she handed me I would receive confirmation of my crossing the date line. I did so and felt thrilled. Although I crossed the international date line many times, It was nothing like that very first flight.

I arrived at Honeda Airport on a rainy night in Tokyo, and there was Fumio Suzuki as a greeting party of one. We bowed, shook hands respectfully and headed for my headquarters, the Tokyu Ginza Hotel. I say headquarters because that's what my room became while I stayed in Tokyo.

It was after 11:00 P.M. when I checked into the hotel, and I went right to my room on the top of the building, the ninth floor. I took a hot shower, turned on the television set, turned out all the lights, and jumped into bed. The television came on and I almost had a heart attack. There was a pretty nude woman doing a lewd dance, making obvious sexual overtures to the T.V. camera. I watched it for a while, afraid if I moved I'd knock the station off the air. I took a deep breath to calm myself down and take stock of the situation.

I turned the dial to a couple of other stations, and they were doing the news or commercials, so back to my naked lady. *Wait a minute; this must be the hotel's closed circuit station,* I thought. I had heard of hotels having their own channel. Boy, those Japanese think of everything.

I started to munch on some almonds I had snitched from the airline and dialed my new interpreter, Fumio. "Moshi, Moshi," I could hear him say. "Hey, Fumio, old pal, this is Eddie-san. Boy, I've got to hand it to you guys for hospitality. There's a lady

176

dancing on my T.V. with the most beautiful boobs I've ever seen!"

I had probably awakened Fumio or he completely missed what I was saying. "Oh, White-san, *gomen nasai*, I'm so sorry. I apologize for my country. The dirty show you are watching is called Pink Mood, and we Japanese people are all writing letters to the newspapers to have this program canceled."

Now Fumio Suzuki had annoyed me a few times before this, like when he tried to imitate Americans or to tell a joke, and especially when he misquoted me or misinterpreted what was being said by others, which happened too often. I choked up with frustration, and all I could say was "Fumio, go back to sleep."

"Pink Mood" came on television every Sunday night, and during my first trip to Japan, I was its most ardent viewer. It wasn't just the beautiful naked dancing ladies; I honestly loved the commercials. The commercials would show a boy and girl in the front seat of a car from the waist down. I didn't understand the Japanese language then, but what I imagined the boy and girl were whispering used to make me passionately crazy. Then, too, the boy would get fresh, with his hands roaming all over the girl's legs and garter belt. You never saw their faces, only the boy and girl from the waist down and a part of the car's dashboard. What they were selling? Oh, they were selling car radios. I used to love those commercials.

Fumio Suzuki showed up the next morning at our prearranged time. I noticed he looked very solemn and waited for him to open up. He started by saying that we were on the threshhold of making history in the business world, that destiny had introduced us and it was our fate to become blood brothers. Fumio used a Japanese word that was to eventually get me into trouble in the future. The word was *giri*.

Giri, Fumio explained, is similar to the American Indian custom of becoming "blood brothers." *Giri*, Fumio further explained, goes deeper and is more binding than family, country, society, and the world. Fumio asked that before we become involved with each other, I take the vow of *giri*.

I asked him if he was nuts, saying no one came before my country and family. Here we hadn't concluded our first business deal and I was asked to swear allegiance to some strange concept. I was becoming suspicious of my newfound Japanese partner.

With all his oratory, Fumio at times would take little pot shots at America, its customs, how we humiliated Japan before, during, and after the war, and the "good time Charleys" who were the Japanese we must beware of, and many times I had the uncomfortable feeling Fumio wasn't always telling the truth. One thing I respected about Fumio Suzuki, though, was his fierce pride in being Japanese, but he was becoming an Oriental Sammy Glick of *What Makes Sammy Run* fame, right before my eyes.

Fumio laughed, which he didn't do too often, and said *giri* was mostly a feeling, that I didn't have to sell out my country or family, but most of what he said was a figure of speech. I told him that if *giri* was good, I was all for it. It sounded like something I felt for my partner Mack Wolfson or my buddy during the war, Art Stringari, or my longtime friend Stanley Adams. It must be a deep emotional feeling more than friendship but less then blood. Fumio liked that explanation, and we said *kumpai* with hot green tea and shook hands on it. I was then sworn to the utmost secrecy on this *giri* between us, which I remember made me feel slightly uncomfortable. The United States government once checked me out on the highly secretive Norden bombsight with far less histrionics.

Giri mission accomplished, Fumio then took out a bunch of papers and said that I had appointments every morning with Japanese music publishers, record companies, electronic manufacturers, and noodle companies—you name it. They all wanted to meet Shiro-san, Mr. Eddie White from America. And meet them I did. For days on end I listened to Fumio interrogate Japanese businessmen who wished to be represented in the United States. How I wished I could understand the Japanese language. Fumio's interpreting always made me feel a little uncomfortable and uneasy, *giri* or not. My suspicions were eventually proven correct, that although Fumio was representing me as an interpreter, he was mostly representing himself. I learned this in a letter I received one morning, written in Pig Latin, from one of the businessmen who had paid me an early-morning visit and who had been insulted and fared badly at the hands and mouth of Fumio-san. This man, who was a music publisher wishing to secure a foothold in the United States, said that Fumio Suzuki had a bad reputation in Japanese business circles, that he was misinterpreting me and only out to promote himself. This gentleman suggested I check Fumio Suzuki's credentials out thoroughly before I proceeded further.

Check Fumio's credentials out? I wondered. Where? With whom? What the hell, Fumio got me to Japan! I doubt if I could have done it without him. I'm a grown man, as sharp as any Japanese "Good Time Charley" like Fumio. I can take care of myself. . . . Wanna bet?

Each day, after our business meetings, Fumio and I would have lunch and then tour Tokyo, with Fumio constantly lecturing me on how to act and how to lord it over the businessmen wishing to hook up with us. He informed me that Japanese men feel and act inferior to anything or anyone American. He told me to be aware of and to be sure to take advantage of this sensitive trait in the majority of Japanese men. I began to think that Fumio was a student of many facets of Japanese and American life, most of them negative.

Something was troubling Fumio about most of the businessmen who came to meet with us. They were too cautious, too conservative, too frightened. They were an inferior lot. Fumio had a great idea, maybe a surprise for me, but it would take time. While he worked on his idea, I started to venture out to see Tokyo on my own.

The elevators in the Tokyo Ginza Hotel were run by young girls. One pretty nineteen-year-old girl would giggle each time I stepped into her elevator. I took this as a sign that she liked me, and I was right. The first two times I asked for a date, she put her free hand over her face and giggled. I soon found out that most young Japanese girls were shy with foreigners and went through the hand-on-the-face giggling routine.

On the third shot, Tomoko painfully managed to squeeze out that I should meet her in front of the theater marquee, across the street, at six that evening. I was ecstatic. When Fumio called me, I diplomatically suggested he get lost for another couple of days, because I was busy doing some research on Japanese history. Fumio gave me another of his "Good Time Charley" lines about too much study making me a dull boy.

Tomoko took me to authentic family-type restaurants, the

kabuki theater, and little places where elderly men sat on cushions, and so did the audience, and the men told funny stories. I seemed to anticipate the punch lines and laughed in all the right places. Tomoko wanted to know if I really didn't understand Japanese. I told her I was beginning to sense the rhythm of her beautiful country.

Tomoko's English was fairly good, and my Japanese was nil. A girl from Tokyo and a boy from the Bronx—movies have been made from less of a setup. Each time I became amorous, Tomoko, Japanese girl that she was, submitted ever so tearfully. Each time, American bastard that I was, I backed off at the last moment. It was too easy. Tomoko was too nice, too fine, too good. I don't know if it was my conscience, religion, fear of my karma, or what. Tomoko looked at me with such respect, dignity and belief. How could I destroy this highly aesthetic relationship of a type I'd never known before?

There were massage parlors almost on every city block and at every hotel at that time. Fumio and I would go to one of the better ones on occasion, and I would give vent to my pent-up emotion. It wasn't easy. As soon as I removed my clothes, a scream of laughter would emanate from the massage girls. The first time it happened, I thought it was a police raid. Soon I learned that they had never seen anyone as hairy as yours truly. First my name was Gorilla to the Japanese massage girls; then they called me Kashiwado, after the current champion Sumo wrestler. Whenever I entered our favorite massage parlor, the girls would get hysterical and the place buzzed with excitement. I thought of charging them just to see my body.

Before I left the States, I had corresponded with the Toho Motion Picture Company, the producers of that first Japanese film that captivated my heart and soul, *Ikiru*. I suggested that possibly Mack Wolfson and I could write a song inspired by this awe-inspiring film. They agreed, we did, and now it was time for me to let the Toho people know I was in Tokyo, if they would care to see me. They sent a limousine for me and rolled out the red carpet. First we enjoyed a magnificent lunch; then I met Peggy Hayama, the girl who had recorded our song, "Ikiru," on the Nippon King Label. Miss Hayama sang the song in English and Japanese, and then she finished in English again. King Records didn't spare any expense; it was gung ho, with a big orchestra full of strings and French horns. I asked Miss Hayama, who was a big recording and T.V. star, how she learned the American contemporary singing style. She replied, "By listening to your Patti Page albums over and over again."

Then the Toho company gave me a rare treat. They allowed me to see the film *Ikiru* in Japanese, the original full-length print. Although I didn't understand Japanese, I knew the story line and I cried even more. I asked if I could see the film again and again, and the Toho company always complied. I kept coming back afternoon after afternoon, and I would see my wonderful *Ikiru* and possibly another Toho feature. None of the other films was in the same ball park with director Akira Kurosawa's masterpiece.

Through the Toho officials, I sent my regards, best wishes, and respects to Emperor Kurosawa, as he is fondly called by those who know him in and out of the theatrical community, and also to the star of the film, Mr. Takashi Shimura. I received. warm notes of recognition from Mr. Kurosawa and Mr. Shimura, and my intense love affair with all things Japanese took root. I stood a little taller after each meeting with the Toho company, I really felt secure with myself and began to negotiate with a more affirmative attitude.

I picked up a few words of Japanese, learned at least a word a day, with Tomoko-san and a few of my newfound friends assisting me, and took on many of the inherent traits of the Japanese. I moved into a Japanese furnished room at the hotel, invariably frequented Japanese restaurants, wore the *yucata* robe (the male kimono), mastered chopsticks and bowing properly, refrained from telling jokes, slept on tatami on the floor, and generally did my utmost to understand and become as Japanese as I possibly could. I even contemplated entering a religious retreat in Kyoto to live sparingly as a monk, possibly for thirty, sixty, or ninety days. Fumio thought I was nuts and put my feelings down to another one of my Yankee weaknesses or failings.

My speaking Japanese at that time was still in the stop-and-go period, but I felt I was beginning to understand a little of this wonderful country's culture and its people. Later on, I realized that the more I knew about Japan and the rest of the Orient, the less I knew. Just when I thought I had something down pat,

With Japanese film superstar Toshiro Mifune for screening of *Yojimbo*.

On Japanese film set in Tokyo. Notice—no shoes.

something would come along to contradict everything I had learned. Then I found a book written by Quentin Crewe, titled *Japan—Portrait of a Paradox*. The book explained most of my feelings and frustrations, and I gave up trying to analyze anything Oriental. I made up my mind I would never be able to unravel the secrets of the Orient so I might as well just take things as they came and enjoy them.

I don't know if anyone ever enjoyed Japan as much as I did. Just going out for lunch or dinner was an exciting event; everything was so new and different to me. Being an adventurer, I wanted to see and try everything. The Japanese people, with their custom of practically always greeting you for the first time with gifts, the tiny cabs with tiny television sets, the old Japanese wearing kimono and *yucata* and the new Japanese wearing miniskirts and doing the twist. To me, it was a scene out of a Walt Disney movie, and I often wondered when they were going to "strike the set."

I also felt a serenity; you might say I experienced some sort of religious feeling. Whatever, I felt ecstatically happy most of the time. The only time I felt unhappy was when I came crashing down to earth now and again when the world of business or finance intruded on my fantasy, usually in the person of Fumio Suzuki. But that all came later.

To say I was falling in love with Japan is an understatement. I was completely smitten and still am, even though I was eventually defeated and broken by their business war lords, lied to and tranquilized by their industrial samurai, and savagely cut to pieces, emotionally chewed up, and spat out by their cunning kamikaze engaged in trade and finance—all this in the land of chrysanthemums, lotus, and cherry blossoms.

It all started one morning when Fumio called and told me to stop the presses, cancel all negotiations past, present, and future, and stand by for the moment of truth. Fumio-san had shown some officials from the Yamaha Company my credentials, and they had shown interest in finally meeting me.

The first meeting was in a local coffee shop, and through Fumio I related my years as a songwriter, record producer, and personal manager in the music-entertainment business. I just happened to have some photographs showing me with a few Amer-

183

ican film and sports stars who were very popular in Japan, such as Richard Chamberlain, Frank Sinatra, Mickey Mantle, Yogi Berra, and a few others. The meeting broke up with a lot of bowing and smiling and some more bowing. Fumio was ecstatically happy. He said I had made just the right impression by being conservative and laying back. Then he took a verbal swipe at John Wayne and loud, violent Americans in general. Fumio-san more and more took on the appearance of an oriental Sammy Glick.

The next morning, Fumio called and said that the wheels were turning, that some chief of music up at Yamaha wanted to meet me. In Japan, almost everyone in Japan who works for a living has a title—chief, chief of staff, manager, head clerk, chief of this, head of that, and on and on. This time we were taken to a fine Continental restaurant and made some small talk, or so it seemed to me. Again Fumio said that I had done fine and we would eventually meet another chief of another department. And so it went, from one chief to another. I asked Fumio, "When do I get to meet Cochise or Sitting Bull?" but he failed to see the humor.

Fumio showed up one early morning, without the usual preliminary phone call, and said I was to be taken to a town outside of Tokyo to meet the president of Yamaha Nippon Gakki, Mr. Genichi Kawakami, the chief of chiefs. The town was Hamamatsu and we soon were on our way. Fumio was overjoyed and so was I, but mostly because I could now see part of the Japanese countryside by train. Fumio and I had our usual argument on the train. He felt I was always being too nice to people he felt were inferior and/or I wasn't listening to him enough. Ours was a strange business association, with Fumio trying to insert the word *obey* into our marriage contract.

When we arrived in Hamamatsu, we were met by the usual group of titled Yamaha officials, all smiling and bowing. Fumio was to stay in the main building, and I was shown to a small Japanese-style house that was to be my home while I was in Hamamatsu. I had an elderly maid who appeared and disappeared as if by magic, and she was assisted by her young daughter. The daughter was pretty, and although I had ideas of an uncertain nature, the possibilities never presented themselves. The house was decorated in a warm old-world Japanese fashion with tatami floors and shogi screens throughout. I wore *yucata* while I was in my house, slept on the floor on tatami mats, and was constantly being served green tea by my two disappearing friends. I told them to call me Samurai Eddie, and I think they are still giggling somewhere.

Coach Fumio would visit to give me pep talks and last-minute instructions on how to play my role. One morning, he showed up and said we were to meet Mr. Kawakami, the president of Yamaha. I changed into my conservative Western clothes and followed Fumio to the main building. We were ushered into a room that was obviously used for meetings. There was a long table with about eight very glum, apprehensive Japanese men already seated there. I was introduced to each man, his title was given, we both snapped to a bow, and I took my seat next to the head of the table. Fumio was to act as my interpreter, and he sat directly to my right.

After about eight minutes of silence, the door opened and everyone, myself included, automatically jumped to attention. President Genichi Kawakami was ushered into the room by two aides, took his seat at the head of the table, and said some sort of a Japanese greeting, and we all sat down. Then Fumio said something and kicked my leg. I jumped up again, as did Fumio and Mr. Kawakami, and we bowed, as I was introduced. Mr. Kawakami pointed to my chair, and again I sat down.

Tea and cookies were served while each Yamaha official made a short speech, as interpreted by Fumio, welcoming me to Japan, Hamamatsu, Yamaha, and the Land of the Rising Sun. Each time Fumio thought I didn't react fast enough to any comment or toast, he kicked me under the table. Mr. Kawakami, through Fumio, interrogated me thoroughly. I answered politely and just hoped that my trusty interpreter wasn't injecting any of his own thoughts into my replies. That night Fumio told me I had again passed with flying colors. I told him to go easy on the kicking under the table.

I was treated royally during my stay in Hamamatsu. The food was mostly Japanese, and it was the finest. They even served me bacon and eggs for breakfast one day, although I would much rather have had the Japanese rice, tea, and tsukudani. Tsukudani

185

is a sweet mixture of smoked baby shrimp, clams, and eel, and it was my favorite for breakfast. Fruit, hot green tea, and seaweed cookies were always available to me, as was anything else I desired. The Japanese are fabulous hosts, especially if they want something.

The second day, negotiations really began. Yamaha Nippon Gakki was represented by President Kawakami, but there were different faces around the table, all asking different questions. This time it was firmly established that Yamaha Nippon Gakki, one of the largest manufacturers of pianos and other musical instruments in the world, which also produced motorcycles, sporting equipment, boats, and electronic equipment, now wanted to obtain a foothold in the extremely lucrative business of music publishing. Yamaha now wanted to control musical copyrights, and where best to start but in the United States, heart of the contemporary music world?

If I could pass all the questions being thrown at me, not mind my past being microscopically examined, and not mind a slight insult here and there, both to myself and my country, then maybe I was their man. I think I passed everything with flying colors except for the latter category. I snapped back at every little innuendo, but I got the weird feeling that Fumio-san was watering down my answers, that he was interpreting with answers he thought I should say instead of what I actually said. When I questioned him on this, on occasion, he looked hurt and said I was wrong. But something in the eyes of my adversaries told me I was right.

The third day, some new faces appeared, and they too examined this *gaijin*, this foreigner—again with the same questions, the same digging and tiny bit of needling. I began to think of something I read or heard somewhere: "Just because you're paranoid doesn't mean they're not out to get you!" Or was it Fumio's interpreting again?

The fourth day, there were some new questions, but it was back to square root one, the same old picking at me, the same old questions. That night I told Fumio, "I think I've had it. If they don't put this show on the road, they can shove it!" Fumio told me that I was doing well and that their decision was forthcoming momentarily.

186

The eighth day was sheer torture, and twice I stood up and told Fumio I wouldn't take this bullshit any longer. Once I stormed out of the room. That night at dinner I was purposely noncommunicative, nodding and smiling like a robot but not saying anything. Then something Fumio interpreted for Mr. Kawakami stuck in my throat. I asked Fumio to repeat what he had just said, and he changed the entire meaning. I was beginning to catch on to this entire shell game and especially to Fumio.

What Mr. Kawakami said, as interpreted through Fumio, was "If Americans are such great humanitarians, as they always maintain, how come a U.S. destroyer had to bomb a small town like Hamamatsu during the war?" Innocent enough. Like hell!

Fumio had warned me never to raise my voice or show anger, "like a typical American gangster." Well, I guess I'm my father's son, and I reverted to character. I showed anger and I raised my voice. "Fumio, you tell these guys that we didn't bomb Pearl Harbor, you did. And if we bombed Hamamatsu, there must have been a reason. What were you manufacturing here? You want me to sell out my country for a fucking job? And Fumio, you'd better quote me word for word. They know I'm mad, so get it right, and stop stepping on my foot!"

Before Fumio could utter a word, Mr. Kawakami had slapped the table and was talking and gesticulating wildly. I noticed all the other officials had their heads bowed, almost as if in prayer.

Fumio turned to me and said, "Well, you did it. Mr. Kawakami says you're his man; he likes you. Tomorrow we will work on your contract. Congratulations." Hot sake was brought out, and we *kumpied* the night away. It was the first time I had seen President Ginichi Kawakami smile. I was a little groggy, bewildered but happy. Rocky Graziano once told me how he was lost and almost defeated, bleeding, and how he had swung wildly at Tony Zale and connected, thus winning the middleweight championship of the world. I now knew how he must have felt.

From that evening on, everyone in the Kawakami compound continually smiled at me. If I thought I was being romanced before, now began a honeymoon I shall never forget. My slightest whim was like a command. I was constantly asked if I needed anything. What I wanted was a contract and getting back to some degree of normalcy. The rich food and sake were killing me.

Finally the contract negotiations were completed. I was to be a vice-president of the new Yamaha Music Corporation, to be located in New York City, offices to be selected and decorated by me. I would own 50 percent of said new corporation stock and control three out of a total of six votes on the Yamaha Music Corporation board of directors. My starting salary and expenses were to be minimal, but they would improve as the firm progressed. Decisions would be made mutually, but the final decisions would actually come from Japan. Yamaha Music Corporation was to be a separate entity but associated and controlled by Yamaha Nippon Gakki.

My stock was to be issued upon my return to Tokyo, at another series of meetings, whereupon I would be issued a *hanko*, which is a stamp or seal that all important Japanese businessmen use instead of their actual signature. Fumio told me only "big shots" get a *hanko*.

Then I was driven to the train station by Mr. Kawakami, and just before Fumio and I boarded the train, the president of Yamaha Nippon Gakki said, in perfect English, "It was indeed a pleasure meeting you, Mr. White. I hope you enjoyed yourself in Hamamatsu. Have a nice trip back to Tokyo." I was stunned and at a loss for words. All I could say was "You speak English!"

It was too late for a lengthy conversation. On the train, Fumio too said he was surprised by this turn of events, but I was recapitulating a few things in my mind. *No wonder Mr. Kawakami didn't wait for Fumio to interpret my blast at the Japanese bombing of Pearl Harbor; he had already known what I had said. Why didn't he speak to me in English? What was this all about? Why?* I didn't accept any of Fumio's feeble answers to my questions, and I swore to observe him more closely in any future negotiations. I had mixed emotions. I couldn't have accomplished any of this without Fumio, but neither could he improve his lot in life without me. I felt uneasy when I thought about all this. If Fumio doesn't interpret properly for me, somewhere I was going to get screwed up. Was Fumio trying to control me completely, as his dupe? *I'll be sure to change all that,* I thought.

Prior to going to Japan, I had called my old friend Mr. Murray "Pop" Sprung, who was an attorney with offices in New York and Tokyo. Mr. Sprung, you remember, was my counselor in the orphan asylum and my father image all during my childhood. Pop had explained to me that there were less than forty practicing American or European attorneys in Japan, granted by special decree by the Japanese National Diet. When the Japanese *bengoshi,* or attorneys, demanded equal representation in the United States and/or Europe and were denied, no more foreigners were allowed to practice in Japan. Those who were already *bengoshi,* though, were allowed to continue the practice of law.

Pop explained that he was one of those *bengoshi,* that he shared an office with two other American *bengoshi* and one native Japanese. Pop Sprung advised me to contact his office in Tokyo if the time came when I would need legal representation. Pop lived in the United States and visited Japan about twice a year, whereas the other two American *bengoshi,* Raymond Bushell and Warren Shimeall, lived in Tokyo permanently.

Mr. Raymond Bushell was a most interesting, highly educated personality. He and his wife, Frances, a Japanese lady, were very involved in the art world in Tokyo. Mr. Bushell also is the world's foremost authority on *netsuki,* the tiny hand carvings Oriental women wear on their sashes. He has written many books on the subject and is the head of The Netsuki Society and their foremost spokeman. Recently one *netsuki* sold for a quarter of a million dollars.

Mr. Warren Shimeall, at first meeting, struck me as the opposite of Mr. Bushell. Whereas Mr. Bushell was conservative and dignified, Mr. Shimeall, although knowledgeable, was more interested in a good time, women, having laughs. He too was married to a Japanese lady, but he often spoke about his ex-wife and Oklahoma, where he used to live, with bitterness and sadness.

Mr. Bushell was very involved when I called upon Pop Sprung's Tokyo legal office, and although he was courteous and nice to me, I was assigned to Mr. Warren Shimeall as a client. Warren Shimeall was overjoyed at meeting me, a bachelor; he could show me his favorite bars and coffee shops and introduce me to all the hostesses he knew. Warren loved my jokes, songs, and outlook on life, and he said I was more than a client, I was his pal.

Whenever I tried to get serious and talk business, Warren would say, "Come on, where's the Eddie I know? This is Tokyo, where the lights on the Ginza never go out. Let's have a good time." And we'd start another whirlwind tour of nightclubs and geisha restaurants. Harmless enough.

What I wasn't informed by the law firm of Bushell, Shimeall, and Sprung, until it was too late, was that Counselor Warren Shimeall could have been the inspiration for the book and film titled *The Lost Weekend*. I learned, much too late and to my sorrow, that my newfound pal, Warren-san, would disappear every so often for six or seven days. He would eventually be found, God knows where, dead drunk, dishevelled, and incoherent. His poor wife would clean him up, dry him out, and send him back to his law office.

Once again, final negotiations began in Tokyo with Yamaha, Fumio on one side of me as my interpreter and Warren Shimeall on the other, as my attorney. The unholy three. By now I was a little more forceful and insisted on certain clauses, which were agreed upon and noted. I was to share in 50 percent of the new Yamaha Music Corporation stock, and I would control three of the six votes on the board of directors. I would leave for the United States immediately, to open offices in New York City. My stock certificates would, as soon as issued, be delivered to my *bengoshi*, Mr. Warren Shimeall. Yamaha insisted that my *hanko*, my signature or seal, should remain with them for safekeeping. Harmless enough, right? Wrong!

After that meeting, there were a few others, to tie some loose ends together, lunches, dinners, and a "sayonara" party given for me. Suddenly Warren Shimeall wasn't to be found anywhere. He had disappeared. I called his wife and she was frantic. The Ginza had swallowed him up. I was upset but had to, according to Fumio, show Yamaha my best face.

I left Japan, never seeing Warren Shimeall again, until my next trip, but hoping that everything would turn out all right. *Surely Mr. Bushell or Fumio or someone will remind Warren to secure my stock certificates,* I thought. *I'll make sure to write him. Where the hell could he be?*

When I arrived back in New York, I found offices with a huge fireplace and an apartment attached. I hired a secretary, and my first letter went off to Warren, reminding him about my stock certificates. I received a letter from Warren, telling me he was

Four champs and a chump!

With songwriting partner Mack Wolfson and Eddie Fisher up at Grossinger's before Eddie and Debbie broke up.

okay now, thanking me for my concern, and saying he would have stock certificates within a day or so. He informed me not to be too concerned; issuing the stock was merely a formality. I had my contract, which assured me of my participation.

I breathed a sigh of relief. Pop Sprung told me that Warren was an alcoholic, but after one of his "Lost Weekend" jaunts he would be good for months. I set about organizing my office, retaining a music-business attorney, informing all the trade papers about the new Yamaha Music Corporation's desire to represent American music publishers and recording companies in Japan, and selling my old apartment.

That week, Paul Case, a longtime music-business publisher and friend of mine, asked me to have dinner with him at Al and Dick's Steak House. He was at a table with a serious-looking young man when I arrived. I was introduced to Phil Spector, an up-and-coming songwriter and record producer who desperately needed an apartment. Paul raved about Phil Spector's talents and said he was a musical giant. How can you say no to a giant? I told Spector the apartment was his, for next to nothing. Then Phil admired my Triangle watch, which I had purchased from Henny Youngman, the comedian. The watch was quite inexpensive, so I took it off and handed it to this musical giant. I could be quite magnanimous. After all, wasn't I now vice-president of Yamaha Music Corporation?

Some weeks later, my friend Tony Corrado brought three black girls up to my new offices. Tony knew Sue, the mother of one of the girls, who sang with her cousin and one other girl. I liked them and told the mother about this new musical giant from Philadelphia. I sent them over to see Phil Spector. Thus Ronnie and the Ronnettes was born. Phil eventually married the lead singer, Ronnie. As I recall, Phil Spector never thanked me for the apartment, the watch, or sending him Ronnie and the Ronnettes. He's divorced from Ronnie but what about thanking me for the apartment and the watch? Par for the course. So much for one of the record producers of the Beatles.

I moved into the apartment adjoining the new offices and starting acquiring musical copyrights, recordings, and publishing catalogues for the territory of Japan. If a recording hit the charts in the United States, I immediately tried to buy the record or the copyright or both for Yamaha, to be released in Japan. I took

192

another apartment, a block away, so that now I had room for any visiting Yamaha dignitaries.

Fumio had been appointed chief of Yamaha Music in Tokyo, by me and by agreement with the Pacific side; he had a stock participation with me personally, and he had one vote on the board of directors. I think I fulfilled my part of our *giri*, but I kept reminding Fumio, "play it straight; let's keep our heads, be humble, work hard, and all that sort of jazz."I said the things we had accomplished would in time be stepping-stones to bigger and better things. Fumio agreed, mostly to get me off all that Western philosophy crap. Fumio was Sammy Glick from *What Makes Sammy Run*, and no one, nothing, was going to change him. I was the dumdum, the square, the *gaijin* pollyanna. I found out, too late, that Fumio's philosophy in life was "Get it all while you can and run like hell." He was living a real corny black-and-white grade "B" movie starring nervous, apprehensive me. I always sensed that Fumio's aftershave lotion was "Larceny," but until I could definately prove it, I said and did nothing. Once in a while I tried, in subtle ways, to let Fumio know I was aware of some of his devious "shtick," but Fumio always felt like he had me in his hip pocket, that he could control me.

We were quite successful from day one. The hit songs and dance of the day were "The Twist" and "The Peppermint Twist." I contracted for those two songs and also sent diagrams of the twist dance to Mother Yamaha in Japan. Before you could say "banzai," I had all Japan twisting. "Roses Are Red," by Bobby Vinton, hit the musical charts big; off it went to Yamaha. As did the records and songs of Paul Anka, Fabian, Bobby Rydell, and so many others.

Personal manager Bob Marcucci, the inspiration for the future! motion picture *The Idol Maker*, became a friend of mine and invited me to one of his clients' wedding. Frankie Avalon and his bride were beautiful and young, and all Philadelphia drank a toast to their future happiness. My contacts were getting to be on a higher echelon, and now I was negotiating for entire catalogues of musical copyrights and recordings. Many music "mavens" came to me for advice. I was invited to benefits and parties and asked to sit on the dais. Business and life in general were all great now.

It was too smooth and beautiful to last. Word was getting

back to me that Fumio was beginning to throw his weight around in our Tokyo office. Cliques were forming, some pro Fumio but mostly anti. Then one of the clerks inferred that Fumio had propositioned her but the situation was quickly squashed. I told Fumio that, whatever problem he had, he was not to let any of these stories get back to Hamamatsu, to President Kawakami.

I returned to Tokyo to visit our new offices on the Ginza, at the Yamaha department store. This time, when my plane let down at Honeda Airport, I returned as a conquering hero. When I reached the top of the plane's steps, I saw many people and children waving little American flags. Was General MacArthur on the plane?

No, it was Lt. Eddie White of the First Sea Search Attack Squadron, Langley Field, Virginia. Fumio met me at the foot of the stairs, and I noted he was wearing an official armband. I was escorted through Customs immediately, straight to a press meeting. Fumio made a speech in Japanese, in which I heard him mention my name a few times, and then he concluded in English, such as it was; "So let's welcome Mr. Eddie White with a big crap," and everyone applauded.

That last word threw me off, and I glanced at Fumio before I spoke. Fumio was smiling as innocently as he could, so I guess it was just a harmless Japanese faux pas. I spoke mostly in English, with a basic Japanese word thrown in here and there. Then I was taken to an elegant restaurant for a party in my honor. I felt Yamaha Nippon Gakki was showing its appreciation for my good work and loyalty, and I felt warm and glad.

There was a round of more meetings with more Yamaha officials, discussing mostly the future standard operational procedures of Yamaha Music. President Kawakami wasn't in attendance, but his presence was felt. I was constantly being informed of what Mr. Kawakami expected of me. Fumio kept reminding me not to let anyone push us around, that we controlled three out of a total of six votes. I never pulled rank nor expected to. No matter what the Yamaha officials felt or said behind my back, they were overly polite to my face.

Business completed, word came down from the top that a holiday had been declared for everyone connected with Yamaha Music. We were all whisked to the seaside town of Ise for its mineral baths. For a week, I was pampered and bathed by beautiful ladies who served me hot sake and sushi. I went completely Japanese, even to wearing my *yucata* robe and wooden clapper slippers out on the street. The Japanese women stared and giggled, and I guess I must have felt like some kind of a missionary.

It was in Ise that I learned that the Japanese men cannot drink as much as the *gaijin*. I'm not a big drinker, by any means. On a scale of one to ten, I might be a two. After two sips of sake, my Pacific side comrades' faces would become flushed and they would become overly talkative. Someone explained to me, true or not, that the Japanese cannot drink as well as Americans because of a lack of fat in their system. At any rate, I feigned being tipsy and listened attentively. Fumio was disliked by practically everyone on the Yamaha Music staff—that was for sure. There had been many confrontations, but Sammy Glick, in the form of Fumio, was able to talk his way out of creating a major war. I was sure that President Kawakami knew all that I was hearing for the first time.

The third day at Ise, we were visited by President Kawakami and Fumio and I were taken by boat to Suga Island, some miles off the coast of Japan. Everyone else stayed at the small inn in Ise. Suga Island was named after Princess Suga, Emperor Hirohito's daughter, whom I was to meet and get to know some months later. The people living on Suga Island were even smaller than most Japanese, and they spoke an unusual dialect. Fumio couldn't understand a word they said.

I was escorted around and couldn't help but note that although the natives and their homes were poor, the sole income derived from fishing and pearl diving, their schoolhouse and playground were immaculate and well kept. The women on the island did practically all the work, and they were built fuller and bigger than the men. I had to laugh when I heard the men barking out orders to the women who were diving for sea urchins or pearls. All the men were sergeants, and all the women were privates.

One afternoon, after Mr. Kawakami and I had gone swimming and were sunning ourselves on a deserted beach, I saw a group of nude women coming toward us. I couldn't believe my eyes. They headed straight for me, and one of them gave me a small basket with some cooked fish and an unusual-looking fruit. Mr. Kawakami told me this was their way of saying "Welcome." I didn't know where to look first. Although the women had young bodies and full breasts, they had bad skin and hardly any teeth. These were the famous pearl divers. Mr. Kawakami told me that their life span was somewhere around forty years.

We lunched on the fish, and I feasted and fantasied on the nude bodies off in the distance. After a while, I became disinterested, which proves sex is mostly in the mind.

I bit into one of the strange-looking fruits and tasted something more heavenly than the best mango, peach, plum, apple, or pear, with a little taste of each fruit thrown in. I went into raptures. "What is this and where did it come from and how can I get more?" Mr. Kawakami laughed and said the fruit was called *nashi* in Japanese and *twentieth century* in English. Embarrassed as I was, I ate two more, skin and all.

The next day, I learned more about Suga Island and its inhabitants. The people subsisted on fish mainly and a green-brown vegetable I saw the women also beat into a powder. Meat was unseen and unheard of, as were candy and some of the other goodies of this world.

The children were curious about me but wouldn't come close. I tried to grab a couple of them, but they teasingly ran off. I missed my son, Peter, and just wanted to hold a child. Finally, I enticed one funny face to come close by holding out some candy Charms. I grabbed him and when he had sat on my lap for a while, all the other children piled on top of me. I gave them all the candy Charms I had and wished I had a truckful.

That night I lay on my tatami bed in the little hut assigned to me and heard a baby crying somewhere off in the distance. I listened to the waves and the wind and wondered what stroke of fate brought me to this remote dot on earth. That baby crying wasn't crying in Japanese. It sounded just like a baby crying in Harlem, U.S.A., or some town in Russia. I swore I would do something for this island, this village, these poor people, these children.

When I told Fumio about my inspiration, he threw cold water on it. He advised me not to mention my feelings to Mr. Kawakami, that everyone up at Yamaha Nippon Gakki would think I was a weakling and I would certainly lose face. How many times did he have to tell me that the Japanese leave unfortunate people alone? He taught me a new expression, "Kankay nai"—"it is there, but it is not seen."

Back in Ise, we had one more sayonara dinner, and after breakfast the next day we headed back to Tokyo. On the train, I had the opportunity to speak to Fumio at length. I didn't let on that I knew about the problems he was having with the staff of Yamaha Music. I told Fumio that I had had what I thought amounted to a religious experience on Suga Island. I told him to go easy with the clerks and office staff of Yamaha Music, because we'd need their loyalty someday. Fumio listened and then nodded off.

Murray "Pop" Sprung had given me the names of two of his friends in Tokyo, Toni and Hiroshi Matsobara. I called them, we met, and we hit it off from the first second. Two more charming, intelligent, cultured people I had never met. We made the rounds of the usual Japanese Continental restaurants, and then they introduced me to a culinary delight called "okari-bayaki," the food of the samurai. The staircase to this tiny restaurant, in the Shimbashi area of Tokyo, went almost straight up. Meat was cooked or seared on a samurai helmet, and they could only serve four people in each of two rooms. After my friends Toni and Hiroshi introduced me to this restaurant, I went back there, with Tomoko, six nights in a row. Just like in the massage parlors, all the girls would giggle as soon as they saw me ascending those dangerous stairs.

Another restaurant I particularly liked was in the Sanno Hotel, which was run by the U.S. Army. Here for two and a half dollars a person you could eat the food of Genghis Kan, a barbequed dish similar to "okari-bayaki." You needed connections to be served in the Sanno Hotel, but I had plenty of those and my adjutant general's card from my air-force days helped.

To be truthful, I never had a bad meal in Japan. The noodle shops, the sushi bars, the kobe steak houses, and the tempura restaurants were delightful, not to mention the "shabu-shabu" places. A diner cooks "shabu-shabu" himself; it is not unlike fondue. You are served platters of meat, fish, and vegetables, and you dip them, piece by piece, into a pot of water boiling at your table. Each morsel of food is then dipped into various sauces and eaten, and when the food is all gone, *"banzai,"* you have a delectable soup to enjoy.

I always found going out to lunch or dinner in Japan an exciting event—the smells, the sights, the anticipation. The Japanese motto is "Feed the eyes before you feed the stomach." That is why so many Japanese restaurants show the actual cooked dishes in their front windows on the street.

The ultimate food of Japan has to be Kobe beef. The way cattle are raised is a cruel one, but I was a hypocrite and partook of the food whenever I could. It seems that Kobe cattle never set foot outside of a cratelike shelter and they are massaged daily and fed large bottles of beer each evening. When they are slaughtered, the meat is so soft that it can be cut with a spoon. The first time I ate Kobe beef was in an elegant restaurant in Kyoto. I was served Kobe roast beef with a dish of white horseradish and a few slices of brown raisin bread. Innocent enough. I personally ate the entire roast beef, about five pounds, not caring what my hosts thought about me or if I died. Now I knew how a junkie must feel.

In time I became friendly with a few members of the National Diet, the Japanese Parliament, and they entertained me royally, mostly at geisha houses. A geisha house is a very costly proposition. A patron usually buys or takes over an entire establishment for one evening's drinking, dining, and divertisement. The latter part consists of the geisha or "maiko-san" girls singing, dancing, and engaging in teasing small talk. The woman in charge, the boss lady, is called Mama-san, the geisha usually use theatrical pseudonyms like Yumi-san or some such name, and the maiko-san, who is a geisha in training, hardly ever talks, raises her eyes, or gives her name. Hanky panky is on the menu if the patron is wealthy or important enough. I was introduced to the geisha house by some wealthy and important businessmen.

At one sayonara geisha-house party, I was being served hot sake by an adorable seventeen-year-old maiko-san. Sayonara or "good-bye" parties are given almost the instant one arrives in Japan. This way all your friends and business contacts get their chance to say good-bye properly, even if you've just arrived for an extended trip. This beautiful "maiko-san" child, kneeling at

198

my side, kept filling my sake glass the instant it was empty. I drank more than I usually did, as I enjoyed her attentiveness, while I teased her to try to make her speak. Much later in the evening, feeling grateful, relaxed, and in my cups, I said to her, "Ako-chan," which means Ako-baby, "what would please you the most?" I felt like I wanted to buy this Oriental Dresden princess, who made me feel like a king, the moon, the stars, or at least a new kimono. Her eyes dropped and she hid her face with her hands. Everyone became silent. "Ako-chan," I repeated, "what one thing in this world would please you most?" When she spoke, either Tokyo had another slight tremor or else it was my imagination—she said, "To please you!"

When my host suggested I go upstairs "to rest," I had to be assisted by my tiny butterfly. Once in the room, she helped me undress and unashamedly placed a *yucata* over my nude body. She eased me down to the tatami bed and, kneeling, kissed my forehead and the corner of my mouth. She asked me if I was happy, and ecstatically I said, "*Hai, hai, hai*," which means "yes." She kissed me again, this time on the lips, and asked me if I liked the Mama-san because she had sold Ako's virginity twice. It seems that wealthy businessmen bid for virginal maiko-sans and our cunning Mama-san knew how to turn a fair deal.

Again Ako-chan kissed my lips, and either the hot sake or the kisses made me slightly dizzy. Ako started to untie the sash on her robe, and I almost passed out with anticipation. Another kiss and she excused herself and went to hang her robe on a screen. I watched her undo her long hair and blew kisses to her. Oh happy day, the bluebird of happiness was surely smiling at me and my cup had runneth over. I could hear the sound of Tokyo at night, the cars, the "charamella" vendor playing his noodle theme song, the mixed voices somewhere in the distance. *What's keeping my beautiful princess so long?* I wondered. I looked her over and Ako was undoing another robe and then another garment. *Soon. Calm down, Samurai Eddie. You'll want to savor this moment for all time. This is a night to remember.*

In the morning, I awoke to the smell of hot green tea and Ako kneeling alongside me. I looked sheepishly at her. What had happened? Could this child-woman have tricked me? She bathed me, helped me dress, and assisted me down the stairs, as I was still a little woozy. My friends were all having their breakfast tea, and they all looked up at me with admiration. We said our good-byes at the geisha-house gate, and as everyone started to leave I grabbed Ako's hand and whispered, "What happened last night?" She lowered her eyes and squeezed my hand. "Eddie-san, you pleased me very much." It's been over twenty years, and I'm still trying to figure this scene out. The mysteries of the Orient.

Pacific business concluded, it was back to the Hawaiian Village in Honolulu for three days, then to Los Angeles and three days with Stanley and Harriet Adams for laughs. Stanley was always a tonic for my heart, soul, and funnybone. We visited the sets of the television programs and movies then being filmed in Hollywood. It did my heart good to see so many movie stars making a big fuss over Uncle Stanley, as they all called him. Each morning for breakfast we ate "pechah," a Russian-Rumanian heavily garlicked gelatin meat dish at the Bagel Deli on Fairfax Avenue. My ascetic soul and stomach fortified, I caught the red-eye express, the midnight plane, back to New York. There were memories to keep me warm in my twilight years.

Back to a normal, sane routine. I had time to meditate on the plane. Two things disturbed me, even though I tried not to admit it. Fumio Suzuki, giri or not, was creating an undercurrent of dissension that someday might devour us both. And the young attorney representing Yamaha Music in New York, who was being paid a monthly retainer, had more on his mind than copyrights and catalogues. He kept telling me how he was going to take over the music business with computers. That was none of my business, but each time I introduced this overly ambitious legal beagle to a potential client for Yamaha Music, he would spend the first half-hour selling himself, his ideas, his office, his attractive equally ambitious wife's ideas for the music industry, and his computers. I vowed to even the score one fine day.

I didn't have to lift an eyebrow. My fine, feathered counselor at law, with the ethics of a Nazi warden, quickly got it in the neck, the pocketbook, and his ass. I had heard, from one of his secretaries, that his wife was playing footsie with one of the other attorneys in the office. It seems that the entire office knew the story but you know who. It was all so hard for me to believe until, oops, she ups and disappears to California with this other

200

lawyer. "Hey, buddy, don't mess with me or you'll get shafted" was the only message she left. I was happy, then sad, when I learned that she took his kid, too. I had wanted to wing the guy, not destroy him.

The songs and records kept flowing from the Western world to the Pacific side. I made the music trade papers almost every week, my stature kept growing, and I felt secure I would spend the rest of my business life with Yamaha Music. The position I occupied fit me like a glove. I was good at it, and I was getting better. I knew practically everyone worth knowing in the music business, and I knew where most of the bodies were buried. I could reach anyone or secure anything musically; everything was just a phone call away.

I remembered my vow or pledge to those children on Suga Island and got busy. At least five letters went out every day to people in the music and other businesses. My request was for a small amount of money, say five or ten dollars. My pal Rocky Graziano pitched in and helped. He invited me to the Sherry Netherlands Hotel for a party given for a bunch of ball players and celebrities. We got Mickey Mantle, Yogi Berra, Milton Berle, Phil Silvers, Rocky Marciano, and a host of others to throw money into a hat.

Each day my office received a few checks, from Andy Anka, Paul Anka's father; Marvin Cane, the music publisher; Art Stringari, my old army buddy who was now a labor-relations attorney in Detroit; Ed Wachtel and Herb Goldsmith, from Europecraft, the Members Only Company; Charley Lester, the Pittsburgh builder; Phil Wanger from Union Underwear; my sister, Ruth, and brother-in-law, Leon; Eddy Manson, the Hollywood Academy Award composer; Dave Dreyer, the music publisher; pal Stanley Adams, the actor and my former partner in comedy writing; and my son, Peter White, who put in two dollars.

We called it The Children of Suga Island Fund. It was now October 1961 and time to decide what to buy for the children. I wanted everything to arrive before Christmas.

Peter White suggested fishing kits and sailboats, inasmuch as the children lived on an island. My heir apparent also suggested candy and pen-and-pencil sets for school. I remembered someone on Suga Island mentioning that the school could use an organ.

201

So be it! I wrote to Mr. Kawakami and suggested all of the above be sent to "The Children of Suga Island" in time for the holidays. Mission accomplished. The Japanese papers got a hold of the story, and it was front-page news for a while. I was called the American Santa Claus. It's a good feeling, being able to help kids. The papers showed a picture of me with my hair slicked back and wearing a bow tie. I don't remember ever having a bow tie, but it was my kisser. Leave it to the Japanese.

Just when I felt the most secure and relaxed, it happened. It started with a phone call from Fumio telling me he was suspended from Yamaha Music, that they can't do this, as I was the boss and, besides, he wasn't guilty of anything. He mentioned *giri* to me and reminded me that most Japanese think of suicide at a time like this. The world spun and so did my brain. What the hell. It had all been too good to be true, too good to last. *"Fumio, you asshole, I told you"* was what I thought I should tell him.

For weeks and weeks, the officials of Yamaha would tell me nothing. My expense money was held up, and I had to negotiate with music publishers and record companies while I was in a state of limbo. I had learned from my Japanese brothers not to lose face. Lose face? Hell, I was about to lose my ass if Yamaha Nippon Gakki pulled the rug out from under me. I sent cablegrams to Tokyo, to Mr. Kawakami in Hamamatsu. "Please, tell me something," I pleaded. Nothing! *This must be some sort of Oriental torture*, I thought.

Finally Fumio called and said I had best come to Tokyo. Yamaha wanted to fire him; they had accused him of accepting a kickback or bribe from one of the radio stations, and he swore he wasn't guilty. He felt he was being framed. There were other charges, but with my presence in Tokyo, Fumio felt he could overcome all of the allegations. He reminded me once again about our *giri*, and he sneaked the word *suicide* into the conversation.

Passport in hand, I flew to Tokyo, with only a momentary pause between planes in Los Angeles and Hawaii. Fumio met me at Honeda Airport, took me to my hotel, pulled the drapes, and told me to be on guard. "Yamaha Nippon Gakki has spies everywhere. Your room could be bugged right now; they might even try to hurt you," he said.

Breathlessly he showed me a few of those gossip or scandal magazines in which Yamaha Nippon Gakki was accused of placing spies with opposition companies, to break down their workers' morale, to steal ideas or patents, and to disrupt them completely and send them into bankruptcy. There was one story of how another Japanese manufacturer, the Kawaii Piano Company, complained bitterly about Yamaha's business tactics and lack of ethics.

Fumio told me he still had the keys to the offices and that he could assemble some real rough guys and we could remove all the files from Yamaha Music Company. After all, it wasn't stealing. "Eddie, you're the boss. They're not playing straight with you. Let's hit them fast and first!"

Sammy Glick Suzuki, my interpreter, my partner in *giri*, my representative on the Yamaha board of directors, Fumio, had seen too many Jack La Rue movies. I told him that I had done nothing wrong. If my room was bugged, "so what? I have nothing to hide." If he was in trouble, I'd use whatever power I possessed to help him, but it wasn't in my nature to grab the files and to antagonize the real powers that be until we found out what this was all about.

I reminded Fumio of how we met, neither of us hungry but both of us looking for direction in our chosen fields, how tough it was to negotiate this affiliation with Yamaha, and now that we had momentum we were about to blow it. I for one valued and enjoyed my association with Yamaha. I mentioned that we should do our utmost to heal this breach and win Yamaha Nippon Gakki's confidence once again.

Fumio ignored my thoughts completely and talked more about Yamaha being a corrupt organization, something the Japanese mass media had known about and written about for years, that we should go into our next meeting with a show of strength, throw our weight around, show them who is boss, and shake them up and that we had as many votes on the board of directors as they had and this was war! Fumio was visibly shaken, frightened, and out for revenge.

It was no use arguing with Fumio. I told him I would know what to do and say once I knew the charges against him. By the way, I said, "What are the exact charges?" Fumio again gave me his double-double talk, and I went to bed knowing as much as I did the day before. *Well, I'll get straight answers at the board-of-directors meeting*, I thought.

The meeting was held at the Yamaha Nippon Gakki's music

department store, in one of their special large offices. Everyone was there, including Mr. Kawakami, the president, the chairman of the board of directors of Yamaha, and every chief of every music department. I tried to smile, but no one else returned the feeling. There was a funereal feeling predominant, and I felt it best to wait and see which way the cookie crumbled. Every Yamaha official had on his samurai "Kankay-nai" face; "you are there, but we don't see you."

We were greeted by the chairman of the board of all Yamaha, whose name I failed to get and whose message I failed to understand. I was seated to the right of Mr. Kawakami and the chairman of the board of directors, with a new Yamaha interpreter on my right and Fumio to his right. The chairman said something about the seriousness of the meeting, and then he passed the buck to Mr. Kawakami, who acquiesced and segued to me.

I looked around at all the glum, hostile Japanese faces and felt like saying, "Shit, men, it's all not worth it! All this energy and hostility. For what? In thirty years no one will know we were ever on this earth. A funny thing happened to me on the way to the shogun's palace." But no one in that room was in the mood for humor, let alone *gaijin* humor.

I took a deep breath and gave my best Academy Award speech and performance. I spoke of how and when I first met Fumio and how he had introduced me to the Japanese way of life, which I admired and respected. I spoke of *giri*, which I understood, and about the Japanese custom, which I had read about, of hiring employees for life. I thought Mr. Kawakami glanced at me benevolently, but I wasn't sure.

A few other people spoke, but the Yamaha interpreter told me very little to enlighten me. Fumio kept looking my way, grimfaced, as if he was trying to tell me something. I truly felt sorry for him. Finally I grabbed the reigns in desperation, cutting the interpreter off in one of his inane explanations.

I asked the board to be lenient, saying if any mistakes had been made by Fumio, he and I would work twice as hard to make up for them. Surely the word *forgiveness* was in the Japanese lexicon, I added. You could hear a *sushi* drop. No one even looked up. It was as if they were praying and listening to the Japanese "Ave Maria." Again I thought that President Kawakami glanced down at me with some paternal feeling. His eyes were not unkind, like those of the others in the room, who stared at me as if I were their lifelong enemy.

Meeting over, nothing was concluded or stated. I was told to enjoy my stay in Tokyo and that eventually, upon my return to the States, I would be brought up to date on any decision. I was told that President Kawakami still believed in me, respected me, and liked me very much, "like an adopted son." That last phrase led me to believe the worst was over and that this tempest in a teacup would soon resolve itself.

That night, I poured my heart out to some friends, over dinner and sake. If only I knew what the Pacific side was thinking. What did they want? Exactly what were they after? Someone suggested I buy a book titled *Japanese Manners and Ethics in Business*, by Boye De Mente. This could help me in my dealings—not only with Yamaha, but with all Japanese in particular.

The book was hard to find. I scoured the bookstores until I finally found a copy. It was less than 200 pages long, and I read the book three times that first evening.

Some of the titles of chapters are: "Why Is Face So Important?," "Are They Really Polite?," "Why Are They Prone to Break Contracts?," and "Why Do They Fail to Answer Inquiries?" Why? Why? Why? Why didn't someone suggest I get and read this book before I went into the dragon's den? Oh, how this little book of knowledge could have helped my ass with Fumio's bullshit and misinterpreting, with the early meetings with all those Japanese businessmen in my hotel room, with waiters and hotel clerks and especially with Yamaha Nippon Gakki.

Fortified with all this necessary additional enlightenment, I ached to go forward and begin this entire Japanese adventure from the start. But no dice. I was locked into a melodrama on life's center stage, and I had to perform in every scene, whether I wanted to our not. The battle lines were drawn, and even though I was an uneager contestant, on a side I didn't particularly care for, there was nothing much I could do but play out my kamikaze role. Loyalty and gratitude are the two most important feelings in my gut. Destiny brought Fumio Suzuki and me together as a team in this charade, and good or bad, I just couldn't get myself to walk away from this guy.

205

Fumio was an educated man who, I think, was a little startled and bewildered by Japan's successful emergence into the industrial world. There were so many new companies rising up, so many new innovations, that Fumio didn't know which way to turn first. His ability to speak English, though not perfectly, placed him in demand at a time when Japan was straining at the industrial bit. Rumor had reached me, more than once, that Fumio had been a double interpreter or a double agent, that he had interpreted for both the Americans and also for the Japanese at the conclusion of World War II, playing both sides. Fumio admitted to me that his life was threatened more than once by his own countrymen.

Still, I had nowhere else to place my allegiance. We were stuck with each other. I was rubbed the wrong way more than once by Fumio, but this East-West odyssey began with Fumio Suzuki and it would end, happily and successfully I hoped, with Fumio and me with our *giri* intact and with honor.

I began to remember that each time I would begin to like something about Fumio, he would invariably throw a monkey wrench into my lap. He was the greatest "opener" I had ever met, but I soon learned he had the mind of an incorrigible guy bent on grand larceny. I felt I could change Fumio. I could win him over; possibly with friendship and understanding I could get him to change his ways. I honestly thought all this was possible, that it was just a matter of time. Maybe I was a little too hard on Fumio in the past? I'd change my attitude; I'd try a new, soft approach.

Hard as I tried, it was no go. Fumio's personality and outlook on life were locked in, and he could not be changed one iota. I refused to believe this for a long time to come, but eventually that was my sad, final conclusion. Then there was the fact that Fumio had never forgiven America for winning the war and Japan for losing the war. He was bitter about many things, but *ichi ban*, number one, was the shame he endured when Japan capitulated.

I made Fumio admit that General MacArthur's introduction of democracy was the best thing that ever happened to Japan. It helped a guy like Fumio rise up above his designated lot in life. Once Fumio remarked that "All Japanese men feel inferior to Americans." Then, in a heated argument, when he was accusing Americans of every crime he could fabricate, I inadvertently and

206

incorrectly lashed out with "The reason you Japanese feel inferior is because you are inferior!" Fumio never held that remark against me—I don't know why—but I held it against myself. I felt I had stooped to a new level in order to win a point. I excused it with "What the hell, I'm human, too." But every so often that one remark jumps into my craw.

Back in New York, I continued negotiating for Yamaha but felt a strange cloud hovering overhead. Catalogues of music and recordings were continually being shipped to Japan, but letters and answers to viable questions were almost nonexistent. Worse still, monthly expense checks stopped abruptly. We received one Telex stating that everything was *dai-jobu*, okay, and that I should continue on and a forthcoming letter would bring me up to date on everything.

I did receive a letter from Hamamatsu, from President Kawakami, telling me that I was like a son to him, that I shouldn't worry, and that everything would be straightened out in time. At this time, I was running Yamaha Music in New York City with my own funds. It was getting sticky, but I believed—oh, how I believed.

Still no explanation. In desperation, I wired President Kawakami to please expedite some funds and instructions. More silent treatment. I read Boye De Mente's chapter again, "Why Do They Fail to Answer Inquiries?" Mr. De Mente states that the Japanese philosophy is that unless there is a meeting face to face, the recipient of a letter doesn't feel obligated to answer, even as a gesture of courtesy. How many face-to-face meetings did we have to have?

More silence, and I could now see and feel and smell the handwriting and calligraphy that hit the proverbial wall. It was obvious that the Pacific side was waiting for me to make a move, maybe commit harikari or walk into the sunset and disappear. *Kankay-nai*: "you are there, but you do not exist!"

I called Pop Sprung and asked that my Yamaha stock, held by Warren Shimeall in Tokyo, be sent to me. The eventual answer was devastating. Yamaha Nippon Gakki had kept promising to mail the stock certificates to Mr. Shimeall but never did. Mr. Shimeall never followed up on his request; his alcoholic mind got in the way. Should I go to Japan and kill him?

More time elapsed; more money was expended by me person-

207

ally. Pop Sprung said that my ace in the hole was that I owned the name, Yamaha Music Corporation, in the United States. The Pacific side would have to communicate some sort of an offer eventually.

In the meantime, Fumio was waiting and calling with "I told you so. Why didn't you go in and chop heads when you were in Tokyo?" Then a letter arrived from Hamamatsu, from Mr. Kawakami's first assistant, saying that I shouldn't be bitter, *shkaht-a-ganai,* which is Japanese for *c'est la vie,* and that everyone at Yamaha Nippon Gakki thought the world of me.

Pop Sprung advised me that if I sued, in Japan, it might take six years or so to adjudicate my case. And then there was the chance I might lose. He thought it best to try to settle quietly and amiably. The Pacific side held all the cards. I thought it out for a few days and came to the conclusion that they not only held all the cards; they owned the deck and the hall.

We settled, as was suggested, and after attorney fees and expenses, it came to less than $25,000. After all past incurred expenses and obligations, it came to zip, nothing. King or millionaire for a day, I was both or none. *More like a fool for a day,* that's how I felt.

For a month I was a nervous wreck, couldn't sleep, lost weight, and withdrew from life. I didn't want to talk to anyone about anything. I relived the past two years, almost day by day—meetings, conversations, trips, agreements, and associations—and finally came to the conclusion that I should chalk the whole thing up to a great adventure on life's huge canvas. Otherwise, this betrayal, as I felt it was, would consume me.

I could almost excuse and forgive all the performers in this comedy of errors except one—Mr. Genichi Kawakami and Yamaha Nippon Gakki, being one and the same, not issuing my participatory stock certificates as promised. This was the reason they suggested and advised me to entrust them with my *hanko,* my Japanese seal or signature. Yamaha made plans, early in the game, to control me completely. When I jumped to Fumio's defense, that was it. *Kankay-nai;* I was there, but I did not exist anymore. *Whaccali-mashta* (I understood), and *oari* (it's over). Roger, willco, and out!

Déjà Vu

Now what do I do with the large suite of offices, the huge rent and overhead? If I wanted to retain some measure of respectability and not lose my American face, I thought it best to remain where I was, to put on a front until I was able to get going again. Fumio was still writing and calling me, saying that Japan was hungry for American jazz stars; I could make it big in the Orient as a concert producer. At this time, I was also offered a partnership to produce Broadway and off-Broadway shows. Which way? Maybe both?

I sublet two of the rooms in the large office suite to the estate of Moss Hart, which was being handled by the late Mr. Hart's very good friend, Joe Hyman.

It was nice seeing Mr. Hart's lovely and talented wife, Kitty Carlisle, come by the offices and say hello every so often.

Then Paul Vance, writer of "Itsy Bitsy, Teenie, Weenie, Yellow Polka-Dot Bikini" and "Catch a Falling Star," rented another office. Paul's constant guest was the popular singer Johnny Mathis, which didn't hurt the office's popularity any. There were always a bunch of kids hanging around to catch a glimpse of Johnny.

I was home free, almost rent free, now my office overhead was minimal, and I could set my sights on other horizons to conquer. Fumio had mentioned something about Japan being hungry for American jazz artists. My friend Leonard Green, who owned Basin Street East, a leading New York nightclub, knew Norman Granz, Ella Fitzgerald's manager. Why not shoot for the top? I called Leonard, he called Norman, and Granz agreed to meet me in New York City, when his pal Duke Ellington was appearing there. With the Duke looking on, at the Americana Hotel, Norman Granz and I drafted an agreement for Ms. Ella Fitzgerald to appear in concert in Tokyo, Kyoto, and other major towns.

I cabled Fumio and he assembled a group of Japanese promoters, under the personal direction of Mr. Masuo Furukawa of Target Productions, Inc. Mr. Furukawa was an interesting man, extremely quiet and withdrawn, but a man of action once he made up his mind. Furukawa-san had the gambler's instinct and

209

guts, I concluded, and I have learned since he went for broke on many a theatrical venture. If there were any Japanese panning for gold in the Klondike, they must have looked like Masuo Furukawa.

Mr. Furukawa had interests in many theatrical fields. He produced his own variety TV show, starring Joji Ishimatsu, the singing idol of Japan. Joji Ishimatsu was endearingly known as Ai George by his many fans in Japan and as I. George eventually here in the United States. I. George was born of a Spanish-Filipino mother and a much traveled Japanese father, which background enabled the young boy to learn many languages. Deserted as a war child, I. George became a wandering street singer to earn his way, eventually cut some records, met his manager and producer Mr. Furukawa, and became a star in films and on TV, and the rest is history in Japan.

Mr. Furukawa also owned talent agencies, and nightclubs and managed many of Japan's budding young singers and entertainers. Yet he was a quiet, introspective man, choosing to allow his many colleagues to follow his policies. Furukawa-san was a handsome man, thin, of medium height, with the air, elegance, and joie de vivre of a true samurai. One never knew what he was thinking, but once I discovered he had a sense of humor, I knew everything would always be *dai-jabu* (okay).

Fumio and Mr. Furukawa came to the States to finalize the Ella Fitzgerald contracts and to have a vacation in New York City. I liked Mr. Furukawa from the moment I met him and in time found him to be one of the most honorable men I had ever encountered. We had future problems with contracts, managers, performers, lighting, and unions but never between the two of us. I instinctively felt we liked each other from that first mutual bow.

It was at this time, while there was a slight lull in my life business-wise and personally, that my entire world was smashed to smithereens once again. Only this time, if it weren't for Peter, my loving son, I might have done something drastic to myself. One dark fall day, sitting at my desk and listening to the news, I heard that my hero, my idol, my president, had been shot while visiting Dallas, Texas.

Dear Lord, don't let this beautiful man die. It can't be. This is all a dream, a nightmare, a hallucination. I thought. *Is it the*

With Suzuki, Furukawa, and "Jazz at the Philharmonic" Norman Granz cooking up the Ella Fitzgerald concerts for Japan.

end of the world? I was paralyzed with fear and apprehension. I chased everyone out of my offices, double locked the doors, and went to bed. The radio said he was dead. John F. Kennedy, forty-six years young, thirty-fifth president of these United States. Statistics. Now the man I thought would be the savior of our world had been cruelly assassinated. That handsome, charismatic young man, Jackie's husband, was now a historical statistic.

I cried for days. Oh, how I cried. I called for Peter; maybe he could snap me out of my abyss. He lay down next to me, and we both cried for days. My bones ached. *God, how could you let this happen?* I asked. *Maybe dear John Kennedy is better off wherever it is he went? Why does it hurt so? He never had a chance; he would have shown them; he would have straightened out this screwed-up world.*

When Lee Harvey Oswald was shown coming out of prison toward the TV cameras, I yelled, "Kill the motherfucker! Shoot the bastard!" Sure enough, a lone hand, a gun, bang, bang, and all that I wished had come true. I couldn't believe it. My God, I

211

was just thinking out loud. Did I have anything to do with this murder? No! Millions of people were thinking the same thing. So was a distant stranger by the name of Jack Ruby.

Ella's concert was now a few months off, and each day the Yamaha experience and President Kennedy's death were healing in my heart somewhat. I could even talk about it without gagging. The Whiteway Production office had become the hub or hangout for people from all walks of show business again.

My old partner Stanley Adams was playing the part of Perelli, the wrestling promoter, in *Requiem for a Heavyweight,* then being filmed in New York. Naturally, Stanley lived with me, and each day he brought over a bunch of people working on the film. The laughs, the stories told, and the practical jokes were legendary. Mickey Rooney, whom I had met once during the war, usually held center stage, and deservedly so. He never ran out of energy or stories, and he was a one-man show every minute.

One evening, we all went over to Mickey's suite at the Warwick Hotel, where the Mick was in his cups from a few hot buttered rums. While telling us of his past, Mickey became sad and held out fourteen dollars. "This is all the money I have on me, and if my ex-wives knew it, they would grab this, too." But then he would smile and say, "Hey, who had more fun than I? Most guys have one-night stands. I married 'em. That's the answer."

Mickey Rooney had more energy, more talent, more ideas, more thoughts, and more dreams than any ten men and not all regarding show business. He had ideas for fast-food restaurants, for children's talent schools, for films, for inventions, and on and on. Mention a subject and America's Andy Hardy was off and running. He mentioned that he had even written a batch of songs, and I stopped him in his tracks. I sang the opening lines to one of his ditties, "Oceans Apart," and he couldn't believe it. I had seen Mickey and Judy Garland in one of their appearances at the old Capital Theater, and Mickey had sung this new song he had written. I had only heard the song once.

I introduced my son, Peter, to Mickey, and the light of my life slapped Rooney on his ass and said, "Hey, how come you always go around machine-gunning innocent people?" Mickey and I couldn't figure it out until we realized that ten-year-old

Peter White was a little mixed up. Mickey had been in a film *Machine Gun Kelly,* and Peter had confused reality with make-believe. Mickey said that my son would be a natural for one of his future talent schools and that Peter would make a good actor. My son chose to go into another field, which was okay with me.

Mickey introduced Peter and me to his wife, and I went away with the feeling that Mickey was happy and in love and the very best of Joe Yule's son was yet to come. Joe Yule was Mickey's father, a well-known clown in old-time burlesque. Just a short time later, the screaming headlines told of Mickey's wife being murdered by someone they both had known. The little envy I had felt for Mickey turned to pity, and I swore not to think the grass was always greener and so forth. My son said, "Daddy, she was such a nice, pretty lady."

One spring day in 1963, a Telex arrived in my offices requesting information about the availability of Carnegie Hall. I checked into the situation and wired Mr. Furukawa dates and prices. I waited, but there was no immediate followup.

Time hung a little heavy at this time, so I started reading scripts from various producers. One, from famous Broadway producer Leonard Sillman, had me laughing from page one till the curtain. There were other offers to produce rock concerts in Sheboygin and Austin, Texas, but Mr. Sillman's script for *The Family Way* had me intrigued. I met with Leonard Sillman in his auspicious townhouse on East 72nd Street and agreed to become a co-producer. I had heard that he was very difficult to work with, but the die was cast. At this stage of my life, I didn't like to think or dwell on the worst.

Then another lengthy Telex from Mr. Furukawa. How would I like to produce a series of Japanese concerts at Carnegie Hall starring I. George? It wasn't a matter of making money but more of introducing I. George, one of Japan's top stars, to the American public. All expenses would be paid by Target Productions of Japan, Mr. Furukawa's production company.

I wired back my assent and again met with the Carnegie Hall officials regarding some alternate availability dates, seating capacity, costs for the hall, insurance, security, and all the other information needed to produce a concert. Mr. Furukawa, Fumio Suzuki, and Gomi-san came over to the States to help select the

213

dates, to choose a music conductor, and to discuss the price of tickets and the rest of the program starring I. George.

I learned from Fumio that Furukawa-san and I. George hadn't been seeing eye to eye for a long time, that they were on the verge of breaking up their association, and that this forthcoming Carnegie Hall concert was Mr. Furukawa's last bid to make amends, if possible, and, at the very least, to show all of Japan that their partnership would go out in a blaze of glory.

This time I wanted all to go well, with no mistakes if I could help it, no recriminations, so I hired a top Japanese newspaperman as my advisor and interpreter. Mr. Sho Onodora was a nisei (American-born son or daughter of Japanese immigrant parents) friend of mine who had served as one of America's top interpreters during World War II. Sho had been on one of the first three American planes that landed in Japan at the end of the war. He also served on Gen. Robert Eichelberger's staff and the war-crimes trials prosecuting Tojo. In mid-1963, when I called upon his good services, Sho Onodera was the top reporter for the *Sankei* newspaper of Japan and had just finished dubbing in his voice for the starring role in the English version of the hit motion picture *Hiroshima, Mon Amour.* I admired Sho, his intelligence, his forthright, no-nonsense approach to matters, and his analyses of world and domestic matters. To me, he always seemed to put a new light on matters.

Contracts were drawn and dates, October 8, 9, and 10, were set for Carnegie Hall's first authentic Japanese concert, starring I. George. I chose Academy Award–winning composer Eddy Manson as conductor of our twenty-five–piece orchestra, augmented with Japan's foremost percussionist, Furuya, playing the huge "taiko" drum.

We originally thought of hiring the Tachibana troupe of Kabuki dancers, but Mr. Furukawa and I. George had one of their staring contests. Sho Onodera took me aside and informed me that I. George had let it be known that unless he had his way, he was about to take a walk. Thus what had started out to be a Japanese concert, starring I. George and featuring various other Japanese dancers and entertainers, wound up as strictly the I. George show.

Mr. Furukawa suggested the I. George concert be filmed and recorded for posterity and Japanese TV and as a two-set album

214

for Teichiko Records. A huge order, but after the usual hassles, staring contest, false starts, and setbacks, it was arranged.

I agreed with Mr. Furukawa and Sho that I. George should concentrate more on singing Japanese folk songs, leading up to the contemporary pop song sung in Japanese, with an English chorus thrown in here and there. Again I. George rebelled. This was his shot at the big time. He was going to wear a tuxedo, not the traditional Japanese *yucata*, and his concert was going to be in the style of Frank Sinatra's and Harry Belafonte's. No amount of arguing on my part could convince him otherwise. The playboy of the Eastern world had made up his mind.

Publicity went out to all the newspapers, invitations were sent to every member of United Nations, ads were taken in all the Japanese-American periodicals, and word of mouth spread the story of I. George, the Soul of Japan, in person at Carnegie Hall, October 8, 9, and 10, 1963. "The Soul of Japan" was a little misleading. A Kabuki or Noh play would have been a little more appropriate. But go fight the shogun.

The week of the concert, everyone checked in from Japan in good spirits except Mr. Furukawa. Upon talking with Fumio, I learned that he was upset because I. George had brought his current lady friend, a geisha girl, with him. Furukawa-san smelled trouble.

The October 8 concert was mostly for the mass media, the press, Japanese dignitaries and businessmen, their families, and theatrical agents, personal managers, and producers. Outside of a weird ringing feedback sound on a huge loudspeaker, which we finally corrected minutes before the first concert, and an argument between the NBC crew videotaping the show and the Carnegie Hall union men as to who was in charge of lighting the show, everything went off reasonably well.

Mr. Patrick Skine Catling of *Newsweek* magazine and other members of the press came by to tell me how much they enjoyed the concert, but "Why didn't I. George concentrate more on Japanese songs? There were enough imitations of Fisher, Sinatra, Eckstine, and Jolson without I. George competing on that level and throwing away his natural advantage." I couldn't agree more but refused to get upset at this stage of the game. We were promised good press, but Edith Piaf had just died and space was at a premium that week.

215

The second night, October 9, was a black-tie affair, with many dignitaries from the United Nations attending in their respective country's native costume. It was a gala night, when we did most of our videotaping and recording of the two I. George albums. Cute eleven-year-old Peter White was all over the TV cameras and recording equipment, wanting to know how everything worked. Peter stole the evening from I. George, and I'm not saying that because I'm his father. (Like hell I'm not!)

Again there were complaints about I. George's selection of material and his not doing enough of the Japanese standard folk songs. I weathered the storm as best I could. Peter White loved his daddy's concert, and that was what mattered most to me. Offers for I. George's services came in from "The Garry Moore Show," "The Jack Paar Show," and a few nightclubs. I mentioned

Me, Count Basie, and "The Soul of Japan," I. George, backstage at Carnegie Hall.

216

this to Mr. Furukawa and suggested we have a round-robin meeting after the last concert. He agreed and said he would inform "the Soul of Japan."

After the third and last concert, on October 10, a "Wasp" dinner party celebration was held in Saito's Japanese restaurant. Everyone showed up but the guest of honor. I. George was late as usual. Then someone arrived and said that I. George had just left for Mexico City, geisha in tow, to visit with his old pals, the Los Panchos Trio. I later learned that Mr. Furukawa and his protégé had exchanged harsh words earlier that evening, and this was I. George's way of punishing his mentor, his discoverer, his personal manager.

I felt sorry for my good friend, Furukawa-san, but samurai that he was, he didn't show any outward emotion that night. More offers came in for I. George's services the next few days, and Furukawa-san and I both came to the conclusion that I. George had hurt mostly himself.

It was now getting time for me to prepare myself for Ella Fitzgerald's concert tour of Japan. I looked forward to going back to my adopted second home. I still loved so much about their way of life. The only pain in my heart was leaving Peter, but I always asked for his permission to make these extended trips and he always gave it. I don't know what I would have done if he didn't. I told him I would call and write and I bring him many surprises. That last thought usually helped us both lose the lumps in our throats. I thought of putting him in school in Japan, but his mother's veto killed that. Then I thought of kidnapping him and both of us never coming back to the States, but it was only a thought.

The day before I left for Japan, I had to make a business decision that had been haunting me for weeks. I had always loved sports, all sports, but especially professional football. I had let it be known to everyone I knew that I had this crazy obsession, this dream of getting involved in pro football. An acquaintance of mine mentioned that cowboy star Gene Autry had the same obsession and was waiting for a new football franchise to come his way. Mr. Autry already owned the California Angels baseball team. Then I got this hurry-up call. It seems that Lady Luck had bypassed Mr. Autry regarding a professional football team, for

217

the moment, but my acquaintance learned the Philadelphia Warriors might be up for sale. A series of meetings was held in my offices with Mr. Basketball himself, Eddie Gottlieb, who was then a stockholder of the Philadelphia Warriors franchise.

Mr. Gottlieb explained that a group of businessmen in San Francisco had made a tender offer to buy the Philadelphia franchise and move the team to San Francisco, thus leaving Philadelphia open for an entirely new franchise. Mr. Gottlieb stated that he intended to retain some of the San Francisco stock and to buy into the new Philadelphia franchise. After all, basketball was his life!

Hell, I didn't care much for basketball; it was football that had me by the proverbial. But here's this guy Gottlieb who had so much faith in basketball that he was willing to buy into two franchises. I called my close friends Ed Wachtel and Herb Goldsmith, owners of Europecraft Members Only Clothes, for solace and/or guidance. Eddie was a high roller, a guy who took a shot. Herb was a sweater; he perspired when he took a chance on a punchboard. They both, in unison, said, "I pass!"

On a wild, crazy impulse, I made up my mind, for once in my life, to indulge myself. On behalf of my heir apparent, Peter White, and myself, I wrote the largest check I heretofore had ever written. I remember how my pen stuttered as I wrote the figure. Chicken feed to some, but a life's earnings and savings to me. I told Peter, "Think of the fun we'll have. Now we can tell our seven-foot center, Wilt Chamberlain, off. That is, if we don't talk too loud." Peter thought the idea was wonderful, but he rather would have had a new bicycle or a fish tank.

With the check hesitatingly mailed to San Francisco, home of the new San Francisco Warriors, name later changed to the Golden Gate Warriors, I left for Los Angeles, to meet up with Ella Fitzgerald and company. In Los Angeles, I stayed with Stanley Adams, who had just finished shooting *Requiem*, and we hung out with Louie Nye, the comedian, and ate most our meals in Little Tokyo. Louie got a kick out of my speaking Japanese, and he was constantly frightening tiny Japanese waitresses by threatening to commit harai-kari with a soupspoon. The laughs flowed and I was so happy to be with Uncle Stanley once again.

Coach Alex Hannum, Mr. Basketball Eddie Gottlieb, and my son, Peter, with the franchise Wilt "The Stilt" Chamberlain the year we bought into the Golden Gate Warriors.

Ella in Japan

Japan Airlines had issued eight round-trip tickets, gratis, for the Ella Fitzgerald troupe's trip to Japan—six economy for myself and the band, and two first class, for Ella and her traveling companion. In return, Japan Airlines could photograph us and publicize the fact that we had used their airline.

At the eleventh hour, we all got word that Mr. Norman Granz,

219

Ella Fitzgerald's manager, who had originally stated he wasn't going to Japan with us, had changed his mind. He was going to meet us in Tokyo, and he was utilizing one of our first-class tickets for himself. I smelled trouble, but it was too late to do anything about it and "Mr. Jazz at the Philharmonic," Norman Granz, was too powerful a man to argue with.

At the airport, Ella looked a little nervous and exasperated. I asked her if anything was wrong, and she said she was upset because she had to fire her maid that day. Ella had discovered that all the butter in the refrigerator was missing. The maid maintained she took it, as it would go to waste inasmuch as no one would be living in the house for close to a month.

Prior to the flight, I got friendly with Tommy Flanagan and the other two members of his trio, Bill Yancey on bass and Gus Johnson on drums. Gus Johnson was the most open and genial of the entire Ella Fitzgerald troupe. "Little Jazz" Roy Eldridge, who had second billing to Ella in the concerts, immediately became hostile and angry, so I steered clear of his person. Roy boozed and gambled and snickered from moment one.

On the flight to Hawaii, Ella got a little lonely, so I sat with her and chatted for an hour or so. Then I tried to send one of the musicians back to first class, to keep her company. Each one said the same thing: "Hey man, that's not my job!"

Joining us on the flight was my old air-force buddy Art "Buck" Stringari, who was now one of the nation's leading labor-relations conselors. He was in awe of Ella, so I sent him back to keep her company. Art had always wanted to see Japan, he needed a holiday, he was proud of my producing the Ella Fitzgerald concerts, and this would be a way for us to catch up with each other for all the lost years. Detroit, where Art practiced law, was an interesting town, but the picture I painted of Japan had Art drooling and panting. It wasn't too hard selling him on taking this trip.

Our momentary stopover in Hawaii over, we were on our way to Japan. Again Ella needed company, and again I had to rustle up some hesitant volunteers to help her idle away the hours. Producer, bullshit! Try baby-sitter.

At Honeda Airport, hundreds of Ella's fans were there to greet us, with banners and cameras. Immediately Ella grabbed

On my way to Japan with Ella and "Little Jazz" Roy Eldridge.

my arm and said, "No flash cameras, Eddie. I have something wrong with my eyes." I thought she was kidding, but she looked stern and dead serious. No flash cameras. In Japan? That's like saying, "No chopsticks."

A press conference was held at the airport, where I begged off on all flash cameras, and all went well until who shows up but Mr. Wonderful, Norman Granz, Ella's manager, impresario extraordinaire, world traveler, dilettante, and art collector. Immediately I noticed Ella and the musicians tensing up, and an air of uneasiness predominated. Gone were the waving and smiles; enter the dragon.

The concert contracts called for Ella Fitzgerald and musicians and myself to live at a first-class Japanese hotel. It was agreed by all concerned, after much discussion and argument by Mr. Norman Granz, that we would stay at the Ginza Tokyu Hotel. We checked in and were assigned rooms on the same floor. Ella, though tired, her maid and road manager professed pleasure and acceptance of the Ginza Tokyu, and we all started to unpack.

Suddenly there was yelling and epithets out in the hall. Norman Granz was prancing around and screaming, "Sammy Davis stayed at the Okura Hotel, and so will Ella." Knowing how sensitive the Japanese were, I tried to calm Norman and reason with him. I explained that the Pacific side had already made arrangements with the Ginza Tokyu. Granz shouted at me, "Don't worry. I'll pay for the Okura Hotel myself!"

Everyone heard that last remark, thank God, which prevented Granz from giving me additional trouble later on. Our Japanese concert associates thought Mr. Granz's antics were an outrageous insult. Mr. Furukawa confirmed, later on, that Mr. Granz indeed was paying Ella Fitzgerald's bills at the Okura Hotel, saying he felt that the issue was then a thing of the past.

This was all an appetizer for Mr. Granz. At each rehearsal, he called the Japanese technicians and lighting men amateurs. He constantly reminded our entire staff that he was the best thing that had happened to jazz in the past twenty-five years. Many times he threatened that Ella wouldn't go on unless he, Norman Granz, had his way and say.

The Japanese were furious but intimidated. As we toured Kyoto and the other cities, they threw lavish parties, mostly to appease Mr. Granz. He repaid them by telling everyone, including the waiters, off, talking about the Black Muslim movement, which he backed wholeheartedly, and shouting that the time for talk was over, that the blood of the white people would start to run in the streets of America, and that John Kennedy had been a big nothing in office, and all this without ever thanking our hosts for their elegant hospitality. A pretty good speech for a fat cat that lived, at that time, in Switzerland. I did all I could to hold my good buddy Art Stringari back from cold conking this ugly American.

During the trip, N.G. turned to me and said, "After these concerts, Ella and I are going to Hong Kong on a shopping trip." When I told this to Mr. Furukawa, he was livid, and rightly so. Furukawa-san found out that N.G. had booked Ella for two days in Hong Kong, against AFTRA (the American Federation of Television and Radio Artists) rules.

Then when Ella's concerts ended in Japan, N.G. demanded payment for the rooms at the Okura Hotel, although he had originally stated he would pay for these rooms himself; plus he wanted to be paid for Ella's 340 pounds of excess luggage. Mr. Furukawa had already paid for Ella's excess baggage from Los Angeles to Japan and agreed to pay for her return trip if Ella and company would continue to fly via Japan Airlines, as agreed. Norman Granz refused and said, "You fucking people stink!"

Dave Carello, who was Ella Fitzgerald's band boy and road manager, confided to me that N.G. had said the same thing and pulled the same routine in South America, Germany, and the rest of Europe. Small consolation. I just hoped the Japanese didn't think all Americans were like N.G.

The concerts over, it was time to think about the future. Mr. Furukawa wanted me to find out the availability of the Gene Krupa Band, the Crosby Brothers, Elvis Presley, Tony Martin, Cyd Charisse, and other name attractions. It was time for sayonara parties and exchanging gifts and swapping stories about Ella's concerts and drinking toast after toast after toast.

Just as I was about to leave Japan to return home, I received the following letter from young Peter White: "Dear Dad, please get me the biggest and the best. Love, Peter." The biggest and the best? What could that chubby little kid mean? I went to Tokyo's

223

ichi-ban department store, Mitsukoshi, and loitered around the toy department. A young lady was doing a magic act, and I remembered that Peter usually hung around the magic counter at penny arcades. I bought the largest magic set available and a small transistor radio for Peter White.

Upon my return to the States, I asked Peter what he had meant by "the biggest and the best." He couldn't remember. I gave him the magic set, and he immediately said that that was what he meant, that now he remembered. After I gave him the little transistor radio, he was back in five minutes complaining it wasn't a Japanese radio after all. "All the stations speak English." Kids, I love 'em!

I wasn't back in New York two days when the old pressures started to take over again. My secretary informed me that the Internal Revenue Department had paid us a visit, stating that I had failed or neglected to pay the taxes on the I. George concerts at Carnegie Hall. I told her that I had mailed a check to the Internal Revenue the very day after the concert as I was leaving for Japan. She said she had told the IRS man but that he had placed a lien against our production company anyway. My accountant advised me not to make waves. Two years later, I received payment for the mistake, the IRS explaining that in moving the files from one office to another, they had goofed. This was democracy at work.

I also had more offers of jobs with major music publishers, theatrical producers, and artists who needed management than I could shake a stick at. But I was committed to do the show *The Family Way* with Leonard Sillman. I made my availability known to Mr. Sillman and proceeded to raise my share of the show's projected budget.

The next few weeks were fun and games with Prince Peter. We went to our favorite dude ranch, took long trail rides, and generally caught up with each other. I knew he missed me terribly, as after our evening wrestling and tickling match, he would fall asleep in my bed.

I had arranged for Peter to be taken to the ranch, in upstate New York, even when I was busy or out of the country. The woman who owned the Sunnycraft Ranch, Sylvia DeMello, loved Peter as one of her own, and Peter had the run of the place. I was quite comfortable knowing Sylvia and another close friend of mine, Leon Duftler, were always on the watch for my son.

The thought crossed my mind that my son was at the age where he needed his father more than ever. He seemed to cling to me more. Also, I noticed a few gray hairs starting to sprout here and there on my head. And then a chance remark by a woman up at the ranch made up my mind. I was home to stay. There would be no more extensive traveling unless my son, Peter, was at my side.

This kind lady had mentioned that she had seen Peter crying one rainy afternoon. It was her opinion that the boy had missed his father very much. I thanked her and requested she don't mention our conversation to anyone. I assured her that I would handle the matter.

Upon my questioning Peter, he failed to look me in the eyes and was on the verge of tears. I quickly came to the conclusion that the woman was correct and vowed to take my son whenever and wherever. Thank the good Lord we have since been on fishing, camping, and vacation trips to the Virgin Islands, Puerto Rico, the Thousand Islands, Canada, Miami, and Key West and have home movies to help us relive all those wonderful memories.

10

Broadway Bound

1964: The Beatles explode on the scene; Sonny Liston becomes heavyweight champion; the mechanical heart is invented; gasoline hits thirty cents a gallon.

IT WAS NOW THE FALL OF 1964, time to meet with the ogre of Broadway, Mr. Leonard Sillman. Everyone by now had warned me that Mr. Sillman was impossible to work with, that I would hate him and probably wind up by beating the stuffing out of him. It was close, but nothing like this happened. As a matter of fact, although we had our differences, ours was more of a mutual admiration society.

Very few people on Broadway had anything nice to say about Leonard Sillman the man. Leonard Sillman the producer was a different story. He had refined the revue type of entertainment to its infinite form, both for the theater and for cafés. His "New Faces" broadway revues are classics, and the performers Leonard Sillman introduced to the theater are legendary.

I felt, from the start, that I could learn much from Mr. Sillman; he was an older man with more experience and the credits to prove it. I made up my mind that the key to getting along with this talented complicated man was "respect."

Leonard Sillman seemed to sense this feeling in me, because although he ranted and raved about everything and everyone, he never raised his voice to me. One day he argued with one of our associates and finished off by saying, "And your lousy cigar stinks!" The poor guy looked around and said, "But Eddie is smoking a cigar, too. Why don't you say the same thing to him?" Leonard smiled at me benevolently and said, "Because Eddie's cigar has a pleasant aroma."

Leonard insisted on artistic control over *The Family Way* from the start. That meant that he had the final say on the matter of casting the show. I acquiesced immediately, bowing to his vast, superior experience in the theatre. But one of our associates stood toe to toe and nose to nose with Leonard, and the arguments and hysterical histrionics were a Broadway show in themselves.

One of the men I cherish meeting through Leonard Sillman was Mr. Al Goldin, the show's general manager. Al looked exactly like Little Caesar or Edward G. Robinson—take your pick—but he was a pussycat. I felt comfortable and content knowing that Al Goldin was at the helm of the ship. Finding out how treacherous it was to do a play, I swore I would never produce anything unless Al Goldin was involved. I spent many memorable evenings with Al and his beautiful wife, Paula. Al was so meticulous about everything. To give you an idea, Al eventually passed away at Lincoln Center while attending the opera, but he made sure it was during the intermission.

Then there was Martha Greenhouse, who was a lovable bundle of nuclear energy all by herself. Martha is not only a capable actress, but she willingly serves on practically every theatrical union committee that exists. To know Martha Greenhouse is to know love. She's fed me umpteen times, she invariably laughs at my jokes, and she thinks that I'm a nice guy. Two out of three isn't bad.

I was close to practically everyone connected with *The Family Way*, especially our star, TV's Jack "Bart Maverick" Kelly, but the years tend to water down many casual friendships made in show business.

I still see Paula Goldin almost every Sunday at comedian Henny Youngman's weekly brunch held at the Carnegie Delicatessen. Paula does all of Henny's administrative work. I run into Martha everywhere, as she is known to be more than one person, especially during the Jewish holidays, when I am usually invited to break bread or matzo with her family, including her husband, Dr. James Sasmore. Martha continually scolds me for telling what she calls sacrilegious jokes during the services, but she laughs louder than anyone else.

When *The Family Way* went into rehearsal, the Shubert brothers allowed us to use their Lyceum Theater, which was the actual theater we opened in after we returned from our tryout in

227

Philadelphia. This was an entirely new experience for me, watching our director, Michael Gordon, coaching the actors and listening to all the backstage gossip. I couldn't help but pick up the morsel that our leading lady, Collin Wilcox, wasn't too happy with Mr. Gordon, although he personally chose her for the starring role. It all started when Michael Gordon told what Collin thought was an off-color joke at lunch. I was there and didn't think the joke was too extreme.

It all came to a head one afternoon while I was sitting in the darkened theater watching a rehearsal. Michael Gordon called a lunch break, and as an afterthought he said to Collin, "I have some notes I'll give you after lunch." Notes are corrections a director gives to actors to help improve a line, a scene, a moment, an attitude, or whatever.

Collin turned to Michael, snapped, "Give them to my maid; I'm not taking any notes from a dirty old man like you!" and started to walk away. Michael shot back, "Miss Wilcox, you're an Equity actress. If you walk offstage while I'm talking, that's a breach of your contract." Everyone froze onstage.

I don't know what got into me. I usually allowed Leonard Sillman to handle the ball in matters such as this. But Leonard wasn't there. I bounded up onstage and in my best General Patton voice said, "Here now, how long has this been going on in the theater? Don't you people realize you have an obligation to the people who invested money in this play? The people who believe in you, and you, and you? Come on now, let's all pull together, become a family, and make this show a hit."

It only took a moment, and then there were shrieks of laughter from everyone, including the stagehands. They all crowded around me, raining kisses on my cheeks. The men, the women, and the children were all kissing me, tears of laughter streaming down their faces.

Michael Gordon made a speech. "Thanks, Eddie. We needed that. Arguments onstage have been going on since time immemorial. But you broke the spell with your comedy relief, and now we will be all the better for it. Thanks, Eddie." And with that he kissed me on the forehead. Sheepishly I went to lunch, vowing not to open my amateur mouth again.

At this time, I received a letter from a fine actor friend of mine, Harold Gary. Whenever I needed solid theatrical advice, I usually turned to the sagacious Harold, and he never let me down. Some months prior to our rehearsals, I had asked Harold to read *The Family Way* and let me know his feelings. I read Harold's letter, thought it was interesting criticism, and put it in my coat pocket. Whatever Harold had to say, good, bad, or indifferent, I was already committed to *The Family Way*. There could be no turning back.

The rehearsals went relatively well, and I noticed that each time Leonard Sillman told someone about the play, he showed more excitement and enthusiasm than the last time. Could it be? Did we have a hit on our hands? Leonard said so and he should know. He'd been to the well often enough. I held back my enthusiasm. *I'll play it cool,* I thought.

There were five children with the show, Michael Kearney, Christopher Man, their two understudies, and my associate producer, Peter White. Try as I may, I couldn't keep my hands off of these five kids. I sort of adopted them, hovered over them, scolded them, and loved them, but, more important, I cared for them.

Once I noticed that nine-year-old Christopher Man looked unusually pale and thin and was yawning. Upon questioning him, I found out that he had to get up earlier than usual to pay his mother's electric bill. A nine-year-old having to pay an electric bill? Where was his mother? "She didn't come home last night." What did he have for breakfast? "A Nedick's hot dog and an orange drink." (Shades of the Hotel St. Moritz.)

I hugged the kid and called a huddle with Collin Wilcox and Martha Greenhouse. I asked them to watch over the boy and please, not send Christopher on errands for coffee and sandwiches. After all, he was one of our leading actors, child or not.

Little by little, I had learned that Christopher Man's mother was a beautiful young woman, currently separated from Christopher's father, a comedian-actor then touring Australia. I tried hard not to make a judgment, but it was a losing battle. I remembered my divorce case, when someone had mentioned that "fathers are secondary parents." Bullshit, horsefeathers, and poppycock!

Off the show went to Philadelphia for more rehearsals; it

229

was scheduled for a January 2 opening at the Walnut Street Theater, the oldest active theater in the United States. The cast mostly stayed at the Bellevue Stratford Hotel, with some members staying at the Benjamin Franklin. Each day, I noticed the show getting tighter and tighter and really taking form. Even though the food in Philadelphia was bad to lousy, except for a place called Frankie Bradley's, I was happy. I was part of a future Broadway show, Christmas 1964 was almost upon us, and my precious son was with me. My heart swelled with thankfulness, and I said prayers every night just to keep the momentum going.

With the holidays upon us, although there were Christmas and New Year's parties for the cast, I threw special parties for all the children. I invited the parents, too, serving champagne and food, and each child received an electric toy, handed out by my son, Peter the magnificent. At the end of the evening, Peter tried to collect all of the toys, for safekeeping, he said, but I told him the toys belonged to the children to keep.

It was at one of these parties that Christopher Man's young mother walked in. I could see how any guy, myself included, could be physically attracted to her. She had on a short, dark dress with sexy sheer black stockings, and she was quite attractive. I was respectful and after a few moments she left Christopher in my care, saying she had a date.

Enter Collin Wilcox. Backstage I began to notice that Collin and her actor-husband, Geoffrey Horne, who had starred in the film *The Bridge on the River Kwai,* were paying more and more attention to Christopher. After rehearsals, they invariably left together, and Collin and Geoffrey, I felt, were surely filling a void sorely lacking in Christopher Man's young life.

New Year's Eve I threw another party for the children, with ginger ale for champagne, and then New Year's Day, we all went out to watch the fabulous Mummers parade, Peter included, and I have wonderful super-8 movies to relive those memorable moments.

New Year's afternoon, word got around that Collin Wilcox was again peeved with our director, Michael Gordon. Claiming she was sick, she emphatically stated she "could not go on." Panic struck my heart. We were supposed to open in just one more day. The production staff called nervous meetings, and we all ran in different directions but resolved nothing.

Finally Field Marshall Leonard Sillman barked out orders. According to Equity rules, the producer has the right to accompany a doctor to examine and question an actor who claims they are too ill to go on, to perform. This information was transmitted to Collin Wilcox at her Benjamin Franklin Hotel field headquarters. A truce was declared for a few hours, and then an honor guard, in the person of Geoffrey Horne, Ms. Wilcox's husband, delivered her ultimatum to our command headquarters at the Bellevue Stratford Hotel.

"Collin Wilcox will allow no one to enter her room, especially and specifically Leonard Sillman, except for the person of Eddie White." A cheer went up from the production staff and actors. "Go to it, Eddie. You can straighten this mess out." I heard the drums roll and the trumpets blare as my commander, Leonard Sillman, gave me some last-minute instructions. Then he gave me a French kiss, on both cheeks, which made me uncomfortable, to say the least.

Bewildered, I trekked over to the Benjamin Franklin Hotel accompanied by a small horde of actors and production people. I made up my mind to play it by ear and to be myself, no matter how forceful Leonard had told me to be. *A woman is a fragile thing*, I thought, *especially an actress*.

Geoffrey Horne escorted me up in the elevator and left me at the door to their apartment, which was slightly ajar. I cleared my throat, straightened my tie, and gently knocked on the door. No answer. I knocked again and then entered a dark living room. I could see a dim light in the bedroom and called out, "Collin, darling, it's me, Eddie White." Upon entering the bedroom, I could sense I was in the presence of some great personage. There was almost a religious aura filling the room.

There was frail Collin Wilcox sitting up in bed, with not a blanket or a pillow with the slightest ruffle or crease. It was Collin's supreme moment, her greatest scene. Her face and lips were chalk white, such as those of a geisha girl or Kabuki player. It was as if Collin were trying to steal a scene from Bette Davis's "Queen Elizabeth" movie. I was mesmerized and truly fascinated.

I repeated, "Collin, darling, it's me." Collin extended a limp, fragile hand, and the bed was so low I had to kneel in order to

231

touch it. I felt like I was being knighted. Collin still hadn't opened her eyes. Again I cleared my throat. "Collin, I don't want to disturb you, but Leonard wanted me to look in on you."

Finally she opened her eyes. "Darling, how good of you to come. Do sit down." I looked around, but there wasn't a chair available. I couldn't help but notice how antiseptic and clean the room appeared, with not a speck of dust and not an object out of place. Again "Darling" and Collin started to cough. (In show business, everyone is called "Darling.")

"Darling, I haven't been myself lately. I've never really been strong, but lately . . . " and she turned her head away from me. I mumbled something about not wanting to tire her any further, and Collin again extended her hand, with her face still turned away from me. I knelt and kissed her hand and knew that this was my moment, my scene, my big speech. I said, "God bless you, dear child. I believe in you, Collin. I love you." Then I started to leave. As I entered the dark parlor, I could hear Collin's last words to me. "Darling, if I make opening night, it will be mainly because of you."

I felt I did it in one take. I was concerned, I was brief, and I didn't blow my lines. Oh, well, I did the best I could. I returned to the lobby, where the cast and crew hit me with questions from all sides. Finally Martha Greenhouse asked, "What did she look like?" I looked at Martha, and everyone grew quiet and tense for my answer. Slowly and with much thought I replied, "She looked like George Arliss in his great death scene in *The Man Who Played God*."

This was all a tempest in a teapot in Philadelphia, because Collin Wilcox, the trouper, was there on opening night and did a great show. It was standing room only in Philly, and we all felt the show was taking shape and had all the earmarks of a hit. We thought of extending our stay in the City of Brotherly Love, but then decided on storming the bastions of Broadway.

Every night I would sit in the back of the theater with the author, Ben Starr, and every night he would clock the laughs. One night it was 152 laughs, the next 157 laughs. I remember when we hit 165 laughs, we folded our tent and headed for West 45th Street, New York City, the Lyceum Theater, Broadway.

It was exciting to be back in New York. My friends received me as a conquering hero. From the audience reaction to our Philadelphia tryout to our New York City previews, it looked like *The Family Way* was a hit. Author Ben Starr clocked three more laughs, and the entire cast was now a tight, cohesive unit. Everyone was "Darling" to each other, and Collin Wilcox had made her peace with director Michael Gordon.

At seven o'clock sharp, the evening of January 13, 1965, the curtain ran up on *The Family Way*. All my friends, family, and well-wishers and my son were in the audience in addition to all the drama critics. I was in a corner backstage as the lights dimmed in the Lyceum. I wanted to be alone at this moment. As the lights faded, I found my hands folded in prayer. I was asking God if he could spare a moment and gaze kindly on our theatrical endeavor.

Then I heard voices and Act One had commenced. I was frozen rigid. Try as I might, I couldn't unclasp my hands. The cast was stiff with their lines. The first laughs weren't as loud or as numerous as they should be, and they came late. If there is anything I truly understand, it is comedy, and Jack Kelly and Collin Wilcox's timing was a little off. *Nerves*, I thought. Still I couldn't unclasp my hands.

I don't know how long I remained in that corner, but I remember thinking or hoping it was me who was off. I was tense, maybe too tense, and possibly I saw or heard things that the audience did not. Sometimes this is called being paranoid. Well, opening night of *The Family Way*, possibly I had a most severe attack of paranoia.

Act One, curtain down, I went out the backstage entrance to get a breath of fresh air. There was little nine-year-old Christopher Man with a look of anxiety on his face and tears in his eyes. After much affectionate prodding, I finally wheedled the story out of him. His father, who was at this moment touring the Australian provinces with a show, hadn't sent Christopher a congratulatory opening-night telegram. I told him it was still early, and I was sure the telegram would arrive eventually (even if I had to send it myself).

Arms around this little man, I walked Christopher back to

his dressing room and consulted with the cast mother, Martha Greenhouse. Not having much time to talk to me, she quickly informed me not to get involved. If I sent the telegram and the boy found out, the ramifications could be disastrous. With a heavy and somewhat chicken heart, I agreed.

After the second act, I had to go through the process again. The boy was inconsolable. Not only did I have the show to worry about, but now Christopher was on my mind. I knew Collin Wilcox loved the boy, but I was afraid to tell her the story at this moment for fear of hurting her performance. The show must go on, you know.

During Acts Two and Three, I still had the feeling that the entire cast, the entire show, was a beat off. It was if someone had slowed down the camera of life. In Philadelphia, the laughs came faster; they were more impromptu, more devil-may-care. This terribly important evening, almost every pertinent scene was slightly forced, almost in slow motion. I hoped it was my imagination.

The final curtain came down to thunderous applause, and everyone embraced each other. Somehow I couldn't get into the prevailing mood. I was like a high roller gambler; I wanted to see the chips stacked in front of me. I shook hands with the investors and my friends with a frozen smile on my face. I went backstage and kissed all the children and the rest of the cast, still in a zombielike state.

It was prearranged that after our premiere show, we, the investors, friends, and cast, would all meet at the famed Sardi's Restaurant. This was an opening-night ritual, and we were following in true theatrical tradition. Then, in New York City, evening papers were still not out, so the investors and cast were invited to Leonard Sillman's East 72nd Street townhouse for a buffet dinner and to await whatever tidings the critics had for *The Family Way*.

As I entered Sardi's, a swarm of well-wishers devoured me. Like in a Fellini movie, it was one unrecognizable face after another, strange people pumping my hand and kissing me. Only one person stood out as huge as life and still does in my memory of flashbacks.

A handsome middle-aged women, coiffed and dressed to the nines and undoubtedly well to do, embraced me like the Queen

Mother bestowing an award. She kissed me on the forehead and said, "Well, Eddie, you did it again!" I was whisked into the dining room of Sardi's and remember thinking, *Who was that strikingly elegant woman?* I had never seen that lady before and never saw her again.

I walked part of the way to Leonard Sillman's house, to meditate and to take a few breaths of fresh air. This night was moving too quickly for me; there was much too much excitement, so much at stake for me. I dare not allow myself to think the show was the hit all the backslappers were proclaiming. *Even if the show was a "smash," did I want all this heavy bullshit in my life?* I asked myself that musical question.

Even the bearded cabbie taking me to Leonard's townhouse got into the act. I recognized him as an actor whom I had seen performing at Freedomland, doing a scene from *Man of La Mancha.* I told him my son had loved his performance. No sooner did I say that, when he launched into a heavy Shakespearean soliloquy, interrupted by another cab making a turn from our right side and cutting us off. My cab driver didn't miss a beat. He rolled down his window, looked back at me, and said, "Excuse me." Then to the other cab he screamed, "You hard-on!" And he finished his soliloquy. *Only in New York City,* I thought.

When I arrived at Leonard Sillman's townhouse, Ruth, his kind and genial maid, was busy serving people from a hot buffet table. I was too nervous and excited to eat, just this one time in my life, and walked around waiting on my group of investors, who were also my dearest friends. I remember I was standing at the buffet table with my air-force buddy Art Stringari when Leonard Sillman, in a husky stage whisper, said, "Get 'em out of here. The show is a flop! A disaster! Get 'em out of my house."

I looked Leonard Sillman right in the eyes and told him, "No way." I had heard Leonard could be rude and cruel, but I also knew there was another side to him, too. I said, "Leonard, if you hurt me or my friends now, this way, I'll never forgive you." Leonard, a little on the effeminate side in his personal life, looked at me and said, "All right, dear boy. I'm going upstairs; I'm retiring for the night." I watched him shuffle up the stairs, a disappointed, stooped, aging theatrical producer, and felt sadness for him. The best of Leonard Sillman, his glory days, were well behind him.

But he had done it all. He showed them. Maybe Leonard had gone to the well once too often.

Closing notice had gone up on the bulletin board backstage at the Lyceum before we even opened. Every show does this as a precaution, so as to protect their bonds posted with the various theatrical unions. If the show is a hit or the producers wish to fight the critics and make a "run for it," the closing notice can always be removed. But a show that doesn't have a prayer protects union bonds by posting a closing obituary and usually uses said bond money to pay off any and all outstanding bills the show may have incurred.

The critics blistered *The Family Way*. The show ran for five performances, and although the cast got its act together and the laughs flowed more freely with each performance, it was too little and much too late. Another show that opened that same evening, *Kelly*, a musical with a huge budget, actually closed their opening night. One other show that opened the same season and was rumored to be a weak show was a smash hit. It was *Any Wednesday*, starring Sandy Dennis.

A few critics actually liked *The Family Way* and a few thought the show had possibilities, but the "big seven," the important New York City newspaper critics, panned the show. To a critic, they especially mentioned and disliked one crucial scene. That was when divorced actress Collin Wilcox's son, desiring a father so intensely, hands out her eight by-ten glossy theatrical pictures to whomever he considers prospective fathers. All the critics thought the boy was procuring or pandering for his mother. Timing. A year later, they were using four-letter words and much more sexually involved situations in Broadway shows. It was bad timing for *The Family Way*.

As director Michael Gordon was taking his leave, to return to California and a drama professorship at UCLA, he said to me, "Eddie, you were the only bright light associated with this entire production." Mr. Gordon may have said that to be nice to me or to lessen the sadness very obvious on my face and in my eyes, but those kind words still ring in my ears to this day. My little dream world was shattering, falling apart. I was drowning in my own self-pity, at that moment, and Michael Gordon gave me the feeling that I had contributed something worthwhile to our show.

His words rekindled the dream and the vision in my heart, and for that and his warm friendship that followed through succeeding years I thank him.

Back again to the drawing board. I didn't want to go back to being a full-time songwriter, although my partner Mack Wolfson suggested it many times. I felt that acid rock, punk rock, disco, and other new musical forms were taking their hold on the industry, and our type of songwriting was still the good old-fashioned melody and lyric. Mack still felt that Burt Bacharach and Hal David were lucky, that we were as good a songwriting team as they were, better, but they had gotten the breaks. Go tell a guy you love, "So what?" I couldn't hurt Mack. Best to leave him with his dreams. I had mine.

Around this time of soul searching, meditating, and taking stock of myself, the business, the past, and the future, word got back to me that little Christopher Man had been legally adopted by Collin Wilcox and Geoffrey Horne. God acts in mysterious ways. I like to think, in retrospect, that this is why we all got together under the aegis of *The Family Way*. This was fantastic! Little Chris had a full-time mommy and daddy finally.

That evening, in a mellow and melancholy mood, I thought about everyone connected with the show, the circumstances, the dialogues, the different personalities, what could or might have been, and suddenly I remembered Harold Gary's letter. I dug it out, crawled into bed, and read.

Ed,
    I think this is one of the most inept plays I've ever read. It's witless, vulgar, the situation and dialogue trite and banal—the Jewish woman a tried stale cliché—and to have the plot hinge on a 10 year old boy innocently or otherwise acting as a procurer for his mother is obscene and dramatically invalid—and who ever heard of an agent named "Brennan"?—and what's most apocryphal is that an "agent" has romantic urges—no audience would believe it! I'd be less than the friend I am to you if I did not urge you to have nothing to do with it.

Hal

Good old Harold. He was always a joker, a real funny guy. Anyway, his letter arrived a few days too late, if I can recall. Good old Harold. I remembered he was a boxer in his youth. My pal Harold never could pull his punches.

For the first time in a long while, time was mine. I no longer had the office staff to worry about; I wasn't committed to go anywhere overseas; my nine rooms of offices were more than paid for, by the Moss Hart estate and my other subtenants; I had enough money to live on, provided I didn't go crazy, and I felt this extreme feeling of exhilaration. I was a free man—no pressures, no one pulling me in any direction, nothing to be concerned with but my son and myself. And possibly my weight. The good living in Japan had taken its toll. The smallest, skinniest kid in the orphanage was turning into a fatso.

So I went shopping for a gym. One evening at Patsy's Italian restaurant, Tony Corrado introduced me to U.S. Congressman Victor Anfuso. Congressman Anfuso liked my jokes that night and asked me to join his staff, to possibly write a campaign song for him and to infuse his speeches with a little humor. Shades of the past, when I wrote the speeches for a few of my Air-force commanding officers.

At one of Congressman Anfuso's political meetings, I sat next to a very old gentleman, Mr. Morris Morgenstern, a tremendously wealthy real-estate operator. Mr. Morgenstern must have been in his eighties then, but he was light of heart and had a wonderful sense of humor. Morris—he insisted I call him that,—suggested I be his guest at the Business Men's Club, a private health club with an entire floor situated in the West Side YMCA. Morris was a sponsor, a contributor, and a member of the BMC's board of directors.

I went there that evening and haven't regretted it since. I've been a member for over twenty years, and currently I am a member of the board of directors. Physically, the club has done me a lot of good, and the friendships I have made have endured through the years. Dr. Milton Brothers and I immediately became fast friends. Milton, his wife, Dr. Joyce Brothers, and I get together for dinner on occasion. Milton and I are both Rumanians, so it's usually Rumanian food. We wait until the heartburn wears off before we ritually meet again. Sometimes Milt's patients bring him *ikra*, a homemade Rumanian dish containing caviar, which he kindly shares with me.

Milton Brothers has one of those way-out of-the-way, fantastic senses of humor, intertwined with his also being a practical joker. Milt's a proctologist and it's not beyond him to take a Polaroid picture of a pal's ass while said pal is in a compromising position. Or, with the proctoscope in place and said pal rigid with apprehension, Milt might have a phony radio announcer state that "the building must be cleared immediately because of a bomb scare." Or, proctoscope still intact, this sixth Marx brother might chat with you, all the time holding a huge phallic symbol. Each time I visit my pal Dr. Milton Brothers for an examination, I never leave his office; I escape.

Then there are actors Harvey Keitel, Jerry Stiller, Joe Pesci, Peter Boyle, Martin Balsam, Elliot Gould, and many others who belong to the Business Men's Club. In the literary and show field, there's Joe (*Catch 22*) Heller, Joe (*Fiddler on the Roof*) Stein, Israel (*Author, Author*) Horvitz, and Charles (*Annie*) Strauss, just to mention a few. In radio and TV, we have CBS's Jim Jensen, ABC's Bill Beutel, Frank Gifford, and Joel Siegel, and WNEW's Ted Brown. Producer Joe Beruh and director Arthur Penn are seen on occasion jogging or swimming at the BMC, and also restaurateur–Mets baseball star Rusty Staub. CBS's Dan Rather joined up and paid his dues, but then when he replaced Walter Cronkite, we never saw him again. Last but not least is my favorite personality at our humble athletic club, "Jumping" Joe Bowden, a spry young man in his mideighties who shows up every morning, rain or shine, dons his sweatsuit and sneakers, and then proceeds to take a nap. Nappy-poo finished, Joe-Joe showers and then goes home. This procedure has kept Joe Bowden, sometimes known as America's Sphinx, in great physical shape. The last time Joe was heard to speak was at the outset of the 1964 blackout, when he uttered these immortal words: "Who did that?"

I had been friendly with Robert Duvall, the motion-picture actor, and whenever Bobby felt the need to get in shape, for a forthcoming film or a tennis tournament, he would be my guest at the BMC. The renowned playwright and author, Mr. Paddy

Chayefsky, had his locker close to mine, and we too became fast friends. Paul Simon, the composer par excellence, had his locker in the next aisle.

Being on the board of directors and possibly because of my show-business affiliation, I was assigned the task of organizing most of the social activities of the BMC. I had to buy the food for the collations, hire the entertainment for the dinner parties, and generally act as host and master of ceremonies for most of said functions. Believe it or not, the most satisfaction I received from these activities was when I was allowed to write and read the benediction or prayers preceding each affair. I know somewhere in me there's a trace of a preacher man. And yet I intensely dislike most of the "Pray T.V." ministers I've seen. I think I would like to preach mostly the brotherhood or sisterhood of men and women everywhere. No boundaries, no guidelines, no divisions, none of the separations that most religious instill. Just one people under one God. Can it be done? Man, wouldn't that be something. Hallelujah and amen!

When time hung heavy at the office and the conversations began to repeat themselves and there was a lull in the air and I just had to get away from it all, the Business Men's Club was a haven or heavenly escape. After a swim and/or jog of a couple of miles, I would lift a couple of weights, shower, go to the steam room, shower again, cool off in the lounge, and then usually take a coffee break in the local luncheonette with the very stimulating Paddy Chayefsky. Many times I thought how lucky I was to know such interesting people, especially Paddy. We never but never got together that we didn't argue over something, but I never left him that I wasn't stimulated, enlightened, or the better for the presence of his company. But argue we did; sometimes I merely fought just for the right to express an opinion. Then Paddy would scream at me, "Go ahead, shoot, let's hear it, Voltaire," and I would forget what it was I wanted to say. Paddy had that soothing, calming effect on some people. Paddy's favorite expression to me, usually in front of someone like Bob Fosse or the like would be "Go ahead, Eddie; tell them that joke you always fuck up!" I usually followed that line by verbally falling on my ass.

The next couple of years I spent supervising my offices and the copyrights for songs that Mack Wolfson and I wrote and the small music catalogues I published. Lunches were usually spent at the Carneigie Delicatessen with Paddy or Henny Youngman or actor Paul Sorvino or a raft of Broadway characters that I wouldn't trade for all the royalty in the world. Early evening, it was off to the Business Men's Club, and then dinner was either in a restaurant or at my home. I could cook up a mean chicken or beef teriyaki with my own secret sauce concoction. Weekends, it was off to the BMC in the morning for a brisk workout and then the afternoon rituals of watching the baseball or football games with Paddy Chayefsky. Our arguments were lengthy, loud, and legendary. I wish I had taped some of them, to warm the cockles of my heart as I slowly walk into the fading sunset.

My offices were usually alive with the sound of music and talk of the boxing world, the theater, or independent film production. Songwriter Paul Vance was either rehearsing Johnny Mathis or some up-and-coming vocalist.

Rocky Graziano had the run of the offices, and he invariably showed up with the likes of Rocky Marciano, Jake La Motta, Willie Pep, Jersey Joe Wolcott, Archie Moore, Sandy Saddler, Joey Giardello, and so on. One of the likable fellows that Rocky brought around was Pete Savage, an ex-boxer whose real name was Petrella. Pete and I became real friendly right off the bat, as we had a lot in common. Pete liked to write, to act, and on occasion, when he could raise the money, to produce a low-budget film. Many an evening we spent together, exchanging ideas, dreaming about the future, and talking about opening a film production office as partners. Pete was one of those guys who dreamed long and hard, and to the surprise of many, most of his dreams came true.

Pete told me about a book he was writing. It was about himself but mostly about Jake La Motta. It was titled *The Raging Bull*. I liked the idea immensely, although I wasn't too crazy over the likes of Jake La Motta. We had a personality clash right from the start. The way he took over my offices, the phones, and conversations annoyed me. I tried to hide my feelings about Jake from Pete and Rocky Graziano as best I could. I later found out that neither one of them had any good feeling toward Jake but that Pete Savage stuck their association out because of the book.

Once when I had an attack of Bell's palsy (a minor stroke),

241

my Detroit friends Art Stringari and Harold "Chuck" Johns sent me down to the Bahia Mar Yacht Club in Florida to recuperate on Chuck's boat, the *Patsy Anne*. I was sick as you can get, with my face all contorted and twisted. While down there, terribly incapacitated, I heard that Jake La Motta, who then owned a bar down in Fort Lauderdale, had been arrested and convicted of procuring for a sixteen-year-old girl.

I further learned that Jake actually was put on a chain gang, fixing roads. Sick as I was, I called New York to inform Pete Savage, Rocky Graziano, Tony Corrado, and a few others that I would go to Jake's aid. I wanted to get some of my Floridian friends and contacts to help get Jake out of this mess—this in spite of the fact that I could hardly stomach the guy. Only Tony Corrado, in no uncertain manner and voice, informed me to mind my own business, take care of my health, and forget this sudden urge to be a dogooder. His final words were that Jake would eventually kick me in the ass so hard I would never forget it.

Then years later, when Madison Square Garden honored Sugar Ray Robinson, they brought in name fighters from all over the world, fighters who helped make the Sugar Man the legend he is. Everyone was mentioned except Jake La Motta. Say what you will, Jake may be a bastard in his personal life, but he was an exceptionally great fighting machine.

That week I met genial Johnny Addy, Madison Square Garden's boxing announcer, at Patsy's restaurant. I told him about Jake, and he agreed that this wasn't fair to Jake and the fight fans. I asked Johnny if I could get Jake La Motta to join me at ringside that night, would he have the guts to introduce him in the ring. He thought for a moment, and then he said, "It'll bring the house down!"

Tony Corrado thought it wasn't such a good idea. The public was still incensed over Jake's testimony before the Kefauver committee, saying that he had taken a "dive" in the Billy Fox fight. Jake was hardly liked by anyone, but I thought it would be sportsmanlike to have him introduced in the ring the night they honored Robinson. After all, they had fought six ferocious bouts, with Robinson winning five times, the last fight by a knockout.

I got three ringside tickets for the memorable evening and breathlessly awaited the arrival of Pete Savage and Jake La Motta.

Twice I ran to the apron of the ring and winked at Johnny Addy, who winked back. I was supposed to inform Johnny when big, bad Jake arrived. Pete showed up and said that Jake had cold feet but that he thought he would show. The festivities started and my head looked like it was a swivel ball; I kept twisting and turning looking for Jake. Finally, when Johnny Addy announced Randy Turpin, I knew that Robinson would be announced next. Jake never showed. After that, Jack never mentioned the Sugar Ray Robinson evening and neither did I. I just shook my head for months.

Heavyweight champ Rocky Marciano hung around the offices for years. Sometimes, when I was ready to lock up and leave for dinner, Big Rocky, as we called him, would tell me he was coming back that night to sleep in the offices. That was okay with me, but he sometimes showed up with guys he collected in bars. A couple of times I had strange-looking characters sleeping on my office carpet whom Big Rocky couldn't remember bringing there.It was weird, but I never really got nipped off bad. The worst it cost me was a couple of overcoats for guys who were real down on their luck. Big Rocky always apologized, but then late at night he would sometimes show up with guys whose names he couldn't recall. Big, good-natured champ Rocky Marciano could handle a left hook but never a soft touch. God love him.

One month, the office phone bills were way out of line. Someone was making out-of-town calls without mentioning it to me. I suspected Jake La Motta and called him on it. In discussing the matter, Pete Savage came to Jake's aid and one word led to another. I finally asked Jake to leave and forget about coming back. Pete said that if Jake left, he was leaving, too. Rocky Graziano heard and saw what was taking place and winked at me and said, "I guess you mean you want me to leave, too" and hurriedly ushered Pete and Jake out of the offices.

Of course I didn't mean for Rocky to leave, or for that matter Pete, but so be it. Rocky came back within an hour and told me that I was better off and now maybe I could get some work done. Pete Savage didn't speak to me for close to ten years, and when we did meet on occasion at social affairs, he shook his fist at me. The one big drawback Pete Savage suffered from was his driving desire to maintain a tough-guy, macho image. He always talked about busting guys up and "getting even" for past ingratitudes and slurs, mostly imagined. But we who really knew Pete, his family and close friends, saw through this facade and indulged the guy by allowing him to blow off steam. Ten years later, Pete Savage and I became the best of friends again and were quite inseparable.

Almost every out-of-work singer or comic would drop by the offices from time to time. The huge kitchen always had coffee brewing, and I left ham, cheese, bread, and milk in the refrigerator at my own risk. It was love, fun, and games, and I reveled in the affection and attention afforded me, real or not. With theatrical people, only your hairdresser or barber is sure. Knowing this, I still enjoyed every moment of those hectic years.

My close friend Ralph Young, who had threatened many times to quite show biz, was now climbing the musical ladder of success as part of the theatrical team of Sandler and Young. Al Gallico, another of my bosom buddies, was now working closely with Tammy Wynette, George Jones, Lynn Anderson, Joe Stampley, and the rest of the Nashville scene. Al was becoming known as Mister Country Music. Not bad for a poor Italian guy from Brooklyn. He published "The Most Beautiful Girl in the World," which was number one all over the world. The song was written by two of my friends, Billy "The Kid" Sherill and Norris "Norro" Wilson. Many's the time I cooked chicken teriyaki for the Nashville "kids," but I told them the food was Deep South Japanese.

Paul Vance was already doing well with his songs "Catch a Falling Star" And "Itsy Bitsy Teenie Weenie Yellow Polka-Dot Bikini" and was investing his money in training horses and pacers, where he did equally as well.

Eddie Wachtel and Herbie Goldsmith had formed an outfit called Europecraft Imports to bring in sport clothes. They put out a jacket called "Members Only," and the rest is clothing history.

Rocky Graziano's life story had been made into a film with Paul Newman, and with his many commercials, Rocky was now known as Mister T.V.

It seemed like all my friends, as we grew older, were moving up the ladder of success. Time hung heavy. I thought of bringing

244

a big, boisterous, buxom extravaganza to Japan, called Blondes U.S.A. That would get those Japanese guys; they loved tall blondes from Norway and Sweden.

Then I thought of adapting *Ikiru*, the sad film I loved so much, the very film that inspired me to drop my job and take off for Japan. I could write *Ikiru* as a play and present it on Broadway. I would bring it up to date, make it more contemporary, with a setting possibly in a small New England town.

I started reading plays again, but none of them had the "look" I was looking for. I loved *The Subject Was Roses*, a low-budget, small-cast, one-set play that made it on Broadway. For months I read everything I could get my hands on. Nothing excited me.

For the record, all the plays I did pass up never made it to Broadway or else failed miserably once they got there. I met with Dore Schary, former head of M.G.M Films, who was involved with a future Broadway vehicle, *The Zulu and the Zada*. It was cute, from a short story, but once you knew the idea, the play went nowhere. To be fair, the odds against coming up with a Broadway hit are quite high.

Someone suggested I produce a revival, *The Front Page, Tobacco Road, Abie's Irish Rose* as a musical, or a contemporary *Julius Caesar* set in Chicago with gangsters.

I actually met with the great Darryl Zanuck to discuss doing a musical of one of Twentieth Century–Fox's former hits, *Cheaper by the Dozen*. I had read the book and liked it, but thought that I would only have to deal with the author. I thought wrong. After a few meetings with Mr. Zanuck, I came away with an agreement that was deemed to be worthless. For allowing me to produce *Cheaper by the Dozen*, which still had to be written, book and music, I would practically have to pay Twentieth Century for the privilege. Thanks but no thanks.

Then producer Don Saxon auditioned a musical for me based on the life of New York's former colorful mayor, dapper Jimmy Walker. Although I liked some of the songs, I remember I didn't care much for the movie, based on the same story and starring Bob Hope. Jack L. Warner, the scion of the Warner Brothers film family, eventually lost $500,000 as an initial investment in *Jimmy*, with a further investment of $450,000. Close to a million-dollar fiasco. The show had one or two good songs and a fine, believable performance by Frank Gorshin portraying Jimmy Walker, but hardly anything else.

There were other shows I read and listened to, but nothing raised the adrenalin like I had hoped. Revivals were out. How could I expect to make a name for myself based on someone else's former hit? Sooner or later, that lucky script would plop on my desk.

There was talk about a play, *Summertree*, which had just closed sold out every night. I was assured this wasn't a revival, that the play was still fresh in everyone's mind. I was also told that the reason *Summertree* closed at Lincoln Center was because it was only booked for a "Limited run" and the theater was needed for something else.

I read the script, written by Ron Cowan, a twenty-one–year–old author, and liked it. The story was about a sensitive, young musician who utterly abhorred violence but reluctantly went to Viet Nam to make his father proud. The boy lies wounded and dying under a tree, similar to the "summertree" in his own back-yard at home, and laments the past lack of communication between his father and himself that led to this final apocalyptical predicament. The play was so timely; the Viet Nam War was still raging, and the play echoed my personal sentiments.

I read the play again and again one evening and then fell asleep. Sometime in the middle of the night, I awoke with a start and the name Harold on my lips. That's it! My rabbit's foot, Harold Gary. I had to write Harold, who was then appearing in Arthur Miller's *The Price* in England and send him the script of *Summertree*, which I did.

More living with the script and waiting for word from Harold. My inner voice told me the play was well written, with tight, crisp dialogue, the message loud and clear, but a tearjerker of the first order. Upon checking as to the origin of *Summertree*, I found out the play had actually been rewritten many times, restructured and worked on, and had been performed originally at The Eugene O'Neill Theater workshop in Massachusetts.

Every time I met someone who knew about the play from its inception, they would mention that they had a hand in the writing of *Summertree*. I thought this was kind of odd until I met the young author, Ron Cowan. At first, he charmed me with his youthful enthusiasm to get the play produced again. But he was overly polite, cooperative but distant.

When word arrived from Harold Gary that he insisted I produce this "Lovely, sensitive play," I broke my neck to get all the necessary legal papers squared away. Harold, while appearing at the Duke of York's Theater in London in *The Price*, had many fellow actors visit him backstage—Ralph Richardson, Lawrence Oliver, Janet Suzmon, Ron Moody, Rex Harrison, and many others. One evening, Mr. Charlie Chaplin came backstage, along with his wife, Oona, and daughter Victoria. While Harold was removing his makeup and getting dressed, Mr. Chaplin glanced at a few pages of the *Summertree* script lying on a table. After some moments, this comedic genius, who entertained every nation on earth for over sixty years, said, "This is a very beautiful, poetic play." That, coupled with Harold's own advice and feeling, was the sign I was looking for.

The moment we were in production, Mr. Ron Cowan became more distant, fresh, patronizing, and uncooperative. Our director, Steve Glassman, who was also in his early twenties, more than made up for Ron Cowan's lack of communication. Steve was a piller of strength and common sense, young as he was, and his directorial taste helped make the day. I'm sorry to say, at one point during rehearsal, I made the comment that I doubted if Ron Cowan would ever again write a deep, meaningful play. I like young people and get along with them, but something in Ron Cowan's distant background was eating at his emotional insides. I'm also sorry to report that my thoughts were most prophetic.

Our production of *Summertree* opened at the Players Theater in Greenwich Village on December 23, 1969, to unanimous good-to-rave reviews. Clive Barnes of the *New York Times* wrote that *Summertree* remained "immeasurably touching; it really must be seen. I think it may very well speak for a generation." I knew we had a hit when I was told that Rocky Graziano stayed awake, a first, for the entire three acts. He came to me after the premiere and sheepishly said, "Hey, I liked it." No producer could ask for a greater plaudit than that.

I also knew we were in for a good theatrical run when after lingering at the cast party until the wee hours of the morning, I instinctively walked past the theater again. There was a woman sitting in a chauffered automobile waiting for the box office to open in the morning. Upon questioning her, I found out that she had heard about the play on the radio and the story of *Summertree* smacked of her own problem with her son. She needed tickets for her entire family.

Things ran smoothly with the cast and the play those first few weeks, while we were selling out each night. Then on occasion we would run into a heavy snowstorm and the cancellations would come in. It was on these nights, when the house was less than full, that we suspected there might be a little hanky-panky going on in the box office. The nightly and weekly money take did not add up properly. Something was fishy, not in Denmark but in Greenwich Village.

One of my associates, the same one who couldn't or wouldn't get along with Leonard Sillman when we produced *The Family Way*, was now arguing with the owners of the theater, the box office, our production staff, and some members of our cast. Maybe this was a small conspiracy to get back at the producers.

We decided to take turns at clocking the people buying tickets against those actually in the theater. Then we hired people to check for us, then went back to our actually doing the clocking ourselves. When it was my turn, I used to get the same nervous upset stomach I got when I had to return to the orphan asylum as a child after visiting my mother on a Sunday. *This is show business? This is petty shit!* I thought. It disgusted me and I couldn't wait to be uninvolved with everyone concerned.

After a few months of ups and downs at the box office, our funds were becoming depleted. *Summertree* was an artistic hit, but financially it was a struggle. The snowstorms were more numerous, and each week we just about met our payroll.

At this time, Columbia Pictures began publicizing Kirk Douglas's Bryna Productions's forthcoming film of *Summertree*, starring his son Michael and Brenda Vaccaro. Why not go to Columbia Pictures for additional financing to keep the play alive and thus help to further publicize the film? My associates laughed at me for being so naive.

At the Columbia Pictures meeting, I made my little spiel, giving them my idea to help publicize the film and my plea for funds. The Nuremburg jury looked at me. It was all quiet on the

Western front. Finally their leader spoke. "Okay. We'll give you $10,000, but it must be spent through our publicity department and only on newspaper ads, radio blurbs, and show posters, and not a red cent more!"

The publicity gave *Summertree* the lift it needed, but still the box office wasn't adding up. Thank God for the free publicity or the show would have closed immediately. Columbia Pictures had given us a chance to catch our breath.

The $10,000 didn't last as long as expected, so I suggested we go back to Columbia's publicity department with another pitch. After I was told I was crazy and more than naive, I called for another meeting.

This time I was really dressed down. "Didn't you hear properly? Not one red cent more!" I left with another $5,000 for our publicity kitty, but I was getting the feeling that the Columbia Picture execs were getting fed up with me. And I was getting fed up with practically having to get down on my knees and sing "Mammy" every time we needed money to keep the show running.

Anthony Newly was assigned to direct the movie of *Summertree* for Kirk Douglas's Bryna Productions. Newley came by one night to see a performance and brought actor Peter Strauss, Charlotte Ford, and six or seven other people with him. A few days later, I received a note stating that he had enjoyed our production immensely, and it had helped him evaluate the future film, and he swore he would stick to the original script as much as possible.

After 184 performances, *Summertree* quietly folded. With all the problems, snowstorms, box-office thievery, artistic and production differences, and actor tantrums—with all the headaches that went into this show—I felt sad when it closed. The feeling lasted for weeks. It's an empty, guilty feeling, as if some member of your family you weren't too fond of died. It was over. They were a part of your life and now it was past history.

11

Circus

1970: Four students killed at Kent State by National Guard; gold falls below thirty-five dollars an ounce; Joe Frazier wins heavyweight championship; Dow Jones below 631.

PETER, MY SON, was eighteen years old now, and this was my opportunity to spend more time with him. We discussed the coming summer—where to go? what to do? I had become quite friendly, at this time, with Jack "Bart Maverick" Kelly, who had appeared in *The Family Way* for me. Jack mentioned he was taking a house out in the Hamptons and encouraged me to do the same. This way, we could pal around together.

After much discussion, I finally decided on an apartment at the Westhampton Bath and Tennis Club, providing they give my son a job as one of their beach boys. It was agreed upon and Peter and I and our chihuahua, Caesar, moved into an apartment directly overlooking the tennis courts. I bought Peter a 1965 Mustang, and we were all set for a happy summer together. As it was, actually, it turned out to be the worst.

Once in a while, I had to borrow Peter's car to go into the city to check on my office, the mail, and my phone service. Each time I left, I noticed Peter had a long, sad face. He was having trouble with the older bigger beach boys picking on him, which didn't happen when I was around. It was the same scene as when he was smaller, when I had to leave him at the ranch upstate. My son wouldn't say anything; he would just look sad, which gave me a heavy heart.

This ominous early Sunday evening of July 12, 1970 at approximately 6:00 P.M., I started to leave for New York City. Peter looked especially sad, so I put off leaving for an hour or two. I tried to cheer my son up, telling him I would surely return by Wednesday afternoon. Finally I was able to get Peter to smile, and around 8:15 P.M., while there was still some light, I left for the city.

I stopped to get a full tank of gas in the town of Westhampton and headed for the Long Island Expressway. At the Riverhead Road, there was a stop sign on the main thoroughfare, with a two-lane highway going in both directions, and not seeing any traffic whatsoever, started across the intersection. Two cars had preceded me, but instead of crossing the road and continuing, one car pulled alongside the other car so that they could chat, necessitating my car still being out on the main road. I blew the horn frantically but neither car moved. By now it was close to 9:00 P.M., twilight but getting dark, and a slight mist falling.

Suddenly, almost out of nowhere, three cars appeared from my right, moving at a rapid pace. I started to pull off the road to the right of the two cars in front of me, but it was too late. All I remember from that moment was a mass of lights, as if I were hit from above by a gigantic UFO, and then I blacked out.

I momentarily awoke in great pain and hearing distant voices. My car was still upright, a few hundred feet off the road on a grassy lane where I had rolled. The voices finally reached me, and I pleaded for someone to please help me out of the car and let me die on the grass. The pain was so intense, I was sure there wasn't any hope for me. A voice answered, saying that no one was allowed to touch me, that help would soon be on the way. Again blackout.

It wasn't my time to leave this earth, because miracle of miracles, a volunteer ambulance, on its way back to its place of origin, happened to pass the scene of my accident. A young reverend happened to be on the ambulance, and he whispered in my ear, "Don't worry; we'll get you to a hospital quickly."

Lying in the ambulance, I kept passing out but again was conscious of voices. I remember calling for my son, and for the first time I felt blood oozing out of my body. The reverend's voice was kind and reassuring as it got dark again.

I awoke in the Central Suffolk Hospital in Riverhead, Long Island, and could faintly see that my clothes were being cut from

251

me with huge scissors. I recall that everyone in the room looked Japanese to me and that the lights were so bright they hurt my eyes.

Again I awoke to my son Peter's voice urging me to hold on and his squeezing my hand. I mumbled some things, and then I awoke all alone in a dimly lit room, coughing and spitting everything out of my stomach.

The next time awoke, I was in another dimly lit room with four other patients and a woman was screaming, "Melissa, don't die. We all love you so much" over and over again. I could just about move my head and glanced to my right. On a highly raised bed, I saw an angel, a beautiful teenage girl. Two doctors came in to consult with the mother, and I got the feeling they held very little hope for this "Sleeping Beauty."

A nurse by the name of MacPherson asked me if I knew my name. I said it was more important that I know her name. She couldn't believe I was making jokes at a time like this, and she asked me if I was hungry. I couldn't think of food and practically fell asleep in the middle of my refusal.

When I awoke, it must have been the middle of the night. I took stock of myself and the rest of the room. I was obviously in the intensive-care unit. To the left of me was a man having alcoholic deliriums, to the right of me was Melissa, and across the room was an old man whose heart was being monitored. I tried to turn towards Melissa's bed, and although my entire body was racked with pain, I now felt a severe, excruciating pain from my chest and right leg.

I remember thinking how nice it would be to die, and then I thought of Peter and told God to forget my last thought. I actually thought, at that moment, that God was making me go through this whole trying experience for a reason. *Possibly to make me slow down in life, possibly to make me a better person?* I wondered. My heart ached, not so much for me but for the beautiful child to my right.

I turned my head slightly, and something possessed me for a moment. I started to speak without knowing what it was I was going to say. "Melissa, you're so beautiful. I know you must be in such pain, but I heard your mother telling you how many people love you and are waiting for you. Try to hold onto life.

252

If you can hear my voice, just move one of your fingers, and this way we can talk to each other." I was sure Melissa was going to move a finger, but she didn't.

The next thing I knew, I was awakened by a slight noise, whispering, and I was conscious of a curtain around my bed. At first, I didn't know where I was, but then I collected my thoughts. I could see shadows moving on the floor. Something was happening around Melissa's bed. Oh, no, they were taking the bed apart.

"What's happened to Melissa?" I screamed. No answer. "What are you doing to Melissa?" No answer. "Somebody, tell me what's happening, please?" Finally Nurse MacPherson said, "Be quiet, Mr. White. You're disturbing everyone in the room."

I started to plead for information about Melissa, but no one would answer me. As the bed was being carted out, I heard the nurses talk about a coffee break and I let go with every curse word I knew. "Melissa's dead and you're all talking about a coffee break, you——."

MacPherson opened the curtain around my bed, and I was shocked when I actually noticed Melissa's bed was gone. She took my hand and said, "Mr. White, we all loved Melissa, too, but it's best it ended this way. She would have been a vegetable had she lived. How can we take care of you unless we continue to function and not get too emotionally involved? We're human, too; give us a break." I burst out in tears for Melissa but also feeling sorry for myself.

I awoke again to find two doctors studying my charts along with a new nurse. I learned for the first time that I had a broken right leg, nine fractured ribs on my right side and one on the left side, internal bleeding, and various multiple contusions and abrasions. There were some other aches and pains, but too technical to mention. For endless days, I was x-rayed over and over again. I was sure I would wind up impotent, from the X rays, should I ever leave the hospital alive.

Each time someone would die in the intensive-care room we shared, they would have a replacement immediately. My right leg had ballooned to twice its size and was held in place by bricks. I swore to God that if He allowed me to get well and stand erect again, I would give back; I would do something for humanity, for my fellow man or woman. I made this same vow to God if He would get me through the past war, I remember. So this would be "two" that I owed. Believe me, I'm good for them.

After seeing everyone die for possibly the third time around, it dawned on me that If I expected to live, I had best leave this room. I rang for the nurse and told her I wanted out. She said she needed a doctor's okay and, this being Sunday, there was no one around. I raised my voice a bit and told her to call my doctor at home. I suddenly just had to leave this dimly lit room, without windows, immediately. The nurse left, but I kept ringing her button to help her remember.

Within half an hour she showed up with an orderly and without saying anything they started to roll my bed out of the room. The orderly asked me how my ribs were and reminded me he was the one I screamed at each time he changed my sheets. "Try getting your sheets changed with ten fractured ribs," I told him. We became friends later, and I told him every joke I could remember.

I was placed in a ward, with three other men, that had two large windows. Each day, Peter would show up and try to feed me, though I had lost the taste for food, but I felt slightly better every time I saw his affectionate face. In a month, I was able to leave the hospital in a wheelchair.

There was MacPherson in the hall as I was checking out. I learned that Melissa had only been eighteen years old, had been crowned as Miss Hampton Bays that year, and had been in a car crash with a boy who had been killed instantly. Coincidentally, the boy's father owned the very gas station where I had filled my tank prior to my accident. Beautiful, beautiful Melissa, I shall never forget you.

I signed myself out of the Central Suffolk Hospital and was informed that a pin had been placed in my right leg, called the Hansen-Street rod. I would have to go through some therapy to strengthen the leg, then I would be on crutches for months, and finally I would wind up walking slowly with the aid of a metal walker to hold me erect. The morphine, painkillers, other medicines, and pills had taken their toll, and I looked like hell, having lost twenty-eight pounds and my pallor being that of a ghost.

I was still on painkillers and pills of all colors, but I had luckily shaken the need for morphine. It took months, possibly two years, but I fought my way back to health until all that transpired in the hospital and afterwards became a fuzzy blur. It is difficult and painful for me to recall many of the details. The insurance company paid my hospital expenses, and after seven years of stalling, my case was finally settled out of court, no thanks to a horribly incompetent attorney.

One ironical note still remains in my hazy memory. The Central Suffolk Hospital eventually sent me a form letter to fill out. "How was I treated?" "Was I satisfied with the food?" "Were the nurses and doctors polite and efficient?" "Did I have any comments to improve the hospital?" I answered all the questions politely and affirmatively until I got to the last sentence regarding my comments. I wrote asking if it was the Central Suffolk's standard procedure to rob patients as they were admitted to the hospital. I had over $350 on my person when I was brought to the hospital. All they ever returned to my son was a measly seven dollars.

I wrote a thank-you letter to the young reverend and his volunteer ambulance corps, enclosing a check. I also wrote a thank-you letter to my nurses and doctors, who cared for me most diligently. All in all, I considered myself fortunate and lucky to have gotten through this dark period of my life. The accident taught me many things. It gave me time to reflect on my life, the past and the future. Much as I always had an appreciation and zest for living, I now saw things in a brighter and proper light. I honestly believe that for someone who takes things for granted to embrace, understand, and hold life to be as dear as it is, he only has to undergo a traumatic accident, sickness, or loss. Lying on a hospital bed sometimes is an unappreciated gift, time to take stock, to think, to plan for the future, to more fully appreciate life. I've heard of heart attacks that actually saved people's lives. They slowed them down, made them take care of themselves healthwise, made them conscious of what might have happened, and gave them another chance at life. That is, if they made the most of their experience. I value my stay in the hospital and feel it was most therapeutic and educational.

The balance of 1970 and a good part of 1971 I spent learning how to walk properly. When the doctor removed the Hansen-

Street rod from my right leg, he told me how this wonder pin had come about. It seems that when the Allies invaded Germany toward the end of World War II, they found German soldiers actually functioning, walking around, using arms and legs only a short time after suffering a broken limb; thus the Hansen-Street rod was discovered. The doctor asked me if I wanted the rod to keep as a memento. When I looked bewildered, he said, "It makes a great martini stirrer." I told my friend Dr. Roger Levy, orthopedics specialist of Mount Sinai Hospital, what to do with it.

The gym I belonged to, the Business Men's Club, was one heck of a place to meet people from all walks of life. After a brisk workout on the track and in the pool, it was a steam bath and then the fun started in the lounge. I held my own pretty good in the joke department with some of the top people from films, TV, sports, and the world of business who congregated in the BMC lounge, not to mention educators and writers.

One of the guys I got friendly with was a man who was not only most difficult to get to know but to understand, the aforementioned Mr. Paddy Chayefsky, writer of many hit plays, films, and books. Paddy got a kick out of my corny jokes, songs, and horsing around and sought out my company for an iced coffee and a long walk sometimes after we left the club. Most members of the BMC were in awe and slightly fearful of Paddy's tongue and argumentative nature. After a while, Paddy and I became close pals and were inseparable.

It was lunch at the Carnegie Deli and dinner sometimes at The Russian Tea Room or Elaine's or other hangouts for the show-business crowd and literati. As usual, he would say, with pride and a twinkle in his eye, "Go ahead, Eddie; tell them the joke you always fuck up."

With Paddy I got to see all the movie premieres and went to the openings of many plays. We would buy strawberry licorice, and when the lights went down we raced each other to see who could eat the most. Weekends we spent at my apartment watching baseball or football games and arguing about anything and everything. The big events in our sporting lives were the weekly fights. Usually we watched them in my apartment, but if the fight was a major championship match, we would be invited over to the office of the head of ABC's sports and news department, Mr. Roone Arledge.

There I got a chance to hobnob with all kinds of celebrities and on a first-name basis. It wasn't unusual to see Woody Allen, Mia Farrow, Frank Sinatra, Henry Kissinger, George Plimpton, Roy and Cynthia Scheider, David and Joyce Susskind, Dick Cavett, Frank Gifford, Phyllis George, and a host of other names all huddled around fifteen or twenty TV sets, rooting for one fighter or the other.

Cynthia Scheider said that I gave the most interesting running commentary of anyone and that I knew the most about boxing. Knowing Rocky Graziano might have helped, although the Rock never gave me a tip on a winner in over thirty years. It got so that each time Rocky picked a fighter, I bet the other way and invariably won.

One evening I was invited by actor Danny Aiello to see the Golden Gloves at Madison Square Garden. Danny's son was fighting on the card. Paddy begged off so I went solo. There I met actors Robert DeNiro and Robert Duvall, who were ardent fight fans. A bunch of the guys were chewing the fat in the back of the Garden between fights when my acquaintance Peter Savage and film producer Ralph Serpe drifted by. I knew that Peter was still angry with me because of that incident when I asked Jake La Motta to leave my offices, so I didn't bother to say hello. Ralph Serpe looked at the two of us and said, "Hey, you two guys mad at each other?"

Peter started to say, "He . . ." when Serpe said, "Come on, you two bums, shake hands." I put out my hand, but Peter started again: "He . . . " I pulled my hand back and turned to see Robert Duvall watching me very closely. Ralph Serpe grabbed Peter's hand and my hand and forced us to shake hands.

I said, "Okay, okay, I'll shake hands, but that means we're friends and we can't badmouth each other anymore." Peter Savage stared at me with mixed emotion but was speechless. Remember that Savage was a former professional fighter, six-feet-two, weighed over 200 pounds, and looked like the movie version of a handsome, mustachioed tough guy. As a matter of fact, Peter did play that very role in many films, including *Raging Bull*.

Peter Savage at first reluctantly shook my hand and spit out something in Italian. Then he grabbed me and hugged my shoulders, still speaking Italian. I went along for the ride, afraid to ask what he was saying. The spell of anger was broken, and our

My future ex-wife—oh, how I wish! Brooke Shields at sweet sixteen.

The Members Only group: Ed Wachtel, me, and Telly Savalas, and Herb Goldsmith.

friendship took on a new meaning.

In a few months, Pete and I were inseparable. We would have dinner or lunch a couple of times a week, and I was his houseguest at his summer home up in the Catskills. Once, while we were driving upstate, he commented that God had brought us together again for a reason, that we should follow our destiny, the Lord's will. It sounded strange, this macho, tough guy who had been a professional fighter, who had done time in jail, who was a pure product of the streets, referring to God. I listened and believed and marveled.

Word got back to me that movie actor Robert Duvall liked the way I handled myself that night at Madison Square Garden. Dustin Hoffman had an office on my floor two doors from my apartment, and one day Duvall came by to say hello to the both of us. Almost at once, a new friendship was cemented between Duvall and myself. Here was this very complex, deeply emotional, highly talented guy acting like a little boy when we were alone or with a few close friends.

Bobby Duvall loved it when I cooked a Japanese dinner or when a few of us got together to "hold mighty court." That was his favorite expression: "Hey Eddie, let's get together and hold mighty court." That and his inimitable laugh were Robert Duvall's trademarks. You could hear him coming from a mile away, like Santa Claus, with his "Ho, Ho" that was half laugh and half Indian war yelp.

Dustin Hoffman and Bobby Duvall were once roommates in their lean early acting years, and although they shared many laughs and memories, either Dustin's instant success in films or the work that sent them in opposite direction over the years seemed to cool their friendship. If anything, they were civil to each other, but there was always this underlying stiffness and standoffish attitude between them. I tried awfully hard not to get caught in any crossfire or to take sides, but one evening the whole world seemed to come crashing down on my innocent head.

Bobby Duvall was then living in a large house in Tuxedo Park with his wife, Barbara, and her two daughters from a previous marriage. The marriage had already been strained beyond repair when I met Bobby, but everyone, all of Bobby's friends, myself included, carried on as if they hadn't noticed. Bobby mentioned that he was going to have a "cookoff" at his home on that

259

With The Rock and Dustin Hoffman on the set of *Kramer Versus Kramer.*

Me and Bobby Duvall in our "Members Only" Jackets.

coming Decoration Day. Would I cook my Japanese teriyaki chicken and make my sweet-and-sour salad?

Flattered that anyone liked my cooking enough to want me to cook for their friends, I immediately said yes. I called Bobby's wife, Barbara, and asked how many people would be there. She said forty to fifty. Okay, I would need certain ingredients, which I mentioned, but the most important ingredient was the Kikkoman soy sauce. I noticed her voice and attitude was a little strained, and she was annoyed that I asked her to repeat the name of the soy sauce. Again, I stated that I couldn't cook unless I had the Kikkoman. Japanese and Chinese soy sauces are very different from each other.

On Decoration Day, everyone played tennis, went bicycling, or rode horses. All I did was decorate the kitchen from morning to early evening. Needless to say, there was no Kikkoman sauce to be had, only some ersatz sauce that wasn't fit to consume, and this was on a Sunday when the stores were probably closed. Off I went with the Duvalls' maid to find the necessary ingredient. At this point, I no longer was neutral in my feelings toward the Duvalls.

Finally, I located thirty very small bottles of the magic elixir in a distant country grocery store. They were the size of those liquor bottles you get on the airlines. By this time, the Duvall maid was cursing under her breath as we hurried back to the house. It was so hot, I stripped down to a pair of shorts and, with a towel around my neck, started to cook. I made four large pots of chicken and ribs teriyaki and two huge bowls of salad with my secret sweet-and-sour dressing. By this time, I was ready to collapse from fatigue and the extreme heat of the day and the kitchen.

Other friends and neighbors brought food to the "cookoff," but the "oohs" and "ahs" were mostly for my two dishes. After the women stopped crowding around me, asking for the recipes, Barbara Duvall came over and stepping on my bare foot said, "I watched you very closely, and I can make the same dishes and better!" That's the thanks I got that Decoration Day. I just hoped the stepping on my big toe was just an accident. Anyway, I surely wasn't neutral anymore. It's going to take some doing to get me into a strange kitchen again.

That dinner party was strange for other reasons. We all ate in three or four different rooms—there were that many people—and it wasn't out of the ordinary to hear a woman scream or a guy curse out loud. The war was raging both in Viet Nam and in the Duvall house. Political differences arose about the war and President Nixon. The wrong people were sitting at the wrong tables. Finally, one woman screamed, "You motherfuckers, you all stink!" and stormed out of the house. Other people followed moments later, but when the only two people I invited became insulted and left, I became heartsick. Al and Grace Gallico weren't that involved in politics. Someone or something triggered Grace's anger. Barbara Duvall never stopped chomping on the honey-soy short ribs of beef. Try as I might, I couldn't contain Grace, and she and Al left in a huff. Man, I was positively not neutral anymore!

Getting back to that aforesaid evening when the world came crashing down on my innocent head, a few of us were sitting around my apartment "holding mighty court" when Dustin Hoffman's name came up. Bobby Duvall casually mentioned that Dustin and Ann Hoffman, Dustin's wife at the time, hadn't been up to see the new Duvall home in Tuxedo Park.

Then the next statement sent me scurrying into the kitchen, where I nervously started to run the water. Someone said, "Dustin and Ann will never go up to Tuxedo Park, and neither will I. We just don't dig your wife, Barbara." Although the Duvall marriage was completely on the rocks, I could sense that Bobby was visibly shaken and hurt. Then came the statement: "Let's face it, Bobby. None of your friends digs Barbara, not even Eddie."

It was if the whole world became still; not a sound was heard. I turned the water up louder. Then I heard Bobby say, "Is that true, Eddie?" I made believe I was busy and didn't hear. "Is that true, Eddie?" The phrase was repeated louder and louder. I turned off the water and prepared myself to meet my fate. "Is what true, Bobby?" I asked with more innocence than Margaret O'Brien could ever muster in any one of her early films.

"I just heard that Dustin and Ann don't care to come up to my home because of Barbara, and I hear that you feel the same way. Why is that?" I first decided to cop a plea and say it wasn't so, but after inhaling a few deep breaths and seeing I was cornered anyway, I decided on telling the truth. "Mostly it has to do with what happened on Decoration Day, the way she treated, or rather mistreated, me and my friends Al and Grace Gallico." I thought that was that, conversation ended. Bobby fixed me with his famous stare. "Go on. What about Al and Grace?"

"You know my friends Al and Grace are very passive and apolitical, not the least bit argumentative. Yet they felt they were insulted at your party, and they thought that your wife was socially rude." The world stopped. It was limbo or vacuum time again. In acting parlance, at least "ten beats," or ten ominous seconds, ticked off. Suddenly there came a scream.

I had once heard that Robert Duvall was a "tantrum actor," but the look on Bobby's face was deadly and he wasn't acting. He ran to the door of my apartment, opened it, and stood holding onto the frame but never crossing over and out of the apartment.

My heart went out to Bobby. Right then, there wasn't any wrong or right or "you said" or "I said." I could see my friend Bobby was terribly hurt. Bobby leaned his head against the left frame of the door, and I nervously said, "Hey, guys, this is my home; I don't know why you picked my place to hash this thing out. I want it to stop right now." All the time Bobby was muttering.

Bobby stood in the frame for another few minutes and then spoke calmly and quietly. "Okay, I'll talk to you tomorrow," he said and left. I sat down with relief, completely drained and confused. Someone said, "Why the hysterics? His marriage has been on the rocks for years." I just sat there shaking my head. What a scene. The orphanage, the war, the plane crash, the automobile crash, the Orient, everything, everything I've ever seen or gone through couldn't shake me up as much as what had just transpired. These were ten minutes that shook the world, at least my world.

Bobby Duvall did call the next day and never mentioned the aforementioned incident. I was all set to apologize, but it wasn't necessary. I learned in time that Robert Duvall never had much patience for sentiment or explanations. He was more like Col. "Bull" Meecham in the film *The Great Santini* than anyone would ever believe.

We picked up our friendship as if nothing had occurred. But then the phone calls started to come in from Bobby's wife, Barbara. Bobby had previously worked in a Western in Nebraska, with Jimmy Caan, and while in Ogallala, Nebraska, Bobby had met an interesting very unusual family, the Petersons. B.A. Peterson was the typical old-fashioned patriarch of this gung-ho, machismo group of knock 'em dead, shoot 'em up rodeo family, and that included the women and the kids. Everyone in the Peterson family could trick ride, fight, cuss, and handle a lariat or a gun. They fought each other often, but more often, they fought for each other. Woe to the individual who mistakenly picked on a Peterson. They'd have a pack of wildcats on their hands and heads.

Bobby Duvall, upon meeting up with the Petersons, was sure he had discovered the true American archpatriarchal family, and he made up his mind to film a documentary on the spot, in Ogallala, in the Peterson's own habitat, their natural environment. Barbara Duvall was the associate producer of the film, with Bobby directing and producing.

I came into the picture as the provider of Duvall's needed background music for their Western documentary. As I said, my pal Al Gallico, although born in Brooklyn, New York, was known in Nashville, Tennessee as "Mr. Country," and through Al I met more country stars and learned more about country music than most people in our business.

One evening, I gave Bobby Duvall a couple of albums by Tammy Wynette and George Jones, knowing he would flip over the music and might wish to include some of their songs in his film. That week by coincidence, Tammy and George came to town and their label, Columbia Records, threw a cocktail party for the sweethearts of country music. I introduced Robert and Barbara Duvall to Tammy Wynette and George Jones, and on the spot Bobby appointed me music consultant on his documentary film.

It was arranged, mostly through Al Gallico's music-publishing firm, for the Duvalls to title their film *We're Not the Jet Set* after one of Tammy's and George's big hit records. Billy "The Kid" Sherrill, the young dean of country-music production in Nashville and a friend of Al Gallico's and mine, also gave Bobby Duvall the okay with the important Nashville music publishers, so the die was cast. *We're Not the Jet Set* had secured all the necessary country background music it needed. The necessary legal contracts were drawn and sent to Nashville.

Then the phone calls from Barbara Duvall. "Why does it take so long? Who do they think they are anyway?" I called Gallico and Billy Sherrill, and they emphatically stated that the Duvalls could go ahead with the music, everything was in order, and all contracts were approved. Some principals were out of town, but they had called their attorneys and said all was gung ho. When Barbara Duvall called again, I told her the contracts would be forthcoming in due time, approval had been given verbally with the Harry Fox office, the agent for the music publishers, and for her to check it out and then to proceed.

Then another call and this time I didn't wait to hear what Barbara had on her mind. I opened up first. I told her that the music business was a close-knit family, that she had the top people in the profession telling her to go ahead with the film's music and I felt she was taking it out on me personally for the disagreements she had with her husband. As I talked, I got a little worked up and finished with "I guess this is the end of whatever friendship existed between us, you, me, and Bobby. So let's slowly walk into the fading sunset and forget we ever met." Her answer still has me puzzled to this day.

Barbara Duvall said, "Oh, no, you may eventually get rid of me, but you'll never get rid of Bobby Duvall," and she left it at that. Never? I wondered what she meant by that and still do. Maybe I tried to read too much into that statement, or maybe I heard wrong.

Needless to say, all the contracts for We're Not the Jet Set were signed, sealed, and delivered in time, I was given credit in the film for being the music consultant, and a special thanks was included for Billy Sherill and Al Gallico. In my opinion, the film is a documentary art classic crying out to be discovered. I predict We're Not the Jet Set and an earlier black-and-white William Faulkner film, adapted by Horton Foote, Tomorrow, starring Robert Duvall, will one day be critically acclaimed. They both have more than a touch of the realism seldom seen on film. Jet Set stands by itself as a documentary and shows Robert Duvall's touch as a sensitive director. Tomorrow can be compared to The Grapes of Wrath and shows the emerging acting genius of an earlier Robert Duvall.

The Jet Set film completed, Bobby moved out of his Tuxedo

Park home to an apartment in the West 70s. It looked like the separation between him and Barbara was irrevocable. Whatever happened in the past between us, I felt still sorry for Barbara and hoped that somehow their marriage could magically be mended. To me, any breakup of a marriage is a tragedy, especially when children are involved. Although Nancy and Susan were Barbara's children from another marriage, Bobby had been a doting, giving father with far more than a passing fatherly interest. With Bobby Duvall, the word *giving* was surely an understatement when it came to his immediate family, and especially those two girls. It wasn't that he couldn't say no or didn't know how; the word just wasn't in his vocabulary.

Bobby Duvall was in awe of most women, but especially the three close women in his life. They overpowered him, not purely by pressure but by sheer numbers. I'm sure Bobby would have settled for whatever their little hearts desired if they would just let him go to "hold mighty court" with the guys. He was more relaxed, more himself, with the guys. Then the stories, the bullshit, would fly, and we could all laugh at words like *clap* and *herpes* and lie about our sexual conquests, myself included.

Whatever I did in life, especially with women, I magnified it a hundred times in order to impress Bobby. I must have succeeded, as I held his interest and I saw it made him happy. Although I am older than Duvall, he always made me feel much younger. He himself had never grown up, and this one fact is the key to his complicated personality. Bobby just wouldn't grow up, and he wouldn't allow me to grow up, if he could prevent it. Before I had met Bobby, I had seen the film *Tomorrow*, and I remember wondering what kind of a man this Robert Duvall was. When I did meet him, I started to stutter that I was an admirer, a fan of his, and Bobby said something that sounded like "Shaddup!" and turned away. Outwardly, Bobby never liked to show sentiment or affection, yet I just know he has strong feelings along those lines. Otherwise, with all the arguments and differences we've had, how could we still remain friends?

Bobby used to discuss his film roles with humor. Why is he always the heavy? How come he never gets the girl? But aware of the fact that he is considered by everyone in the business as an actor's actor; he was never too concerned about the type of roles assigned him, only their importance. One of his primary concerns is his physical shape. He tries to maintain a steady weight and can invariably be found on the closest tennis court. Robert Duvall was once rated the number-one tennis player amongst celebrities, and he actually won the first celebrity superstar TV competition, outdistancing much younger challengers in tennis, swimming, and cycling.

Occasionally, Duvall loses a tennis match to a local club professional, and it bothers him for days. He won't rest until he gets a rematch, and he usually beats the younger pro the second time around. It takes Duvall a couple of days to reflect on the other guy's game and to figure out his new strategy. It works more times than not, but once in a while, some steady kid with unlimited stamina has Duvall's number. Then Bobby just good-naturally cusses him out for days and the incident is forgotten.

In the summer of 1975, Bobby Duvall signed to do a film, *The Killer Elite,* costarring his buddy James Caan and directed by Sam Peckinpah. Before he left, Bobby asked me to join him in San Francisco, where the film was to be shot. Bobby had rented a house in Sausalito and said there was room for me. He glowed while talking about the different types of restaurants in and around San Francisco. "We'll eat up a storm in Frisco, Eddie. They have these big crabs, and you'll get to meet Francis, and we'll hold some mighty court." Francis was Francis Ford Coppola, who directed Bobby in his most successful role so far, in *The Godfather.*

It all sounded so tempting and inviting, but I knew Bobby would be busy with the film and I didn't want to be just another "hanger-oner" or freeloader. I had just finished studying acting with Jack Waltzer, Bobby and Dustin Hoffman's friend, and after eighteen months of classroom work, Jack said I was ready. He encouraged me to go out to San Francisco, but I was still hesitant.

Paddy Chayefsky spent one weekend in my apartment watching the baseball games and fights early in April of 1975. He said he was just finishing writing a screenplay and Bobby Duvall was up for an important part. The name of the forthcoming film was *Network.* Paddy thought it would be good for me to go out to the Coast, see some of my friends in Los Angeles, and visit

267

with Duvall, and Paddy was sure once I was there and Sam Peckinpah saw me he'd use me in the film. "Personally, I hate the whole fucking place, the people, and their asshole culture," Paddy said, or words to that effect.

That night, I made up my mind to go, and then I couldn't sleep so I stayed up all night packing, even though I wasn't leaving for another three weeks or so. I wrote letters to Al and Grace Gallico, who now lived in a Taj Mahal in Beverly Hills, telling them I was coming. I wrote to my friend Rue McClanahan, who was fast becoming a star comedienne on the "Maude" TV show as Vivian, Maude's best friend. I wrote to Stanley Adams, comedian Louie Nye, and a few of the young girls and guys who were in my acting class and were trying to make it in Hollywood. This way, I'd be surrounded by familiar faces out in Cult City and any rejection or loneliness I might suffer wouldn't hurt me too much. With all the traveling I've done, with all the towns I've been in, all the dots on the map, places I've visited, Los Angeles is the only city I have felt instant loneliness. Sometimes the feeling engulfs me even before I arrived there.

It is my humble contention that people change once they have lived out in LA for any length of time. I know my friends from New York City don't sound or look like they once did. People hardly ever look you in the eye when they speak out in LA. It's almost as if they all have become a race apart. I am mainly speaking about theatrical people, but some of this strangeness has also affected friends of mine who are not in show business.

A young rabbi friend of mine, while he lived in New York, adored his wife and children. When I heard he was leaving to live in Los Angeles, I pleaded with him not to go. The last thing I distinctly remember saying to him was "Please don't let the place get to you. Don't go Hollywood!" He laughed and assured me that could never happen. Silly boy.

It happened; it happened. The first thing he did was buy a big house in exclusive Beverley Hills, the second was take up with a beautiful "shiksa," and the third was divorce his wife and leave his children and the big house. "Now that could happen anywhere," you say. Right. But out in LA it happens faster, so much faster, and more often.

My friend the rabbi is now a legend out in Hollywood. He's famous, or infamous, take your pick. He's still the same sweet guy I knew, but different, as only Hollywood can make 'em. He's now a screenwriter, a personal manager, a friend and confidant to the film stars, and a part-time rabbi. The story might make a good film with *Part-Time Rabbi* as the title, except for the fact that his ex-wife is devastated, as are the rabbi's parents. The last thing my friend's father said to me, before his death, was "Please tell Jerry to return to his calling. Tell him to go back to the rabbinate." I told him, to no avail. Whereas I was once considered the man of the world, my friend Jerry who used to look up to me as a knowledgeable person now looks at me with affectionate pity. Hollywood can do that to you. Incidentally, I met the "shiksa" while out in LA and found her not only beautiful and friendly but also very intelligent. Hollywood can do that to you.

While in Hollywood, I made the rounds with my friends. Al, Grace, and the wonderful person and singer Patti Page, and I went to Le Restaurant and then wound up at Patti's house for drinks. Patti had just gotten divorced, and I couldn't help but think that this lovely lady, with two beautiful children and this big house and a successful career in front and back of her, had such a sad, wounded look in her eyes. Someone or something had done Patti wrong, and it showed through all her laughing and graciousness. Hollywood can . . .

Rue McClanahan took me to a party at Anita Gillette's house, and I met Rue's current flame. My dear friend Rue wears her heart on her sleeve, and you can notice a little patch here and there. Rue not only loses her heart to the wrong guys but sometimes her savings, too. The love and company of her son saves her from a complete emotional wipeout. I couldn't help but think of how much Rue reminded me of Patti, in many ways, and then it occurred to me that they both came from Oklahoma.

With Stanley Adams and Louie Nye we visited LA's Little Tokyo, and Louie flipped when I spoke Japanese to the waitresses. I enjoyed his encouraging me to say more and more, and finally I ran out of things to say. Louie did his famous samurai hara-kari routine, and everyone was hysterical. It was good to be with Stanley again, now that he and Harriet were divorced, and to see

269

him laughing it up like the good old days. Stanley and I did our old routines, many of them not unlike the Mel Brooks–Carl Reiner two-thousand–year–old–man routines. As always, Uncle Stanley brought tears of laughter and happiness to my eyes. Still, I couldn't help but notice that Stanley didn't look well on this trip. Upon questioning Louie and his lovely wife, Anita, I could only get the usual "nothing to worry about" answers.

Upon prodding Stanley, I learned that while he was in a hospital "drying out" from some drug overdose, he had met and fallen for a lovely seventeen-year-old girl. They were now having a relationship, and Stanley was ecstatic about how things were going. I warned Stanley about the huge gap in their ages and finished with the warning that as soon as this nymphet's parents found out about them, there would be hell to pay. I never questioned the drug overdose, as Uncle Stanley never volunteered an explanation. On that issue Stanley considered me a square, as did the late Lenny Bruce and a few other friends of mine. I'd rather have it that way than preach and be told to mind my own business.

I went out to Hamburger Hamlet with a few of the kids from Jack Waltzer's acting class and caught up on the happenings of some of them who were making it out in Hollywood and some who were still struggling. Pretty Pam Dawber was fast becoming a star in "Mork and Mindy," handsome Parker Stevenson was in *The Hardy Boys*, Claudia Brown had landed a part in *Saturday Night Fever*, beautiful Connie Sellecca was one of the fly-away girls for "All-American Hero," and talented Sandra McCabe was due to costar in a film titled *The Dogs*. I told them I was on my way to San Francisco to join Robert Duvall and I might possibly land a part in the film *The Killer Elite*. Most of Jack Waltzer's class was busy, busy, busy.

We all exchanged our current phone numbers, and Sandra McCabe mentioned she was staying at actor Glenn Ford's home. It seems that Sandra's twin sister, Cynthia, was engaged to Mr. Ford, but when I called a few days later an irritable Glen Ford angrily asked, "Who is this and what do you want?" when I asked for Sandra. I gave one of my favorite actors the stock question to his question, "Who do I have to be to speak to Sandra?," and hung up. Now that I think of it, he wasn't that good in *The Blackboard Jungle*.

Tiring of hanging out at the Polo Lounge bar and the pool at the Beverly Hills Hotel and listening to the frantic banter at Nat and Al's deli and seeing the same faces at Cantor's Restaurant and having been to The Farmer's Market twice, I left LA vowing not to come back too soon, if I could help it. It was that same strange, lonely feeling in my gut that no one and nothing was for real in that town. I read somewhere that a "Manson mentality prevailed out in LA," and I couldn't agree more. The place again left me with a melancholy, empty feeling.

I found San Francisco exciting and bustling as soon as I arrived. Bobby Duvall let out his patented Indian war cry when he saw me and made me feel wanted and at home in his little house in Sausalito. His expense check was quite substantial, as was Jimmy Caan's, and evenings it was off to the best restaurants in town, where a bunch of us "held mighty court." The ironic part of it all was that most restaurant owners refused to give us a tab after dinner, feeling honored to have two such distinguished actors in their establishment. We would return another evening to repay the gesture, but the same thing always happened, no tab. The captains and waiters had a field day, though, as they were more than compensated for their services.

One particular restaurant, The Imperial Palace, was especially nice to the James Caan–Robert Duvall gang of six. Tommy Toy, the owner, was once a friend of the late kung-fu king Bruce Lee, and he would regale us with stories of Bruce's prowess and how he got started and how he died accidentally. The food was great at The Imperial Palace and so was the service, but try as they might, Jimmy Caan and Bobby Duvall could not pay one single bill for our elaborate dinners.

One night after a sumptuous dinner, we all went over to director Francis Ford Coppola's house in San Francisco. I was very impressed that Mr. Coppola was so down-to-earth, what with all that he had accomplished in life and at such a young age. He immediately insisted I stop calling him Mr. Coppola, and we were on a first-name basis from the beginning. Francis liked me because I was the only one there, other than himself, who smoked cigars. He delighted in showing me his humidor and insisted I smoke a stogie I could just about lift.

A few nights later, we all went back to Francis's house again, this time for dinner. Francis did all the cooking. There was pasta, salad, chicken with all the trimmings, and we all had seconds. Francis's house was one of those old-fashioned homes the whalers must have built in San Francisco around the late 1800s. It had stained-glass windows befitting a cathedral and high ceilings, and every room was built as if Paul Bunyan lived there. Down on the lower floor Francis had his playroom, a full theater, a complete screening room, with large, soft plush divans and every fun appliance and/or gadget you could think of—popcorn and Coke machines, jukeboxes, games and a built-in device that quietly told Francis that there was a telephone call or someone was at the front door while he was screening a film. A tiny warning light would appear in the lower left corner of the screen. A complete phone system was to the left of Francis's throne, where he could talk to any corner of the world while he and his guests were watching a film.

This night, Francis showed us the first film he made, with James Caan and Robert Duvall and costarring Shirley Knight. I loved the film and everyone's performance, although I heard from Bobby Duvall that *The Rain People* hadn't received acclaim from the critics and didn't make any money when it was released theatrically. Jimmy Caan gave an excellent performance as a brain-damaged ex–football player, Shirley Knight played his wife, and Bobby Duvall was a psychotic motorcycle cop who sexually harassed Miss Knight. Francis Cappola's direction and writing were taut, tight, and terrific in this quiet little film that I found most believable, entertaining and fulfilling. Every time I tried to express how much I enjoyed the film that night, Francis would shove a cigar in my mouth.

At one of our fiestas at Francis's house, I heard Bobby Duvall mention a role that was tailor-made for him. The more I heard, the more I was convinced. I had never seen Bobby get so excited about playing a particular part, and I was sure his instincts were correct. I asked if I could read the script, and Bobby threw what looked like a paperback book at me. I went into a quiet room and started to read *Apocalypse Now,* by John Milius and Francis Ford Cappola. When I got to the part of a weird macho character by the name of Captain Karnage, I was sure this was not only the part Bobby was referring to, but this was Bobby. I read the rest of the first draft of *Apocalypse Now* and hurried back to tell

Bobby that the part of Captain Karnage was tailor-made for him.

Bobby smiled and told me that Francis was after Al Pacino or Jimmy Caan or Gene Hackman. The result was that all the above mentioned super stars had priced themselves out of the stratosphere, asking for $3 million as a starter. Bobby Duvall eventually got the part of Karnage, as he longed for. For some reason, they changed the name from Karnage to Kilroy, which disppointed me. After all, the guy loved war and the smell of napalm in the morning, and the dictionary says that *carnage* means "massacre, massive slaughter, as in war."

While we were in San Francisco and visiting with Francis occasionally, Bobby was held in limbo as to his getting the role he so deserved in *Apocalypse Now*. He was almost resigned to the fact that someone else, possibly Gene Hackman, would wind up playing Karnage. We, all his friends, kept telling him that Francis was just toying with him, that he couldn't possibly consider anyone else but Bobby for the offbeat, nutty role of a warsick officer infatuated with war. Anyway, while it lasted, it was fun for me to help Francis Ford Cappola thread the film machine down in his basement and to smoke his huge black Cuban Churchillian cigars and just to be in his company. I don't know why, but Francis's character and personality reminded me of Rudyard Kipling's classic poem "If."

When Bobby wasn't working or due on the film set, he naturally was on the tennis courts. He had a friendly vendetta with Jimmy Caan and invariably toyed with and eventually would beat Jimmy. One afternoon, Jimmy had had enough and suggested a doubles match. He would team up with a close friend of Bobby's, actor Paul Gleason, and Bobby would have me as a partner. Although tennis is one of my favorite sports and I was always considered more than a fair athlete, I wasn't in a class with these three highly competitive macho jocks. The match was to be held at the San Francisco Tennis Club, a very prestigious court, and the odds on winning were on Caan-Gleason beating Duvall— what's his name.

Before he started, Bobby lectured me about playing the net, telling me about being caught in no-man's-land, and about loosening up, not being tight. Then he fixed me with the Duvall stare that could only mean one thing: he wanted to win this match come hell or high water. I asked myself, *How did I ever get caught in this predicament? If only I were ten years younger. Who do I have to sleep with to get out of this match? Lord, let me be good for Bobby's sake; it means so much to him. It's not enough that he's a star and rich and I'm a little nothing; he has to make my life miserable like this. Now I realize what Job went through.*

The prayer and Bobby's backhand worked. We killed those two young upstarts Caan and Gleason in straight sets, and I made match point with a net shot that handcuffed Gleason and hit him in the balls. I was about to jump over the net in victory, but thought better of it and shook Bobby's hand. Bobby embraced me by mistake and instinct, for the first and last time ever. He wasn't one for much sentiment or affection, remember. Jimmy Caan and Paul Gleason shook my hand, but I swear I could read the work *prick* in their eyes and on their minds.

That night, I asked Bobby why it was always so important to win, win, win. I reminded him that he usually beat Dustin Hoffman 6–0, 6–0, whenever they played. Friends don't do that to friends. Why not let Dustin or Caan win once in a while? I remember Bobby's answer before he dozed off; it was so poetic and profound. The words still ring in my ears to this day. Robert Duvall said, and this is verbatim, "Fuck off!" If only Tennessee Williams could come up with dialogue like that.

It was fascinating watching the filming of *The Killer Elite* in San Francisco's Chinatown. Special permission had to be secured from the city of San Francisco and from the Chinese community in order to close off certain streets during filming hours. There were specified "do's" and "don'ts," but inasmuch as the director, Sam Peckinpah, was always high on something or other, or both, the "don'ts" were forgotten. There began a rumbling in the Chinese community and in the newspapers that the film crew was taking advantage of the situation. Chinese businessmen let it be known that this would be the last film company to have any privileges, that from now on they would have to post bigger bonds and pay for any damages incurred. Having lived in the Orient and knowing just a little of the Oriental mind, I sensed the growing resentment and tried to warn the people in the production office, but no one listened.

I gave a sigh of relief when the shooting shifted to the San

Francisco airport. By then I had made friends of quite a few of the film crew, especially young Jim Bloom, one of the assistant directors, and Mako, the fine actor of Japanese ancestry who was nominated for an Academy Award for his performance in *The Sand Pebbles*. Then there was Ronny Caan, Jimmy's younger brother, and colorful but shy Burt Young, who later would make a name for himself in the "Rocky" movies.

Hot off our win in the Caan-Gleason tennis match, Burt asked me to teach him how to play the game. With all the terrific tennis players around, San Francisco being the center of tennis, professional and amateur, I was honored Burt asked me. We had a few sessions, and I realized why he had chosen little *moi*. Burt showed up looking like Emmet Kelly, and he had the coordination of Gene Kelly, in reverse. He used the raquet like a butterfly net, and he slid all over the court like those kids on a smooth dance floor, after a bar mitzvah. Burt had forgotten to wear sneakers.

Jim Bloom and his lovely girl friend, Janet, were on the production staff of *The Killer Elite*. They worked so hard, constantly on their feet during the day on the set, and then at night they had to attend production meetings. Then it was up at 6:00 A.M. the next day to go through the same routine all over again. I marveled at their stamina and how they constantly maintained their sweet, even dispositions.

Finally, one day on the set Ronny Caan and Burt Young asked me if I wanted to be in the film. I thought they'd never ask. I said okay and was told I would have a bit speaking part as a cop at the airport, trying to stop some kung-fu killers from assassinating my newfound friend, Mako. Each day I showed up on the set only to be told to come back tomorrow. It was rough for me, coming from Sausalito to the film set at the airport and then being told to come back the next day. I began to think there was no such part and that I had set myself up for this emotional letdown.

One afternoon at lunch, I did some "shtick" and had the manager of the Golden Gate Holiday Inn in stitches. She said, "Why aren't you the star of this film?" Which gave me a chance to tell my story. Ms. Pat Alexander said, "If they told you you're in the film, you're in!" She advised me to move to the Holiday Inn with the rest of the cast and told me everything, including food, would be charged to the production company. I did and the waiting continued, only worse.

Now it seemed to me that my part was forgotten. Jimmy Caan's friends were all given small parts and shooting schedules, and the days came and went. Now I was itching at the bit, to coin a pun. I mentioned my predicament to Bobby, but he didn't pick up on it. Someone said that I should walk up to Sam Peckinpah and ask him point blank if I was in the film, to get it over with. Suddenly I was back in the air force. I was Lt. Eddie White, bombardier, navigator, gunner, the tough orphan kid with the chip on his shoulder.

I could hear a distant bugler blow "Charge," and I angrily marched up to Sam Peckinpah's trailer and banged on his door. Liz, his sweet English secretary, opened the door and, veddy British-like, said, "Yes?" I could see good ole Sam sitting there with glazed eyes and a small paper cup in his hand. I said, "I know this is not terribly important, but I'm Bobby Duvall's friend from New York and I'd just like to know if there's a part for me in this film?" The both of them stared at me for what seemed like an eternity, whereupon I did an about-face without saluting, and returned to the hotel.

As I entered the lobby, I shook hands with Mako and a few of the other guys and said good-bye, saying I was returning to New York. I kissed Pat Alexander farewell and remember her tearful kisses tasted salty. She insisted on buying me a couple of drinks and swore she would look me up in New York.

I went to my room with terribly mixed emotions, one of them relief. At least, now I knew what Marilyn Monroe must have gone through with all this Hollywood bullshit. After packing, I thought of calling Bobby but then thought better of it. *Let him be shocked by finding me gone*, I thought, forgetting that nothing shocks Bobby Duvall.

As I hit the lobby, two of the *Killer Elite* stunt men asked me where I thought I was going? They picked up my bags and escorted me back to the elevator and to my room. As they left, one guy said, "Be on the set at 8:00 A.M. tomorrow. They're shooting your scene, Jocko." I sat on the bed for an hour trying to figure this whole thing out. Either that guy told me the truth or else I was being held as a hostage.

When I came down for dinner that night, everyone in the cast knew that tomorrow was my big day. Pat Alexander had a funny catlike grin on her face, and I was sure she had more than something to do with it all. She advised me to eat a good dinner and get a good night's sleep and kissed me for luck. You'd think I was Lawrence Olivier and we were shooting Cathy's death scene in *Wuthering Heights*.

I was up hours before the bus left for the film set, practicing my Bogart and Garfield in the mirror. I kept telling myself to relax, and I kept nervously answering, "I am relaxed." *How come the time moves so slowly?* I kept thinking. Although I had a watch, I kept checking with the hotel operator. I didn't want to show up in the lobby too early or too anxious. Two hours before the bus left, I was nonchalently standing and waiting. I'm sure I didn't tip my mitt.

Finally the lobby filled up with cast and crew and dozens of stunt men and women. Mako said something about breakfast, and I sat there not eating or hearing a word that was said. My stomach was making strange noises, and I was hoping the pretty stunt lady sitting opposite me didn't hear or notice. She gave me a smile, either of pity or understanding. *Why did I have to be a fucking actor?* I thought. I remembered the haunting, hallowed words of Robert F. Kennedy; "Because it was there."

And in the Center Ring

On the bus, heading for the San Francisco International Airport, where my scene was to be filmed, the heavy kibbitzing started with me as the foil. Burt Young, Mako, and some of the stunt people and crew started kidding that I was going to try to steal the picture. I took it good-naturedly, as it relieved some of the pressure on me. After all, I was walking into the unknown, a new challenge, a whole new world. I tried to act as cool and nonchalant as possible, but the old heart kept pumping away in swingtime.

The actual set was the Western Airlines terminal in the San Francisco International Airport. I was to play a bit speaking part, a principal role nonetheless, as a security guard inside the terminal. The stars of *The Killer Elite* were James Caan, Robert Duvall, Arthur Hill, and Gig Young with Bo Hopkins, Burt Young, and Mako making up the supporting cast. The major female role was being played by a young beautiful Vietnamese girl, Tiana, who, although she was only five feet two and weighed ninety pounds, was a brown-belt karate expert.

Once I was on the set, no one was there to greet me or tell me what to do. As matter-of-factly as I could, without drawing too much attention to myself, I ran around looking for Jim Bloom. Warm, friendly, affectionate Jim wished me luck, patted me on the back, and told me to report to Wardrobe, then to Makeup, then back to him on the set. How I loved that boy.

In Wardrobe, they outfitted me in a cop's uniform, complete with a rubber gun and a holster. Makeup was mostly pancake powder, and I pleaded and talked them out of using lipstick on me. When I looked in the mirror, I even fooled myself. Darned if I didn't look like a chicken-shit officer of the law. When I appeared on the set, no one took special notice of me, which relaxed me a bit and made me feel more comfortable. Jim Bloom suggested I get comfortable and wait in the upstairs lounge until they finished a kung-fu scene they were shooting in front of a huge Western Airlines passenger plane. I opted to hang around and watch them shoot the scene.

After an hour or so, something finally dawned on me. I waited for a break in the action and then asked Jim Bloom for my script so I could study my lines. His answer floored me. "What script? You're to improvise. Didn't anyone tell you that? Eddie, don't look so scared. You can do it; now go upstairs and relax."

"Improvise? Improvise what?" If only someone would tell me what the scene was about! My drama teacher, Jack Waltzer, once told me I was terrific at improvising. *Calm down*, I told myself. *You can do it. You can do anything. Bullshit! You'd better find out what this scene is all about.*

As I walked around trying to smell things out, I talked to Mako, who was too busy and couldn't help me, Jimmy Caan's brother Ronny, who was involved trying to make out with a chick, Burt Young, who said I shouldn't worry and asked when I could give him another tennis lesson, and the first assistant director. He was busy with a scene and said he'd tell me what to do before we shot my scene. Great! By then I'd be a nervous wreck.

Someone delivered a message to me. Mr. Robert Duvall had left word I was to use his trailer dressing room. As the crew was setting up for another outdoor scene at the airport, I went to Bobby's luxury trailer and washed up, stretched out on a sofa, and tried to read a magazine. I heard the sounds on the set and realized I was too lonely, being by myself, so I returned to the Western Airline lounge where my scene was being set up. As I walked around, still photographers started taking my picture and some passengers, between planes, actually asked for my autograph.

A couple of other bit players, Johnny Weismuller's son included, started kidding me, stealing my cop's cap and my gun. I was fascinated. One guy actually bounced my rubber gun, and it hit the ceiling. I started to relax and laugh it up with the crew, the bit players, and the extras, of which there were hundreds. With the actual passengers in the airport terminal, it looked like one huge mob scene.

Then a huge voice from heaven, or rather the loudspeaker system, boomed out that lunch was now being served. Everyone was to report to another designated lounge and will "Eddie White, please go to the head of the line, as he has to be on the set directly after lunch." I started to laugh. *Hey, you guys, is this another one of your gags? I didn't come from Squaresville, you know,* I thought.

Then I saw Jim Bloom motioning for me to follow him. He rushed me into another lounge set up with a huge buffet to the left and long tables and chairs to the right. He said I had half an hour to eat lunch, then I was to report to the first assistant director on the set. This was all a daydream. Here I was, dressed as a cop, the center of attraction on a movie set, and everything, for the moment, was revolving around me. I just couldn't believe it.

I went down the line of food, looking at the great array of delicacies. *Boy, they feed you good on a movie set,* I thought. When I arrived at a table, all I had on my tray was a container of milk. For once in his life, Little Orphan Eddie wasn't hungry. The air-force chowhound had lost his appetite. I tried to pay attention to the small talk at my table, but all I could think of was *This may be my first and probably my last film, but today, this very moment, I'm important as hell.* All eyes and attention were focused on me. I laughed when I thought of "Star for a Day." *Man, I had better make the most of these fateful hours when time stands still. If Peter, my son, could see me now.* I told myself I wanted to do good, I had to do good, for him.

After fifteen minutes, I couldn't stand the suspense and headed back toward the set without drinking my milk. There was much movement, setting up of cameras and lights, marking the floors, and the taking of still pictures. Again the crew started on me, stealing my gun and my hat, telling me my scene was cancelled. I smiled like the veteran movie actor I had become. Who were they kidding? United Artists was spending a small fortune, half a day's shooting schedule, to shoot my film debut. *Who knows? Maybe I'm another Bogie or Mitchum. I don't even know myself,* I thought.

Lunch over, the first assistant director, Newton Arnold, approached me and casually said that my scene was an improvisation, that it hadn't been written and I would have to ad lib the lines as I went along. *Jack Waltzer* [my acting teacher], *where are you now that I desperately need you?* I thought. Then Arnold asked me what I had done with my hat and my gun. I didn't want to squeal on the crew so I just looked dumbfounded. He barked out on a bullhorn, and my gun and hat miraculously reappeared.

By now, all the extras were assembling on the set. I could see that this was going to be a mob scene with lots of violence, confusion, and movement, but I was told that the three cameras that were being set up would be trained mostly on me. My limited area of movement was marked off, and I was briefed by Mr. Arnold on what to do. What I had to say was up to me, as if I had been doing this all my life. I looked around for director Sam Peckinpah and saw that his eyes were closed. He was dozing, or out of it, in the director's chair right in front of the cameras.

My assignment, as the security officer at the airport, was to first stop Yuen Chung, or Mako, and his daughter, Tommie, together with their bodyguards, from entering the main lounge at the San Francisco International Airport. They were escaping from Ninja assassins who had tried to kill them in a previous outdoor scene. I would question Mako and ask to see his credentials. When an elderly Chinese gentleman vouched for them and showed me a document, I would allow them to pass.

Then the Ninja assassins, in hot pursuit of Mako and his group, would run through the lounge. I would stop and question them, and then all hell would break loose. Hundreds of extras would start screaming and running in confusion as a mutilated man's body appears on the baggage carousel. Hundreds of actual airline passengers, passing through the San Francisco terminal, were included in the scene.

I noticed Sam Peckinpah, our beloved director, sitting up with his eyes actually open. He motioned for me to approach, and I had to kneel. Sam whispered in my ear, "Kid, don't act, react!" and dozed off again. Good advice. React. I understood and would follow through.

I prepared myself for the scene by making believe I was back in the air force and the ranking officer at this airport or military installation. I tried to get serious, but the crew was still playing practical jokes on me, stealing my gun again and telling me that Mr. Peckinpah wanted me to play the scene as a homosexual cop. The kidding around kept me loose and didn't allow me to take myself too seriously.

I noticed three cameras were trained on me and tried not to look in their direction. I swear once while I was a little boy in the orphan asylum that I envisioned this was going to happen to me someday. Wherever this experience would take me in life, I made up my mind I was going to enjoy and make the most of the moment. I felt proud I had the guts to go through with it. I remembered, as a child, you couldn't get three words out of me. I remembered "Broadway" Jack White, my old man, asking my sister, "What's the matter with him? Is he dumb? Has the cat got his tongue?" Hey, Pop, it's me, your kid. Take a look at me now. Aw, what the hell.

The first assistant director, Newton Arnold, yelled, "Ready," and a thousand people froze. Then "Action" and we were rolling. Everything went exactly as I had hoped: my lines came easy, I hit the marks made for me on the floor, and I felt the adrenalin flow through my veins. I heard Mr. Arnold yell, "Cut!" and I looked at him for some words of praise or correction. He never looked my way but yelled out, "Okay, let's do it again."

We did the scene again, and again he yelled, "Cut!" and "Let's do it once more." I felt something was wrong and asked Jim Bloom if I was okay. He said, "Sure, you're doing swell, but each time we do the scene we move the cameras to get different angles and closeups." By now there was no stopping me. *Watch out, Brando; here I come* was my feeling.

On the third take, the crew, Sam Peckinpah, the actors, the extras, everyone, were all out to get me, it seemed. Suddenly everything changed, the timing, the people, and even the dialogue. In the middle of the scene, while I was speaking to a nun, a man wearing a wig and a trenchcoat appeared and said, "Officer, look at this" and opened his coat and exposed himself. He was stark naked except for his socks and shoes. I almost swallowed my tongue and gave a "take" Jack Oakie would have been proud of. A little dizzy, I followed through with the rest of the scene until suddenly a huge, ugly gorilla of a guy tried to break through one of the security barriers. I thought he was one of the airline passengers who got caught up in the movie scene and stage-whispered, "Hey, buddy, get out of here; we're shooting a movie and you're on the set." All this while, the cameras were still grinding and the microphones were open. He replied, fag style, "That's all right, gorgeous, I'm one of the actors."

When the scene was over, everyone broke out into laughter. I said to myself, *Okay, you guys want to play dirty*, but I noticed they started taking the set down. I ran to Jim Bloom and pleaded that I wanted to do the scene over, that I hadn't known what was happening, and that I could react much better if given another chance. He laughed and patted me on the back. "Eddie, they got just the right take they wanted from you. Don't worry; now you're a member of the Screen Actors Guild."

With a sigh of relief, I walked around the set, not wanting to take my uniform off or leave the airport lounge. I went back to Bobby Duvall's dressing room trailer and hung around for a while, reading magazines, turning the water on, and looking out through the curtains. *I guess that's it, it's over, I'm done, finished, finito, kaput*, I thought. I took a shower, changed my clothes, locked the trailer door, and brought my uniform back to the wardrobe trailer.

At the Holiday Inn, Pat Alexander greeted me with kisses and said she was proud of me. She invited me to dinner in the hotel's dining room, saying I would then meet her close friend Anita Wood. That name rang a bell. Anita Wood?

"Does she have anything to do with the Golden Gate Warriors basketball team?" I asked.

Pat answered, "Yes, she's the owner, Franklin Mieuli's, private secretary."

I said, "She may be his private secretary, but he isn't the owner of the team—maybe the majority stockholder and chief honcho but not the sole owner of the team."

I told Pat about investing my life savings, as a limited partner in what was then the San Francisco Warriors, a group of us having bought the franchise from Mr. Basketball himself, Eddie Gottlieb, and his partners, in Philadelphia. This was in 1962, when professional basketball was at a low ebb. I told her that my son, Peter, was my partner and how excited and thrilled we were to be associated with the team, but my living in New York City precluded my attending the team's business meetings. Our interest, Peter's and my own, wasn't very large, but it represented all the money we had at that time. This was when I was vice-president of Yamaha.

I related how the team was moved to San Francisco, as all of the limited and general partners, including Mr. Franklin Mieuli, came from that area, except me. I told how and when Wilt Chamberlain joined the team and of the years of building and suffering at the box office. Then there was the year we finally won the championship with Rick Barry and I told how I thought we were out of the woods moneywise.

Every few months, I would get a letter from someone connected with the team, one of the investors or Anita Wood, saying that Franklin Mieuli would contact me when he was in New York City and he would personally bring me up to date on the status of the Warriors. Even Mr. Mieuli wrote many times informing me of some future meeting. He never kept his word, I never received any calls, and I never met the man.

I told Pat Alexander that I felt slighted, discouraged, and left out, and in a moment of pique and anger, I sold out to Mr. Mieuli. The ink wasn't dry on the paper when I realized my mistake and tried to undo the agreement, but too late. I realized too late that my investment in the Warriors was more than financial. Peter, my boy, and I were having fun rooting for our own team.

Pat Alexander was most sympathetic, as always, and said if anyone could straighten this situation out properly, it would be her friend Anita Wood. I felt happy and relieved that the least that might happen was that my emotional dilemma would be brought to the attention of Mr. Mieuli. The sale of my interest in the Warriors had been eating me up all this time. Being able to discuss the situation with the proper people and possibly being able to resolve it, I thought, was a tremendous coincidence. God works in mysterious ways.

Ms. Anita Wood showed up, remembered who I was, and sympathized with my situation after hearing my tale of woe. We had a delightful dinner, at which I sang a few of my songs and told my best jokes. Before the evening was over, Ms. Wood repeated most emphatically that she would attend to the matter.

We had a few more dinners, Pat Alexander, Anita Wood, and myself, and I sparkled and entertained my two girl friends all evening long. Each time Anita Wood reminded me that Mr. Franklin Mieuli was out of town but as soon as he returned, she felt my situation would be settled properly. After all, "Franklin's a lot nicer than people realize."

I felt it was time to return home before I had worn my welcome out on all fronts. I had seen my pal Bobby Duvall, lived in Sausalito, gotten to know San Francisco, made many new friends, appeared as an actor in a movie, made progress in resolving my investment in the Warriors basketball team, and spent time in Los Angeles with my friends Stanley Adams, Louie Nye, and Rue McClanahan, and I had the pictures and memories to keep me warm in my old age.

I no sooner got comfortable back in New York when a headline screamed out "Peckinpah Booked In Airport Fracas." It seemed that a young passenger agent's jaw got in the way of our hero Sam's fist at the Los Angeles International Airport. I predict this won't be the last scuffle for Fighting Sam the Man Peckinpah, but I also predict one day he will be cold conked but good.

One afternoon, I was relating some of my experiences out on the West Coast to a few actors who chanced by my office.

Aleta St. James, a fine actress and the sister of Curtis Sliwa, the originator of the Guardian Angels, mentioned that I should join the Screen Actors Guild immediately, inasmuch as I had been a principal in a major film. She stated that the guild would accept me now whereas if I waited too long I would not be eligible. I hopped over to the guild pronto, showed them my contract from Universal Artists, and was formally ushered into the world of acting. Some gal at the Screen Actors Guild cracked, "This card entitles you to be out of work and to authentically starve as an actor." She didn't know that once upon a time, Starve was my middle name.

I was further advised by some of my fellow actors to send glossy eight-by-ten pictures of myself to a few of the casting agents. As my nephew Steve Strauss was a respected fashion photographer, I allowed him the honor of shooting his Unc, as he and his younger brother, Cary, affectionately call me. Mission accomplished, I sat back and waited to see what surprises life now had in store for me.

Before I knew it, I had appeared in a couple of "Kojak" episodes on T.V., been an extra in Woody Allen's *Annie Hall* and *Manhattan*, and played the lead in an off-Broadway play, Clifford Odets's *Waiting for Lefty*. If you look fast, you can see me in back of Woody Allen in *Annie Hall* as he and Diane Keaton have this heated argument while they are waiting on a movie line. Did I get to meet and know Woody Allen? Many times I got to meet Woody Allen, on the film sets, at ABC's Roone Arledge's parties to watch championship fights, and on West 57 Street, but no one—repeat, no one—gets to know Woody Allen. I think he's a genius, in a class by himself, but I doubt if Woody Allen knows Woody Allen.

By this time, Bobby Duvall had firmly secured his longed-for role in *Apocalypse Now* and was knee deep in mud somewhere in the Philippines. I felt sorry for Francis Coppola, as I had heard that a monsoon or hurricane had wiped out his set and a couple of months' shooting schedule. We heard that Harvey Keitel, who had one of the lead roles was unhappy with the on-again, off-again shooting schedule and he was either let out of the film or he had quit, whichever story you believe. It was said that Francis Coppola had lost over fifty pounds, that he was in the hospital with a

285

nervous breakdown, that his wife had left him, that Marlon Brando showed up weighing over 250 pounds, that the Philippine air force was demanding heavy graft from Francis to fly those helicopters, and on and on and on.

Bobby called and asked me to send him a pair of cowboy riding spurs, which he used in that famous "I love the smell of napalm in the morning; it smells of victory" scene. Bobby told me he might use the country song the two of us wrote, "If God Can Forgive Me (Why Can't You Forgive Me, Too?)" in the film if Francis Coppola doesn't insist on holding the copyright. My luck. Francis did so Bobby didn't.

Poor Francis, I thought. Such a nice "haimisha" man, so intensely talented, doing so much, too much, by himself! From what I could learn, Francis Ford Coppola had co-written the screenplay of *Apocalypse Now* and had not only raised money for this film with an enormous budget, but had hocked his house and all his properties, which were eventually devoured by the film and was producing, directing, filming, editing, distributing, and suffering with this monumental obsession. Just the idea of it all would have sent an ordinary man to an asylum. I prayed for my newfound friend, more for his health than anything else.

Bobby once had mentioned that if I showed up in the Philippines, he was sure I could get a small part in the film. With all the problems on Francis's shoulders, I wasn't about to become another one. It didn't sound good or ring true. Pay my own way to the Philippines and hope to land a part and watch Francis emotionally disintegrate? I once made up my mind that acting was going to be fun and games for me or no dice. I most emphatically was not going to give another pound of flesh to this or any other business. I gave already! At the office and on the battlefield of life.

I came to that decision once when I arrived at a casting agent's office to read for a part in a gangster film. I dutifully gave my eight-by-ten composite picture to the secretary and sat down next to three other hopeful mafiosa thespians. The man sitting next to me offered his hand and told me his name. I did likewise and we got to talking. He asked me if I had any kids, and then he told me he was a widower with two kids. He asked me if I knew how much money it took to feed two growing kids. All I could do was shake my head, and then he hit me in the solar plexis. He said, "If I don't get this job, I'm really in trouble. I need the money."

Without thinking, I went over to the secretary and requested she return my picture. She assured me that the producer and director were expecting me and if I couldn't wait, she could arrange for me to be seen right away. I most seriously and emphatically asked her to return my composite picture, which she did with a bewildered look on her face. I walked out of the office with a feeling of complete relief and a solemn vow on my lips. This auditioning or reading for acting parts was for the birds, as far as I was concerned. I made up my mind that there would be no more acting jobs for me unless producers, directors, or casting agents called me for a particular role because they knew me personally or had heard about me. I'm not wealthy, but I surely have enough money not to compete with a poor actor trying to make a basic living. I enjoy acting, but it wouldn't kill me if I never got another part in a film or a play. So far, the producers, directors, and casting agents haven't beaten a path to my door. Shows you how much they know.

Bobby Duvall came back to New York fresh from *Apocalypse Now* and the Philippine Islands to appear in my friend Paddy Chayefsky's film *Network* with William Holden, Faye Dunaway, and Peter Finch, directed by Sidney Lumet. Paddy and I had been friends over a period of years, meeting mostly on the West Side Athletic Club's running track, in the swimming pool, or at the Carnegie Deli for lunch on occasion. Around the time they were filming *Network*, in the M.G.M. building directly across the street from where I lived, Paddy had been spending his weekends at my apartment watching all the ball games and the weekend fights. The fact that they were filming *Network* across the street from me and that my good friend Bobby Duvall was in the film was a coincidence. I had nothing to do with these happenings, happy as I was that it was so.

It was exciting to visit the set and meet Faye Dunaway, or hear Bill Holden expound on the wonders of Africa, or listen to Peter Finch explain how he and his wife escaped from Jamaica in the middle of the night and by the skin of their teeth. Mrs. Finch is a beautiful black lady, and the Jamaican natives were

287

restless and out to do Peter Finch in. At any rate, that's what he believed.

When lunch was announced, we would all march across the street to my friend Bill Funaro's restaurant, mostly for their great hamburgers. That is, all but Sidney Lumet, who I heard expended so much energy during the morning's shooting that his lunches consisted of napping. When I inquired why Mr. Lumet didn't join us, I was asked if I had ever seen or met Sidney's wife, Gail. Gail Lumet was Lena Horne's beautiful daughter. Again it was repeated. "Sidney needs all his strength; he needs his afternoon nap."

At lunch we were regaled by stories, told mostly by Peter Finch. He almost always held center stage, and I was mesmerized by his dynamic personality. Even Paddy Chayefsky, who could enthrall an audience when he so chose, took a low profile while Peter was on. When I heard that Peter Finch had suddenly passed away shortly after *Network* had been an astounding box-office success and won its share of Academy Awards, I was distraught. It reminded me of my feelings during World War II. It seemed that every time I got to like someone from a distance, they would get killed or die somehow. I told Paddy Chayefsky my thoughts, and he said I was sick in the head.

After his performances in *Apocalypse Now* and *Network*, coming after the two *Godfather* films, Robert Duvall's career was at its zenith and his price went up to well over a million for a film. He pretty much could have had his pick of any film or play just for the asking. Bobby felt it was time for him to return to Broadway, and he chose a small off-beat one-set play, *American Buffalo*, written by David Mamet and to be directed by Bobby's close friend and sometimes mentor, Ulu Grossbard.

American Buffalo had two other actors in it, Kenneth McMillan and John Savage, and the three actors made up a friendly, close-knit group. I spent so many nights in Bobby's dressing room, lying on his bed with the lights out and listening to the dialogue onstage, through a small loudspeaker in the room, that I knew all three parts by heart. After the first act, I would throw the lights back on again and greet Bobby as he came offstage. After the show, Bobby and I would usually go across the street from the Ethel Barrymore Theater to Del Somma's restaurant for some Italian food. Most times John Savage would join us.

Sometimes Bobby was too relaxed or happy to make his first entrance on a particular night and would ask me to shake him up and make him mad. If I was at a loss as to what to say, I usually got him with one stock line: "Bobby, I think you're a fag." He would grab me by the shirt and say, "Yeah? Well, I think you're a fag!" and enter seethingly angry, which is what the part called for.

Around this time, Bobby was still going through his divorce and he really wasn't interested in anyone. One evening I got a phone call from a woman I knew who had appeared in a couple of Broadway musicals, Maggy Gorill. She told me that there was a woman in her acting class who was anxious to meet Bobby and asked if I could arrange it. When she mentioned the woman's name, it rang a bell, sort of. Lindsay Crouse. As it turned out, her name was a combination of two former legends of the Broadway theater, Howard Lindsay and her own father, Russel Crouse. *Great credentials; now if the chemistry is A-okay,* I thought. I put Bobby and Lindsay in touch with each other, and children, that's how World War III began.

The chemistry was there all right. Most of the time they were lovey-dovey, starry eyed and oblivious to anyone around or in their company. I thought to myself that this might be it for Bobby, but only for a moment. The arguments and doubts began to increase until one day, after *American Buffalo* closed, the fur really flew during one hectic argument and the Duvall-Crouse romance was ancient history.

Lindsay Crouse eventually married David Mamet, the author of *American Buffalo,* and they now have a daughter, Willa. I sometimes think that I was responsible for this marriage, as I was the unknown catalyst who indirectly brought this all about. When their daughter grows up and possibly becomes a famous actress or marries some prince of industry, I will have been long forgotten. I don't know why these thoughts cross my foggy mind.

Hanging around backstage during *American Buffalo* was John Savage's kid sister, Gail Youngs, a shy, adorable actress-singer. I could tell that Gail had a crush on Bobby, but at the time she hardly ever uttered a word. She just looked at Bobby in that funny, longing way, and you just knew there was something

289

behind that look. I mentioned this to Bobby a few times, never dreaming that years later he would eventually marry this adorable woman.

Before *American Buffalo* closed, author Paddy Chayefsky mentioned to me that he would like to see the show. I called Bobby and he arranged for two courtesy tickets to be left at the box office. On the prearranged night, Paddy and I showed up at the box office and I asked for the two tickets under my name. The clerk said there were no tickets under my name, so I suggested they might be under the name of Mr. Paddy Chayefsky. Again the clerk gave me a negative answer and asked me to move off the line. I refused and insisted there had to be some mistake. In anger the clerk sarcastically asked me if Mr. Chayefsky was with me, and Paddy, who had heard this whole commotion, showed his face. The clerk thereupon threw a ticket at Paddy, which fell to the ground. At that point, an actor who had appeared in the film *Network*, and who also was on the line for tickets, greeted Paddy. The entire crowd in the theater lobby froze for an instant. Paddy picked up the ticket, handed it to the actor, and said to me, "Let's get out of here." As we left, I noticed actor Roy Scheider staring at us from the line.

Outside the theater, Paddy suggested we go over to the Russian Tea Room for dinner and then come back to Bobby's dressing room when the show was over. Jokingly, he said, "We'll tell Bobby that we saw the show and it was lousy." At the Russian Tea Room, we were joined by opera star Robert Merrill and his wife, Marion. I worried all evening and pleaded with Paddy not to joke with Bobby about the lack of tickets but to tell the truth.

Backstage, Bobby greeted us with a smile and lots of energy, like he usually generates when he's happy. He looked at Paddy and said, "Well, what do you think?" Paddy said, "It was great, we heard; only we didn't get to see it." Bobby still had a half-frozen smile on his face when he asked me to explain what Paddy had just said.

I knew that smile and that look, but explain I did. Half a truth was still a lie to Robert Duvall, and lies were something you didn't deal in with my friend. The half-smile now disappeared, and Bobby whispered something to Ulu Grossbard, the director of *American Buffalo*.

The dressing room was now filling up with people, and who walks in but the co-producer of the show, Joe Beruh? Bobby convulsively swings a punch at Joe and then picks up one of those heavy, old-fashioned square wooden chairs and starts to bring it down on Joe Beruh's head. Joe by this time was heading out of the room, and the chair crumbled as it hit the frame of the door. Ulu Grossbard thereupon jumped on Bobby's back and rode him until Bobby calmed down a little. Paddy Chayefsky looked at me and shrugged. "I'm going to use this scene in my next picture," he said.

It took a half-hour for Bobby's dressing room to calm down and get back to some semblance of order. The show's publicist was taking notes furiously, and I just knew this entire episode was going to wind up in all the Broadway newspaper columns, which it did, all with different variations as to what actually happened that evening. Roy Scheider came backstage but didn't come into Bobby's dressing room. Instead he sent in a note that read: "Bobby, sensational! Good luck—I loved it. Roy Scheider (You were having a few words with Joe.)" "A few words"—what an understatement.

For months after this incident, I harbored a grudge against the producer of *American Buffalo*, Joe Beruh. Then one day I happened to meet him in the lounge of the West Side Athletic Club and we shook hands and got to talking. After that, we became friendlier, and I can honestly say I never met a nicer, more down-to-earth and honorable gentleman. That incident at the Ethel Barrymore Theater's box office was none of Joe Beruh's doing, and I've come to the conclusion it was all just a horrible mistake.

Try as I might, I couldn't get Paddy Chayefsky to go back to see *American Buffalo*. His health was beginning to fail, and he continually complained that he didn't have much energy or patience to sit through an entire play. Going to the gym for a workout or a swim was a big effort on Paddy's part, and his afternoon naps were increasing. Paddy had started work on his last motion-picture project, *Altered States*, and the arguments that ensued with the film studios, Warner Brothers, and the director, Ken Russell, and the disagreements he had with the co-producer of the film, Howard Gottfried, proved to be too much for Paddy Chayefsky's health, argumentative and garrulous as he was.

The one time-comsuming thing that Paddy refused to give up was afternoon lunch at the Carnegie Deli. We would meet on a daily basis, many times with director Bob Fosse, playright Herb Gardner, author Noel Behn, producer Irving Mansfield, and myself in attendance. the small talk, show-biz gossip, latest jokes, and gentle but for real ribbing helped Paddy forget his ailments, if only for a while.

Paddy was a battler; he loved an argument, especially if it was on an intellectual level. I remember one friendly argument at Elaine's restaurant with newspaperman Pete Hamill's brother Dennis about whether actress Vanessa Redgrave had the right to air her political convictions on the Academy Awards show. Actors Darrin McGavin, Ben Gazzara, and Dyan Cannon were in attendance, hovering around, listening to the friendly but cutting remarks by both sides. I took Paddy home that night, he being heavy of heart and wishing he had had more strength to defend himself. From what I gathered and heard, Paddy felt he had lost the Vanessa Redgrave argument from its inception. Too many film notables, newspapermen, and organizations came down heavily on Paddy's credibility at a time when he didn't have the "zitz fleish" (patience) to defend himself properly.

Although I too argued with Paddy, about everything under the sun and moon, I started to ease off as I noticed his strength and patience beginning to wane. I went in more for funny stories and jokes to try and make him happy, if only for a few moments. Sometimes he gave me a sad "take" or look as if he knew what I was trying to do.

One of the last really heavy, hysterical arguments that Paddy Chayefsky engaged in took place on the phone in my apartment. Paddy and I were watching our usual Sunday ball games and boxing matches when Paddy's partner and co-producer, Howard Gottfried, called. The discussion between Paddy and Howard started slowly, and then Paddy's blood pressure started to rise and he began shouting, "This is all a trick. I don't want to meet Ken Russell. You're trying to shove him down my throat. I know what you're up to." This went on for close to forty minutes and left Paddy exhausted. I insisted he take a nap for the rest of the afternoon, which he did. He left for home ashen-faced, exhausted, and terribly sad. I said very little.

The arguments continued with Warner Brothers, but English director Ken Russell was eventually hired, over Paddy Chayefsky's protestations. Paddy told me personally that he was sold out by his associate Howard Gottfried and if *Altered States* was ever finished, he, Paddy, was finished with Howard. I felt bad because Howard was also a friend of Paddy's.

The differences became so heated with all who were concerned that I felt certain *Altered States* would never see the light of day. As Paddy was preparing to go out to the Coast, he invited me to go, too. We were to stay in a bungalow at the Beverly Hills Hotel. Paddy let it be known to me that he hated Hollywood, the people and the studios, with a passion and a vengeance. We would stay in mostly, even have our meals at the bungalow, go to the pool, and watch the ball games and films on T.V. I said, "Okay. I'll come out after the film started rolling and Paddy was settled in at the bungalow" as I felt if Paddy had a change of heart after he was involved, I didn't want to feel hurt.

My instincts were on the button. The arguments were too much, and Paddy was either banned from the set or arbitrarily agreed to leave town to allow director Ken Russell more say in the film. The deal with Warner Brothers was for them to send Paddy the "dailies," the filming for each and every day. This way, Paddy could present his thoughts by phone and there would be less wear and tear on everyone concerned. The "dailies" were to be sent to Paddy by air express and on videotape. Paddy swore me to secrecy, and each day we would have lunch and watch the rushes or "dailies," while Paddy took notes. Paddy also asked me to please not express an opinion unless I was asked.

As Paddy watched each previous day's "shoot," his blood pressure rose higher and higher. He disagreed with almost every scene, the acting, the direction, the concept. He would turn white with rage and call Hollywood and spill out his gall and his guts, mostly to his co-producer, Howard Gottfried. For days I would sit there, neither of us talking, and poor Paddy would just stare out the window.

It got so bad, so depressing, that I thought of not showing up when Paddy called me. But I had this gut feeling that I provided some sort of service for Paddy, that he needed a little bit of my strength, my friendship, my company. So I sat there every day and "Yessed" him on everything that was directed my way, just to keep him going. Paddy suffered—oh, how he suffered—and ranted and raved, and I listened and said nothing, but oh, how I suffered, too. One day, after the screaming and threats of a one-hour telephone call had died down, I finally and bravely made my first suggestion. I practically ordered Paddy to lie down and take a nap. As I left the office, Paddy hoarsely whispered that he was taking his name off *Altered States* as the screenwriter, which he did. He used the pseudonym of Sidney Aaron in the screen's credits, Sidney being Paddy's real name.

In spite of all the confusion, hate, and hysterics, *Altered States* was actually getting done. Paddy was getting used to the idea of having to play a distant and lesser role in this, his own film. Changing from a hard-ass, no-nonsense, get-off-my-back nonsentimental intellectual, Paddy Chayefsky began saying nice, almost affectionate things to me. He asked me about Peter, my son, and he would talk about Danny, his son.

We talked about out war experiences and sports. I told Paddy I was undefeated in thirty-one bouts as an amateur boxer, and Paddy told me he was a pulling guard on his college football team. Many times, in the middle of our conversations, Paddy, who would always be sitting in the comfortable recliner in my living room, would fall into a deep sleep for close to forty minutes. I would sit there studying this complex near-genius who was so successful and had such an intellect but was obviously suffering, emotionally unhappy, and highly discontented with almost everything in his life. Soon I and the world would find out that Mr. Paddy Chayefsky was also suffering from many physical ailments beyond repair.

Those last few months I tried to make the happiest and most fun-filled since I first got to know Paddy. We saw all the championship fights in Roone Arledge's offices up at ABC or in his entire floor suite at the Plaza Hotel. Although the food and wine flowed freely at all of Roone Arledge's get-togethers, Paddy would not partake of a thing. While I was scouting the huge buffet table and selecting a few of Mr. Arledge's fine cigars, Paddy would be talking in a corner with Bob Fosse, Woody Allen, David Susskind, or even Henry Kissinger. After the fights, I would rush Paddy home in a cab, as he was usually exhausted.

One of our last enjoyable evenings was at the preview of *Raging Bull*. Paddy and I had looked forward to this night because the film was about fights. As we approached the Sutton Theater, I could see a line forming, waiting for the doors to open. I went to the manager, hoping to seat Paddy immediately, as I knew he wasn't able to stand on line. As soon as the manager saw Paddy, and before I could say a word, they greeted each other warmly and we were ushered to our seats. It seems that all of Paddy's films, including *Network*, had been previewed at the Sutton. Before the lights went out, Paddy sent me to the candy stand for red licorice, which we both loved. There we sat like two kids, teasing each other, seeing who could eat the red licorice faster, and reminiscing about the names of all the old-fashioned candy. It was a candy shootout. Paddy would say, "Buttons on paper" and I would say, "Rock candy"; Paddy would say, "Jaw breakers," and I would answer, "Chocolate twists," and on and on until *Raging Bull* was on the screen. The film was about Jake La Motta's life, and although he sat alongside Paddy and myself, I wasn't too thrilled, being a Rocky Graziano man myself and with Jake La Motta being from the enemy camp. It's hard to explain about Rocky and Jake, but I kept my thoughts to myself, as Paddy was having the time of his life.

The lunches with Paddy at the Carnegie Deli were now becoming fewer and further apart. I couldn't help but notice that Paddy, who had had little tufts of dark hair in his beard and hair, was now white-haired and his face was becoming gaunt, as he was losing weight. I still thought that whatever was ailing my friend was just a passing thing. Paddy, who had written the film *Hospital* and obviously despised doctors, was now becoming very involved with them and was at their complete mercy, to hear him tell it.

In the past, whenever Paddy had to go to the hospital, he let it be known through the media that he was on a cruise or a vacation. This time, all was ominously silent. Paddy had a variety of things wrong with him, but again, I just knew he would pull through, I would see him again, and all things would be the same.

Sure enough, after a number of weeks Paddy left the hospital, and one afternoon he called me to meet him at the Carnegie for lunch. It was then I knew that the end was not too far away, but

With Paddy Chayefsky and strawberry licorice at screening of *Raging Bull*.

like a little child, I was still hoping for a miracle. As much as I've seen and known of death, before, during, and after the war, I still can't accept or get used to the idea, especially about Paddy Chayefsky. Surely God realized this man's contribution to the world of theater.

Paddy was more gaunt than ever, had no appetite, and was now losing his hair. It was whispered that he was undergoing chemotherapy treatments, which usually result in the loss of hair. That afternoon, as we said good-bye, I had the feeling this was the final curtain. Paddy reentered the hospital and shortly thereafter expired. As I entered a restaurant on a Saturday evening, the bartender expressed his sorrow on the passing of my friend. He thought I knew, but shocked as I was, I asked no questions. I just knew he was referring to Paddy, my friend Paddy Chayefsky.

12

So Long, Paddy

LAST MONTH—AUGUST 1, 1981, to be exact—my friend Paddy Chayefsky passed away. I had been able to speak about his passing, but more importantly, hadn't been able to write about it, till now.

Paddy, so full of life, of ideas, questions, solutions, advice, opinions. It was Paddy's idea for me to write this book. When I kept putting it off, he actually threatened me.

And then he stayed on top of me when I dodged it or stalled on finishing a certain chapter. Then when I did finish a painful difficult episode, Paddy would buy me lunch at the Carnegie Deli, pat me on the back, and say, "I knew you could do it!

At the funeral, I was especially touched by the sadness shown by Paddy's very close friend Bob Fosse. Bob kept breaking down. At the graveside, when the Kaddish was being said, Bob walked a little way off to sob by himself. Their friendship, Paddy's and Bob's, was such a private, personal thing that I thought Bob might have wanted to keep his bereavement the same way. I kept watching Bob the entire day, as I was worried about him. He didn't look too well himself, and although we had never been that close, I somehow felt close to him the day of Paddy's funeral.

This was Bob Fosse's second loss of a close personal friend within one year. First it was his friend and collaborator on *All That Jazz* playwright Robert Alan Arthur, and now it was Paddy.

The day before the funeral, I had spoken to writer Noel Behn and asked him whether he was going to say a few words at the funeral ceremony. Noel asked me if I wanted to speak, and I said emphatically that I did. I took his question and my answer to mean that he would arrange for me to speak. Noel was handling

Rob (Meathead) Reiner, Paddy, me, and Bob Fosse in happier days.

a few of the funeral affairs, along with Herb Gardner and Bob
Fosse. Herb and Bob were actually Paddy's two closest friends.

Evidently, my request never got to the proper people, as I
never got to speak. I was crushed momentarily, but then actor
Harold Gary, who was sitting next to me in the chapel, said,
"Eddie, it wouldn't bring Paddy back, so forget it." This is what
I wrote as my eulogy to Paddy Chayefsky. This is what I was
going to say:

> When I first heard that Paddy had passed away, I was
> very surprised. I just didn't think that Paddy would allow
> such a thing to happen!
> Paddy and I were pals. . . . We used to go to the gym
> together almost every day. . . . We'd swim, lift weights . . .
> and mostly jog around the track . . . arguing all the time . . .
> about everything . . .
> Then weekends we'd watch the ball games at my
> house—baseball . . . football . . . sometimes the fights . . .
> still arguing all the time . . . I said that Paddy didn't know
> the difference between a middle line backer and a squeeze

298

bunt . . . and Paddy agreed . . . he didn't know. . . . And he asked me what the difference was . . . and I didn't know. We were the gang who couldn't shoot straight when it came to sports. Just to give you an idea . . . Paddy picked the Mets to win the pennant this year.

Paddy and I were miles apart intellectually . . . but he never said anything . . . and *I* wasn't about to embarrass the poor guy. . . .

I'm going to miss Paddy . . . the arguments . . . the close friendship. . . .

I know Paddy didn't like corn . . . but I have to say this. . . . My pal Paddy isn't dead. . . . He lives on in the hearts of his family . . . all of us . . . his friends . . . and surely in all the things he's written.

I sent a copy of my little eulogy to Sue Chayefsky, Paddy's brave wife, as I wanted her to know how I felt. I also sent a copy to Herb Gardner and Bob Fosse. I then received a call from Rabbi Jerome Cutler of the Sholom Aleichem Synogogue in Hollywood, California. He asked me to kindly send him a copy of the eulogy, which was read at a memorial service in honor of Paddy.

The services in New York for Paddy were held at the Riverside Chapel on 76th Street and Amsterdam Avenue. They were the most auspicious and dignified services I had ever attended, and it seemed to me that everyone who had spoken to Paddy or come into contact with him was there, except one, William Holden. Everyone wondered why he hadn't attended. I guess there's an explanation. I know there was talk of an air controllers' strike.

Historian Arthur M. Schlesinger, Jr., said that for all his satire, Paddy never abandoned hope in humanity. Director Sidney Lumet said that Paddy was irreplaceable, and then he completely broke down and couldn't continue. I thought of the first time I had met Mr. Lumet, when Paddy and Bobby Duvall would take me over to the set while they were shooting *Network*. We'd eat hamburgers with William Holden and Peter Finch. I once asked where Mr. Lumet was having lunch and someone answered, "Sidney? He's taking a nap; he always does during lunch!" Now Paddy and Mr. Finch were gone.

David Shaw, the playwright, talked about himself and Paddy

in television during the '50s and how Paddy had such high standards.

Bob Fosse talked about "auditioning" before he could become Paddy's friend. His speech touched me the most, because I sometimes thought I too had to audition in order to become Paddy's confidant and friend. Also, the things Bob talked about were things that I already knew, and all I could do was keep nodding my head in assent. I also kept thinking, *Here's a side to Bob Fosse that he hardly ever shows. A very sensitive, loving side. I guess it isn't too good to show such qualities in the mercenary arena known as show business.*

Some memories filled my heavy heart and head. I thought of how Paddy had sworn me to secrecy. I was not to tell anyone that I had seen the dailies or rushes on his film *Altered States* or to mention the trouble he was having with director Ken Russell, or how awful he thought the film was turning out, or how disappointed he was in his partner Howard Gottfried's not walking out on the film, along with Paddy, as he had wanted him to.

Then Fosse broke down and cried and I fell apart, too. I thought I had done all my crying at home and on my slow walk up to the chapel. I hoped it was true that "tears are good for the soul."

Playwright and close friend Herb Gardner described Paddy as he saw and knew him. Herb said that he rarely ever got the last word in whenever they spoke. I thought, *No one ever got the last word in when Paddy spoke.* And I say that with affection. When Paddy spoke, I didn't dare interject my prosaic thoughts or ideas. When he stopped speaking, I would sometimes overpower him with my jokes and corny philosophy. I must have hit a soft spot somewhere, as Paddy always listened to me and there often was a touch of kindness in his gruff manner. Whenever he shouted at me, there was still a smidgen of good nature. Oh, I yelled back at Paddy sometimes, but the difference was, I made sure he knew I was only kidding around. Then Paddy's brother Winn spoke emotionally of Paddy's love for his family, saying that whatever he was, Paddy was always a brother.

As Paddy's coffin was being wheeled out of the chapel, past me, I touched it, saying, "So long, Paddy." Out on the street, I heard a woman say, "They packed a lifetime into forty minutes."

There was much shouting and arranging for the trip to the cemetery. I just stood there, not knowing which way to turn, until Bob Fosse told me to get into the third limousine, the first two being for the immediate family. I looked into the car and saw Mr. and Mrs. Arthur Schlesinger sitting on jump seats and Noel Behn and two unidentified women sitting in the back. I didn't feel like sqeezing in anywhere, so I asked the chauffeur if I could ride up front with him, and he agreed.

The ride to the cemetery upstate took close to an hour, and not a single word was uttered by anyone. I thought it strange, but then my mind went back to Paddy and all the funny times and outrageous things we did together. Suddenly the silence somehow got to me and I turned around to Mr. Schlesinger and asked, "Are we permitted to speak?" It was a terrible attempt at humor, the line falling like a lead hockey puck. No one answered me. It looked like everyone was terribly embarrassed. I thought it was funny, though, and could almost see Paddy stifling a laugh somewhere up in Writer's Heaven. Paddy was always irreverent, I thought, but the stillness in that long automobile ride showed me I was no Paddy Chayefsky.

After the services in the cemetery, most of us went back to Winn Chayefsky's home in Scarsdale for lunch. I took hold of Sue Chayefsky's hand, kissed her, and told her how sorry I felt. She said she wanted me to stay in touch and after I come back from my Montauk vacation, she wanted to take me and and all of Paddy's pals out for "some fun." I kissed her again and went into the bathroom and cried. Now that he was gone, there would be this tremendous gap in my life. Whenever I watched a professional fight or a baseball or a football game or a debate in the past, Paddy was there to explain everything. Whether I agreed with Paddy or not, It was reassuring to know his tremendous mind was at my disposal. And there was this wonderfully warm friendship, Paddy always asking for jokes and more stories about my past life. And what about the book?

I thought that death wasn't fair. It just doesn't give anyone time to say good-bye. How I loved my little nephew Bebop (his real name was Peter and my son was later named after him), and his life was snuffed out in a bus accident. I remember thinking then I would just like to hold him once more and kiss him and say good-bye. So many things were left unsaid between Paddy and myself, so many things left undone and unresolved. Again maybe I was crying for myself? This life-and-death thing sometimes gets you all mixed up.

Paddy used to take me everywhere: to film screenings, to parties given by the top celebrities, to closed-circuit fights right in ABC president Roone Arledge's offices, complete with gourmet food and butlers serving us, to the openings of new Broadway plays, to ball games at Shea Stadium (never to a Yankee game, Paddy was an inveterate Met fan!), to The Russian Tea Room, to Elaine's—you name it, we were there. We sat with the most important names in and out of show business, or they would come by to chat with my pal Paddy. He sometimes gave me such a big buildup I would turn around to see whom he was talking about.

Me, I would play the court jester, the jokester, for Paddy, and I loved it. His usual favorite expression being okay "Eddie, tell them that story you always fuck up!" And I would act out my part of getting mad and he would play out his role of getting my goat and everyone came out ahead. Abbot and Costello never got more laughs than we did at the Carnegie Deli. But then, that was my room—such lighting, the sound. I always did well there.

Then there were the somber times, most times after we worked out in the gym. A newspaper headline would disturb Paddy, and he would become incensed. Over iced coffee, we would discuss the situation, and after listening to Paddy's feelings on the subject, I would sometimes walk home from 63rd Street and Central Park West and think how lucky I was to know such a brilliant person. As I look back now, I think that a good deal of who I am and what I know I got sitting at the feet of Paddy Chayefsky.

Then there were the laughs, like the time we went to a screening of Paddy's film *Network* A woman came up to Paddy and asked him to please write something on her program. Paddy picked up the pen and turned to me and said, "Eddie, what should I write?" Sensing a rare opportunity in my life, I milked it for all it was worth. I said, "Paddy, what did you say?" Paddy, annoyed and impatient by now, said, "What should I write?" I said, "Paddy, no one will ever believe me. You actually asked me to tell you what to write. I have to tell my son; I have to savor

302

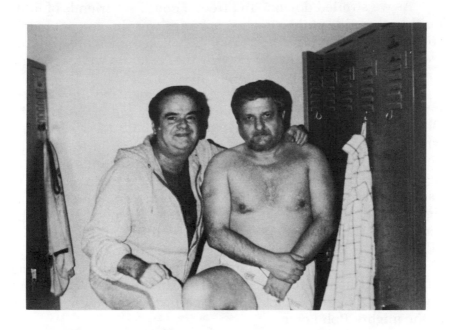

With Paddy at the gym. His illness is starting to show.

this moment, if you don't mind." Paddy told me to shut up and mentioned something that rhymed with "sunnuvabitch."

Then there was the time when Paddy, Bob Fosse, Noel Behn, and I had one of our Deli lunches. On the way out, we decided to walk Fosse back to his offices in The Director's Building on West 57th Street, between 6th and 7th Avenues. Bob suggested we all make a little wager of a dollar a man. Whichever of the four of us got the first greeting from anyone, be it man, woman, child, or animal, would get paid a dollar each from the other three men.

Easy money. I had the best of it. I was the unofficial mayor of that entire neighborhood. I knew every storekeeper and every bag lady by their first names. Some people who might recognize Bob Fosse or Paddy Chayefsky might not dare speak to them. But anyone would approach and speak to me, especially when I was in such elite company. I was the clear favorite. Noel Behn was the dark horse, known to only a select few.

As we strolled down 57th Street, I could see friends of mine on the other side of the street. Fosse kept warning me not to talk so loud and not to wave, and Chayefsky asked me when I started walking like Charlie Chaplin, saying that I should walk a straight line. No matter, I knew I couldn't miss.

As luck would have it, nary a soul recognized any of us. It must have been one of those days. Finally we arrived at the Director's Building, and just as we were about to say hail and farewell we all noticed a ballet dancer standing in front of the building with her feet spread out in opposite directions and holding onto the obvious tutu bag. Fosse tipped his trademark hat to us and started to do this shuffle off to Buffalo into the building, right past the young woman. Upon seeing someone dancing, she screamed, "Why, you're Bob Fosse. Please discover me. I'm good; I'll show you."

Fosse continued his dancing back to the three of us, holding out his right hand, and we all shelled out a buck apiece. I said it wasn't fair, but for a buck I wasn't going to argue with the likes of the mighty Bob Fosse.

The next day, Paddy and I had one of our tête-à-tête lunches where we shared a white turkey sandwich with no mayonnaise and swore we would both go on a diet and lose twenty pounds each, starting the following Monday. It was always manãna with our diets; those Mondays came and went, and we never lost any weight.

Again it was a nice afternoon, so we strolled down to a bookstore on West 57th Street. Paddy used to buy books like most people bought the staples of life. I think he read everything that was ever written. I know he did every crossword puzzle they ever printed.

Strolling down 57th Street, we chanced to meet a lovely young thing, Missy O'Shea, who was just getting set to appear in John Travolta's new film, *Blowout*. Missy screamed the usual show-business greeting, "Eddie, darling, how are you?"

I turned to Paddy and said, "Well, what do you think? Isn't she gorgeous?"

Paddy looked at Missy and then at me and said, "Yeah, yeah, but where the hell was she yesterday?"

A few days before Paddy passed on, the way I heard it, he

had asked Herb Gardner and Bob Fosse to give him sort of a farewell party the night of the funeral. So all of his friends gathered that evening at Herb's house for our "Paddy party." We were told to tell Paddy stories with no tears, but lots of laughs, and there would be great food and plenty of booze. I was still a little bewildered and tired from the huge funeral. I had a heavy heart, knowing I would never see Paddy again, and was generally out of sync from meeting and greeting so many people. Barbara Gardner, Herb's beautiful and very sweet wife, said she hoped to see me at the party, and knowing and adoring her from the moment we first met, I showed up. Before marrying Barbara, Herb had gone with Marlo Thomas for years, and they were considered quite an item. I had met Marlo on occasion, and although we had never really gotten to know each other, I had always respected the things for which she stood, the things she had written and said. I rated her with other women I looked up to, such as Jane Fonda and Erma Bombeck.

I may not have always agreed with these women on everything, but they usually put up such a strong, sensible argument that they could win me over to their side more times than not. But Barbara Gardner was all of these women plus apple pie, cotton candy, and the American flag. I would surely follow her into battle.

At the party, besides Herb and Barbara Gardner and Bob Fosse, there were actors Charles ("Chuck") Grodin, Roy and Cynthia Scheider, Bob Dishy, and Rose Gregorio, directors Elaine May, Robert Altman, Ulu Grossbard, Sidney Lumet, Arthur Hill, and Arthur Penn, writers Peter Stone, Noel Behn, and Peter Maas, agent Sam Cohen, and a host of other theatrical dignitaries I can hardly recall. Greeting me at the door of Herb and Barbara's apartment was Herb Schlein, the genial host of the Carnegie Deli.

I immediately had myself a stiff drink in order to relax in front of all of these famous and familiar faces. It never took much booze to get me feeling happy and loose, and before I knew it, I was telling funny stories and reminiscing about Paddy and there was a little crowd of people hanging onto my every word. The laughs were coming in the right places, and I opened up and went for broke.

My loudest laugher was Cynthia Scheider, and my biggest

heckler was Robert Altman, who was very good-natured in spite of having had too much to drink. Bob Fosse heckled me a bit, but I expected him to, as he was a carryover from our Paddy days. I played the buffoon and loved it. Little Orphan Eddie had all these big-name celebrities sitting up and listening to him, if only for a moment. I remembered thinking that If I bombed out, I could always blame it on the booze. I held center stage and did great, but Harold Gary's words kept popping into my head: "So what? It won't bring Paddy back!"

I left the "Paddy party" at the height of all the laughter and stories, but not before I got to listen to a wonderfully warm guy by the name of Charles "Chuck" Grodin. His plea and message, simply put, was: "Why can't people everywhere be nice and civil to each other?" I couldn't agree more and shook his hand until we were both embarrassed.

Drunk with mixed feelings of happiness and depression, I walked all the way home, a distance of over a mile and a half. *Paddy, Paddy, Paddy, where the hell did you go? You sure gave me something; you left with a fucking headful of thoughts,* I mused. *For one thing, Paddy, you opened me up quite a bit.* A couple of Paddyisms I recall: "Eddie, don't fall in with the commies; most of them weren't nice people to begin with" and "Hollywood is a great place if you are a Mercedes-Benz." Still another was "Don't you know you're nobody in America unless you're indicted?" And there was "Don't count your net worth until high noon."

13
More Memories

WHEN PADDY passed away, I had most of this book unfinished; I had only written about five chapters. the manuscript was lying on a small table next to the couch where I usually slept. Every time I looked at the manuscript, I got these little pains. The more I looked at the manuscript, the more I hated it.

My sister, Ruth, called me from Florida to see how I was feeling and to offer her condolences regarding Paddy. Something in my voice told her all wasn't right, She said she didn't like the way I sounded and would be on the next flight to LaGuardia, even though there was a controler's strike imminent.

For three days, sister Ruth lectured me on being a quitter and not being loyal to Paddy's memory and generally laid all the heavy Jewish guilt on me she could muster. She didn't realize it, but all the time she was lecturing me she was sitting in Paddy's recliner, the chair he always sat in. I took it as a sign from on high and thought I had best finish the book post haste or Paddy wouldn't rest in peace. I could just picture Paddy saying to me, "You always fuck up all the jokes you tell, and now you're fucking up your book!"

I made up my mind I would go to Gurney's Inn out in Montauk, rest up from all this trauma, and then attack the book head on. Better still, I'd take all the pads and notes out to Montauk with me and write as much as I could, block out some chapters, make some notes, and write down some ideas.

A friend who was the owner of a fine New York restaurant had rented a limousine to take me to Gurney's. His wife was an actress, had this terrible facial virus, and we felt the fifteen-day rest would do us all a world of good. Nothing could be truer.

My room at Gurney's overlooked the ocean. I had to pay for a double room even though I was only one person. The tab came to around $150 a day, which included breakfast and dinner. After three days, I didn't want to look at their Italian menu ever again. Everything tasted like it was cooked in a Horn and Hardart restaurant on Mulberry Street.

My friend, his wife, and I were so bored with the menu that we devised a little scheme. We were permitted by the inn rules to each order a dinner worth up to fifteen dollars. Anything over that amount would be added to our bill. So we would spend an hour going over the menu, picking out all the appetizers, which by then tasted much better than the entrées. For forty-five dollars you order a lot of appetizers, and with bread and butter and hot coffee we turned a dull Italian dinner into a Roman grand buffet. Some days we got bored of the appetizers so we would send out for Montauk Episcopalian fried chicken. It was better than nothing, but their chicken actually had no taste. I think it was seasoned with neuter herbs. Montauk could use a good eating place.

My restaurateur friend knew Bob Entenmann, the famous cake entrepreneur. Bob and his family had recently sold their huge pastry empire to Warner Lambert, and although Bob Entenmann was still under contract to the firm, he was now busily buying land and racehorses to breed. Bob had this huge ranch in Riverhead, Long Island, which we visited, and I learned a thing or two about the breeding of horses. I found it to be one of the most interesting, educational, and entertaining hobbies, and I longed to be involved with horses and ranches for the rest of my life. I've always been drawn to the outdoors, horses, fishing, camping, and that sort of thing, but "the best laid plans of mice and men . . . "

Robert Entenmann also had this beautiful yacht, the *Jacqueline II*, moored out off Montauk. We spent a few days fishing ninety-two miles out in the ocean, at a place called Block Canyon. It was an adventure with wonderful memories. I caught enough fish—one was a 235-pound "big eye" tuna—and ate enough Entenmann cake to last me two lifetimes. That Entenmann chocolate coffee crumb cake should be a felony, a crime. A human being should not be subjected to such immorality, such temptation.

Needless to say, the two weeks we spent out in Montauk

was so relaxing that I didn't write a single word. I swore I would attack the book once I got back to the city. It took twelve months, a full year, to write this book. I am certain that if my pal Rocky Graziano didn't show up for breakfast at least three times a week, if I didn't go to all those long Henny Youngman brunches at the Carnegie Deli, if I put more time into writing, if I thoroughly applied myself, I could have written this book in six or seven months. But all the interruptions were good, too: they sometimes stimulated and inspired me; they gave me a breather, a time to recollect, to take stock of myself and events, to formulate a plan of continuance to finish the book. Besides, all the interruptions were fun and games, and man cannot live by bread or work alone. As my business card reads: "Only doing the things that are personally satisfying."

As the Sugar Ray Leonard–Tommy Hearns fight date drew near, I constantly thought about my pal Paddy Chayefsky. This would be the first big championship fight in six years that we wouldn't be watching together. I thought that it wouldn't kill me to skip the fight altogether, to ignore it as if it didn't exist. And that's what I tried to do.

Having breakfast almost every morning with Rocky Graziano at my apartment-office didn't help any. All The Rock did was talk about the upcoming fight. The excitement started to build, and I thought of calling Mr. Roone Arledge's office up at ABC TV and asking him if I could attend the usual private screening over at the Plaza Hotel. I soon dropped the idea, thinking I might be imposing on Paddy's memory. Who was I to Roone Arledge anyway—"Paddy's friend, what's-his-name?" The insecurities of yesteryear always worked their old black magic.

The fight was scheduled to go on at 10:30 P.M. on Wednesday, September 16. Here it was the day of the fight, and the hours seemed suspended in time. At six-thirty, I had a leisurely dinner with casting director Joy Todd and her parents at one of our usual restaurants and all the waiters kept asking my opinion of the fight and wasn't I going to see it, et cetera. I told them I had something else I had to attend to and I could miss a championship fight without falling apart.

Not this one I couldn't. I said good-bye to Joy and her parents and went home to see if there were any messages on my answering machine. Maybe Bobby Duvall wanted me to join him somewhere, he being another tremendous fight fan. Maybe someone had a stray ticket to Madison Square Garden and wanted me to join them. I could go to one of the theaters by myself and try to get in, but I heard this time everything was sold out. Besides, I didn't like watching fights by myself.

The time was now nine-thirty, and the fight was set for an hour away. I turned on the TV to relax and forget, but all anyone talked about was the big fight. Finally, I just couldn't take it any longer.

I jumped up and dialed the Plaza Hotel and asked for Mr. Roone Arledge. The woman answering the phone said he hadn't arrived as yet and "Who's calling?" I mumbled my name and immediately she said, "Oh, Mr. White, I'm sorry about your friend Mr. Chayefsky. Are you coming over to see the fight?" A piece of cake.

I flew over to the Plaza and actually arrived before most of the distinguished guests got there. It was like old home week with one exception. Everyone mentioned how sorry they were about Paddy.

As usual, the food was sumptuous, the fine wine flowed, and Mr. Arledge's Don Diego cigars never smoked better. I couldn't have been more excited anywhere else in the world at that moment but in that suite of rooms. Mr. Arledge came in a short time later and welcomed me with open arms. *What a class guy!* I thought. *The bigger they are,* et cetera.

Cynthia and Roy Scheider sat on the floor, and we shared a running commentary about the fight. Bob Fosse sat alongside them in his usual fastidious black outfit, and we awkwardly shared some pleasantries, trying hard not to mention Paddy.

All the usual faces were there, authors Peter Stone and Peter Maas, David and Joyce Suskind, Walter Cronkite, Dick Cavett, George Plimpton, Woody Allen with Mia Farrow, and so on.

There were also some new interesting faces. To my right not five feet away sat Mr. and Mrs. Henry Kissinger and Lil Ole Blue Eyes himself, Frank Sinatra.

I should think that would be excitement enough, but forth-coming was the fight of the decade. I could see Sinatra's face tense with anticipation. I'll bet he had a bundle on Hearn or Leonard. Everyone knows that Frank Sinatra is a high roller, a real sportsman.

I didn't make a bet on this fight, as I really didn't have a strong opinion. As I previously said, Rocky Graziano hadn't given me a winner in over thirty years, so I waited for him to pick a fighter, a potential winner. For a week he talked about Sugar Ray Leonard being too smart for Tommy Hearns, but then he was invited on the Warner Wolfe CBS TV show and publicly picked Tommy Hearns to knock Leonard cold. Now I was confused. This fight was exciting enough without having to make a bet. I thought of talking to Frank Sinatra to remind him of the old Hank Sanicola, Benny Barton, Solly Parker days when we shared adjoining offices on the fourth floor of the Brill Building. I'm sure he didn't want to hear anything about my writing a song he recorded or anything else that evening except the upcoming fight. And here it was: the fight was on and everyone tensed with anticipation. I forgot myself and started a running commentary about what was happening. Suddenly I realized what I was doing and was about to shut up when Cynthia Scheider said, "Keep going, Eddie. You seem to know more about what's going on than anyone else here." I continued to explain what was happening as the fight progressed, mostly in lay terms for many of the women in the room. I remembered how hyper I felt, but I couldn't stop now; I was on a roll. Then too, no one tried to stop me and it seemed that everyone was listening. The fight was thrilling, the evening was a huge success, and I didn't fall on my face, if I must say so myself. As I was leaving, lovely Cynthia Scheider remarked, "You were so interesting, Eddie. No one even knew that Dr. Kissinger was in the room tonight!" Talented, beautiful Cynthia—from your honest lips to God's ears.

On March 10, 1982 I went to see a good friend of mine at Mount Sinai Hospital. He was recuperating from two delicate kidney operations. It seems he had tried to get his name into the *Guinness Book of Records* by drinking fifty-three bottles of beer in a ten-hour period. Those are the hazards of being a restaurateur: you're always susceptible and exposed to demon booze. You're always hanging around your own bar. While the two of us were making small talk and catching up on each other, my friend suddenly remarked that Irving Berlin was in the next room. I asked him if he was kidding, and he said, "Go look for yourself."

I wandered out into the hall and read the name on the door of Room 730. It was M. Berman. *My sick friend probably made*

311

a mistake, I thought. At that point, a sweet, elderly, well-dressed lady came to the door, which was slightly ajar, and asked me if she could be of any help. I recognized Mrs. Irving Berlin, the former Ellen Mackay. For a moment, I was at a loss for words. *Is this nice great grandmotherly-looking person the wife of that terrible ogre Irving Berlin? I wondered. The man who unknowingly destroyed my Fort Dix army show, who set my writing career back ten, fifteen, twenty years?* She told me that Mr. Berlin was terribly grumpy about being in a hospital, that his appetite was fairly good under the circumstances, that he didn't want anyone to know he was in the hospital, and that she was on her way out to fetch him his favorite Baskin and Robbins ice cream. I quickly volunteered to go fetch the ice cream, but she said it was all right. She wanted to go herself. Before I knew it, I was shaking her hand and telling her I was a former songwriter and a member of ASCAP, too, that I was a friend of Mr. Hal David, the president of ASCAP, and that I was an ardent admirer of Mr. Berlin, and I told her a story I had picked up just a few days prior: "Someone had mentioned to Fred Astaire that it must seem wonderful that Cole Porter had written so many great songs for him. Fred thought for a moment and then said, 'Yes, it was wonderful, but Irving Berlin had written more!' " Mrs. Berlin benevolently smiled, shook my hand warmly again, and headed for the elevator. I watched her for a moment and then thought of walking into the room and greeting the dean of American songwriters. I just touched the door, the closest I ever came to Irving Berlin, and then I chickened out. What happened to my vendetta against Mr. Berlin? Where was my past hostility and anger for this man? It actually never existed. It was a tempest in a crockpot. The truth came out that early evening in front of Room 730 at the Klingenstein Pavillion of Mount Sinai Hospital. Irving Berlin was ninety-three years old then, God bless him. I thought, *Long live the king, the king of popular music the world over.* I was thrilled that night and still am to think I came within ten feet of Mr. Irving Berlin.

On Saturday morning, February 27, 1982, I had just returned from visiting my son and sister in Florida and chanced to bump into my pal Henny Youngman, of "Take my wife, please!" fame. Henny grabbed me around the shoulders and insisted I join him

The Carnegie Deli mob. That's Larry King of radio fame, our host Leo Steiner, King of the oneliners Henny Youngman, and me.

for breakfast at the Carnegie Delicatessen. Knowing the sumptuous, ritualistic, mouth-watering spread I was about to partake of, I didn't put up too much resistance. I could start my Pritiken diet on Monday.

The Carnegie was jammed and noisy, as always. Our host Leo Steiner had four or five tables put together to take care of the usual Henny Yongman Sunday morning brunch entourage. This Sunday, Henny had invited a few gorgeous women from the Playboy musical revue, a couple of comics, some publicists, Larry King, the WOR all-night–talk-show host, and one serious-looking young man who sat directly in front of me. I didn't catch his name, but I did hear that he had recently written an article on Henny Youngman for the *New Yorker* magazine.

Some talk was exchanged from one side of the dining room to the other; loud greetings and the usual screams when theatrical

313

people meet after not seeing each other for half a day could be heard a block away. This young man sitting in front of me said he had heard that I was a good friend of Paddy Chayefsky. I nodded, more intent on and involved with the sturgeon, cream cheese, and bagels. He went on to say that he had heard that Paddy, before his death, was involved with a play dealing with Alger Hiss. Again I nodded absentmindedly, not being able to deal too well with the food and the conversation.

"From what you heard from Mr. Chayefsky, did he consider Alger Hiss innocent or guilty?"

I went on noshing, saying, "You'll never be able to guess."

The serious looking young man replied, "I think I can. Paddy Chayefsky thought that Mr. Hiss was guilty."

"Correct," I said. "This was the basis for one of our last disagreements between Paddy and me. After much research, Paddy came to the conclusion that Alger Hiss was guilty. I maintained, mostly on gut and emotional feeling, that Alger Hiss was innocent." The young man extended his hand, and I automatically shook it, saying, "What's that for?"

He said, "I'm Tony Hiss, Alger Hiss's son. My father was and is innocent, which will surely be proven someday."

I almost choked on my bagel.

There was a side to Robert Duvall's nature that I had always known existed. I had seen him lose his temper in my apartment when he was told that Dustin Hoffman never wanted to return for a visit to his upstate home; when he had become incensed at the producer of the film *The Killer Elite*; when he threatened the producer of *American Buffalo* for failing to leave tickets for Paddy Chayefsky; and on other highly charged emotional occasions.

Many times he screamed at me, mostly for minor things that he mostly imagined. I was beginning to learn to roll with the punches, and the smoke would eventually clear and time would pass and our friendship would somehow weather the storm.

I wasn't ready for what was to come, and in no way was I going to take the insults hurled at me, for no apparent reason. In the fall of 1982, I got caught in a jigsaw from which there was no escape. The only way out, as I saw it, would be for me to squeal on someone, and then I possibly would be in the clear. I say possibly, because when Robert Duvall gets angry, he never has a clear head. Not even remotely.

Bobby had become engaged to this lovely girl, Gail Youngs, the sister of actor John Savage. Everyone was happy, as Gail was sweet-natured and a talented actress and singer, and would surely be a good influence on our friend Bobby. "Maybe he would become more settled," most of us thought out loud.

One day, I received a call from Bobby's secretary inviting me to a stag dinner in honor of Bobby's forthcoming marriage. There would be twenty to twenty-five guys there, and Bobby's future father-in-law was throwing the bash. The party was to start at 8:00 P.M., and Bobby would show up around 9:00 P.M.

The afternoon of the party, I received a phone call from the owner of the restaurant, who was also a distant friend of mine, and he was quite agitated. "Who was paying for this party?" he asked. I mentioned that I was told that Bobby's father-in-law was picking up the tab. The owner said the whole thing smelled and that he didn't like the way "this thing" looked, and he mentioned how many times he had been stuck by actors. (The owner's wife happens to be an accomplished actress.) He insisted that I come over to his restaurant at 6:30 P.M. so that we could discuss this situation.

When I showed up, the owner was more than agitated now, and since I was the one who introduced him to Robert Duvall, it was my duty to see that this tab was paid. I actually said that if it wasn't paid I would make it good, knowing that Bobby Duvall probably wouldn't stand for that.

When Bobby's future father-in-law showed up, he immediately put a pained expression on his face. "Twenty guys, maybe twenty-five? They told me there would be six or eight guys here." The owner looked at me and said, "See? I told you!"

It was agreed by the owner of the restaurant and Bobby's future father-in-law that each guest was to chip in fifty dollars to pay for the party. All the guests knew me and my closeness to Bobby, and they surely would agree to this small amount. I would be the patsy and collect the money. Why the fuck I ever agreed to this dumb arrangement has haunted me ever since.

The first guy who walked in was a close friend of Bobby's who practically owed his entire acting career to Robert Duvall.

Bobby saw to it that this guy always had a part in his films. Upon hearing my suggestion that we all chip in fifty dollars for Bobby's party, this guy almost took my head off, "Shit, man, I was invited to this party by Bobby's secretary. I heard Gail's old man was paying for this. Bobby never liked him anyway. He's a shitheel he does this. Me, I'm not paying a cent. I was invited and that's that!"

The next few people who showed up were divided. Some said they would pay, and others said they didn't have any money on them. I began to come apart at the seams, realizing I didn't look too good suggesting everyone pay for the party. After facing seven or eight bewildered faces, I realized it was all hopeless. I even threatened to leave if the owner of the restaurant didn't figure out another way to get paid.

Finally the owner of the restaurant whispered in my ear, "You're off the hook. I have Gail's father's credit card. I'm going to hit him with a $600 charge for this thing." I let out a sigh of relief, and the party went on about an hour later.

Having introduced Bobby Duvall and many of his friends to this particular Italian restaurant, I was naturally concerned about the food and the service, which turned out to be really bad. The restaurant wasn't busy that evening, so there was no excuse. I kept trying to get waiters to take proper orders and then ran to the kitchen to see what was holding everything up, all the time trying to be cautious and diplomatic to all the workers.

During the evening, the owner whispered in my ear, "I'm gonna make the tab $800." It was none of my business, so I didn't have any comment. I kept the party going, made most of the speeches, kidding Bobby and some of the guests and generally injecting some life into Robert Duvall's stag party. Frankly, without me that evening would have resembled a dinner with Calvin Coolidge.

When it was over, everyone patted me on the back, including Bobby, who said, "Man, you were very funny. That line about Danny Aiello's film festival—ha, ha, ha!" On the way out, Bobby's future father-in-law held out his hand, asking me how much I had collected. Very embarrassed and really not knowing what to say or do, I walked past him muttering that the owner of the restaurant said he would handle the situation. I knew then that this man would never hold me in high esteem.

That night, I got a call from the owner of the restaurant asking me why I had upset his maitre d'. I said I was very respectful all evening, but that the service was painfully slow and now that he mentioned it, his maitre d' was the biggest asshole and wasn't good enough to be a busboy. The owner of the restaurant was an alcoholic who also suffered from diabetes. He was warned many times that his next drink may very well be his last. I got the impression on the phone that Mr. Restaurateur had dipped into the sauce, but good.

A few days later, I heard that Bobby Duvall's future father-in-law was charged $1,000 for that little repast. The owner of the restaurant didn't hand him the tab; he hid in the kitchen while the maitre d' took all the heat and insults. Well, this weird episode was thankfully over, and I made up my mind never to return to that dining establishment again.

But was it over? Not by a long shot. The first one who called me was the actor who owed his career to Robert Duvall, the one who cursed me out when I suggested we all chip in fifty bucks for our mutual buddy's stag party.

He wanted to know why I was so distant, why didn't I go to Bobby and "rat" on the owner of the restaurant? I told him that "ratting" wasn't one of my accomplishments; besides, the owner of the restaurant was once a friend of mine, too, I had been a guest more than once in the establishment, the Bible says if you break bread with someone, et cetera, et cetera. I was emphatically told that the only way I could clear the air with Bobby would be to "rat" on this restaurant individual.

Now, although I had been a guest in this restaurant many times, I also performed a tremendous public-relations service for them, besides bringing many customers and celebrities to the place. Although I didn't drink, except for maybe an occasional brandy, I enlivened a hopelessly dead bar with my jokes, songs, and snappy patter, if I must say so myself. I was the one who introduced Robert Duvall to this Italian restaurant. As a matter of fact, Duvall was a square when it came to good food, and I introduced him to many fine restaurants, all of a different nature. Today he's a maven, a connoisseur of epicurean delight, if you must.

317

14

That's How It Goes

I REMEMBER A FUNNY STORY told to me during my songwriting days. It seems these two hungry songwriters were anxiously demonstrating their prize song, "That's How It Goes," for a famous artist and repertoire director long since deceased. Nothing was said after the first runthrough or demonstration, so the songwriters eagerly went through the motions again and then again. Finally they finished singing "That's How It Goes" for the fourth time, and the A and R man looked into the pleading, expectant eyes of the two songwriters and said, "That's how *what* goes?"

What may have been a joke to me once isn't so funny now. I can't say I didn't get a great deal of satisfaction out of writing my memoirs; I surely did. Now I again ask myself the musical question, "Is that enough?" Who am I to write a book? What right do I have to request a publisher to expend his time, money, and energies on the ramblings of practically a little "Mr. Nobody"? Angrily I again answer, "Who do you have to be to write a book?" We don't have royalty in America. Thieves, murderers, hookers, disgraced politicians, terrorists, phony celebrities, and porno stars write books today. Why can't a poor kid born in the South Bronx, brought up in three orphanages, with only an eighth-grade education, who lived in a furnished closet and supported himself as a teenager on nine dollars earned every ten days, who, miracles of miracles, became a commissioned flight officer in the U.S. Air Force during World War II, who thereupon wrote songs for Frank Sinatra, Tony Bennett, Patti Page, Guy Lombardo, and many other stars, who actually created and was the very *first* independent recording director in the early '50s, who produced shows on

Broadway, off Broadway, at Carnegie Hall, and in Japan, who had bit acting parts in a few motion pictures, who introduced Japan to the American copyright music business in 1960, and who met royalty, major celebrities, and bums but "who never lost the common touch"—someone like that—write a book? Well, he did. Good, bad, or indifferent, Little Orphan Eddie, the painfully shy, skinny, sickly kid who wasn't given much chance to live as a child, let alone write a book, lived and did!

I like the title I chose, but I had others in mind. *Hey, I Wrote for Sinatra* was one. When I thought and wrote about my son, Peter, I wanted to title the book *I Was the Father I Always Wanted*, as I honestly consider myself, if nothing else, a superior parent. Like the usual Jewish father, with more than a tinge of guilt, I think I was always trying to make up for the inadequacies I suffered as a child. I also thought of the title *Slow Fade*, but friends told me it was too theatrical, too "In." Then there was *Requiem for a Lightweight*, which I still like, but I'm glad and satisfied I settled on *Yesterday's Cake*.

And I'm glad, too, that I have so many memories to entertain and tickle me as I slowly ride into the sunset. I don't hate anyone, even those bastards I strongly and often differed with. I never could carry a grudge, and some of those guys sure made life a lot more interesting. Who was it who said, "You only pass this way once"? Hey, I'm not going anywhere for a long time. I missed too many meals in those early orphan asylums, so I still have a lot of catching up on tomorrow's "yesterday's cake."

2

1

3

4

5

In Memoriam

1. Lt. Robert Schratwieser, killed on his seventeenth mission, the first U.S. Air-Force low-level bombing of the Ploesti oil fields of Rumania. Bobby laughingly always called out to me, "Rodger dodger, eh, Eddie," and my answer would be "Wilco and out, Bobby boy!" Bobby wanted to become a priest when the war was over.

2. The man who encouraged me to write when I was eleven years old, Leo Grachow, editor of the (orphanage's) *Rising Bell*. Leo died in his early twenties fighting the fascists in Spain in 1935 with the Abraham Lincoln Brigade.

3. That's me on the left, in happier days, with Lt. Mike Maskaron from Chicago. Mike was killed on his last scheduled and fiftieth mission over Germany.

4. Ens. Rubin Keltch, my Fox Street buddy, was awarded the Congressional Medal of Honor posthumously for "duty above and beyond." A mini-park in the Bronx is named after Ruby who wanted to be a veterinarian one day.

5. The *best* soldier at Fort Dix, Sgt. George Lloyd drilling our outfit, Headquarters Company. Tank Commander Lloyd bravely died in Germany in 1944.

Index

Greenhouse, Martha, 227, 229, 232, 234
Gregorio, Rose, 305
Gregory, Dick, 111
Gregory, Lieutenant Colonel, 80–83
Grodin, Charles ("Chuck"), 305–06
Grossbard, Ulu, 288, 290–91, 305
Gurney's, 308
"Gyp" the Blood, 4

Hackman, Gene, 273
Hall Johnson Choir, 153
Hamill, Dennis, 292
Hamill, Pete, 292
Hannum, Alex, 219
Happiness Boys, 125, 152, 154, 158–59, 171
Hardy, Andy, 67
Hardy, Judge, 47
Harrison, Rex, 247
Hart, Moss, 209, 238
Hayama, Peggy, 180–81
Hayes, Gabby, 48
Healy, Dan, 33
Healy, Eddie, 33, 38, 42–43, 45
Healy, Jack, 128–29
Hearns, Tommy, 309–11
Heflin, Van, 161
Heller, Joe, 101, 239
Hemingway, Ernest, 44
Hepburn, Audrey, 48, 172
Heyman, Sgt. Edward, 62–63
Hikan, Nat, 128
Hill, Arthur, 278, 305
Hirohito, Emperor, 195
Hiss, Alger, 314
Hiss, Tony, 314
Hoffman, Ann, 262
Hoffman, Dustin, 8, 259–60, 262, 267, 274, 314
Holden, William, 287, 299
Hollander, Harry, 65
Hoover, John Edgar, 111
Hope, Bob, 245
Hopkins, Bo, 278
Horne, Geoffrey, 230, 231, 237
Horvitz, Israel, 239
Hyman, Joe, 209

Ishimatsu, Joji, 210
Itzkowitz, Adele, 3
Itzkowitz, Esther, 3
Itzkowitz, Sophie, 3

Jack Dempsey's restaurant, 158, 161
"Jack Paar Show, The," 216
Jenkins, Bill "Moose," 42–44
Jennings, Cpl. Blanche, 97–98
Jensen, Jim, 239
Johns, Harold "Chuck," 242
Johnson, Gus, 220
Jolson, Al, 19, 215
Jones, George, 244, 264

Kawakami, Mr. Ginichi, 166, 184–86, 194–96, 202, 204–05, 207–08
Kearney, Michael, 229
Keaton, Buster, 53, 172
Keaton, Diane, 285
Keitel, Harvey, 239, 285
Kelly, Jack "Bart Maverick," 227, 233, 250
Keltch, Ens. Rubin, 321
Kennedy, John F., 211, 223
King, Dr. Martin Luther, 111
King, Larry, 313
Kissinger, Henry, 257, 294, 310–11
Knapp, Bert, 110, 112
Knight, Shirley, 272
Kovacs, Ernie, 131
Kurosawa, Akira, 170, 181

La Guardia, Fiorello H., 93
La Motta, Jake, 241–42, 257, 295
La Scala, 130
Lantigua, Johnny, 42
Latin Quarter, The, 130
Lawrence, Jack Seligman, 109, 112–13
Lee, Bruce, 271
Lembeck, Harvey, 128
Leonard, Sugar Ray, 309, 311
Leroy, Doris, 19
Leroy, Mervyn, 19
Leroy, Warner, 19
Lester, Charley, 201
Levy, Dr. Roger, 256
Lewis, Jerry, 59
Lindsay, Howard, 289
Lindy's, 158, 161
Livingston, Mary, 34
Lloyd, Sgt. George, 103, 321

326

327

Rael, Jack, 152–53
Rather, Dan, 239
Raye, Martha, 39, 136
Redgrave, Vanessa, 292
Regan, Paul, 112
Regan, Phil, 43–44
Reiner, Carl, 172, 270
Reiner, Rob (Meathead), 298
Reynolds, Quentin, 44
Ricardo's Restaurant, 120–21
Richardson, Ralph, 247
Richtoven, Baron, 71
Rickenbacker, Eddie, 71
Rickles, Don, 48, 132
Robinson, Edward G., 227
Robinson, Sugar Ray, 242–43
Rockne, Knute, 7
Rohm, Harry, 117, 120
Ronnie and the Ronnettes, 192
Rooney, Mickey, 47–48, 109, 172, 212
Rosales, Sgt. Marco, 103
Rose, David, 102
Rosenberg, Charley "Phil," 1, 107
Rosenbloom, Slapsie Maxie, 133, 142
Roth, Broadway Sam, 39
Rothstein, Arnold, 1
Ruby, Jack, 212
Rugel, Yvette, 41
Russell, Ken, 291–93, 300
Russian Tea Room, 256, 302
Ruth, George Herman "Babe," 19–20
112
Rydell, Bobby, 193

Saddler, Sandy, 241
Sager, Carole Bayer, 160
St. James, Aleta, 285
St. John, Fuzzy, 90
Salinger, J.D., 74
Sanicola, Hank, 311
Sardi's Restaurant, 234–35
Sasmore, Dr. James, 227
Savage, John, 288–89, 315
Savage, Pete, 241–44, 257
Savalas, Telly, 258
Saxon, Don, 245
Schary, Dore, 245
Scheider, Cynthia, 257, 305, 310–11
Scheider, Roy, 257, 290–91, 305, 310
Schisgal, Murray, xiii

Schlein, Herb, 305
Schlesinger, Arthur M., Jr., 299, 301
Schratwieser, Bob, 98–99, 321
Schrier, Mr. Morris, 116
Second Sea Search Attack Squadron,
92
Segal, "Champ," 1
Seidel, Ted, 110, 112
Seligman, Jack, 110
Sellecca, Connie, 270
Serpe, Ralph, 257
Seymour, Robin, 152
Shaw, David, 299
Shaw, Wini, 39
Sherill, Billy "The Kid," 244, 264–65
Sherman, Joe, 121
Shimeall, Warren, 189–90, 207
Shimura, Mr. Takashi, 181
Shimura, Takashi, 170
Shore, "Toots," 9
Shubert brothers, 227
Sica, Master Sgt. Alphonse, 59–60
103
Siegel, Joel, 239
Sillman, Leonard, 19, 213, 224, 226–
28, 231–32, 234–36, 248
Silvers, Phil, 9, 128, 201
Simon, Paul, 240
Sinatra, Frank, 8, 35, 129–30, 147, 155,
165, 175, 184, 215, 257, 310–11,
318, 319
Sliwa, Curtis, 285
Smallwood, Sgt. Arthur, 70–72
Smith, Kate, 123
Smith, Keely, 39
Somma, Del, 288
Soo, Jack, 150–51
Spector, Phil, 192
Sprung, Murray "Pop," 14–17, 29,
188–190, 192, 197, 207–8
Stampley, Joe, 244
Stanwyck, Barbara, 34
Starr, Ben, 19, 233
Staub, Rusty, 239
Stein, Joe, 239
Stein, Jules, 117
Steiner, Leo, 313
Stengel, Casey, 142
Stevenson, Parker, 270
Stiller, Jerry, 239
Stone, Dick, 157, 161